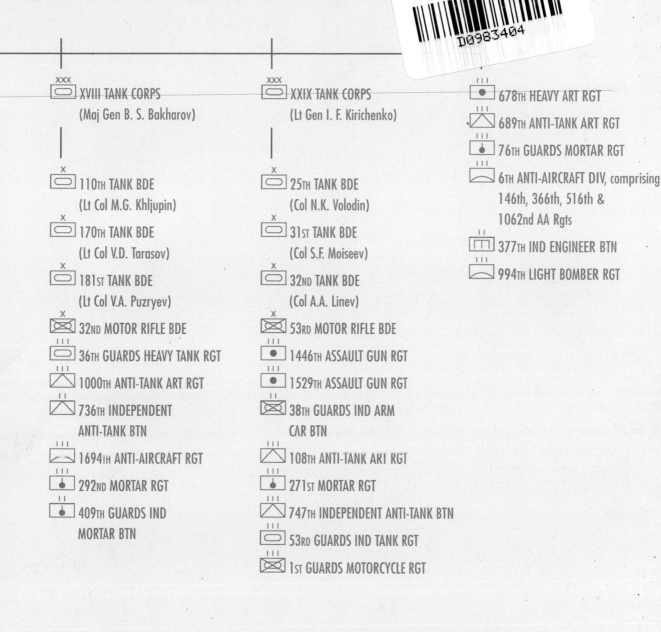

XVIII TANK CORPS
(Maj Gen B. S. Bakharov)

110TH TANK BDE
(Lt Col M.G. Khljupin)

170TH TANK BDE
(Lt Col V.D. Tarasov)

181ST TANK BDE
(Lt Col V.A. Puzryev)

32ND MOTOR RIFLE BDE

36TH GUARDS HEAVY TANK RGT

1000TH ANTI-TANK ART RGT

736TH INDEPENDENT
ANTI-TANK BTN

1694TH ANTI-AIRCRAFT RGT

292ND MORTAR RGT

409TH GUARDS IND
MORTAR BTN

XXIX TANK CORPS
(Lt Gen I. F. Kirichenko)

25TH TANK BDE
(Col N.K. Volodin)

31ST TANK BDE
(Col S.F. Moiseev)

32ND TANK BDE
(Col A.A. Linev)

53RD MOTOR RIFLE BDE

1446TH ASSAULT GUN RGT

1529TH ASSAULT GUN RGT

38TH GUARDS IND ARM
CAR BTN

108TH ANTI-TANK ART RGT

271ST MORTAR RGT

747TH INDEPENDENT ANTI-TANK BTN

53RD GUARDS IND TANK RGT

1ST GUARDS MOTORCYCLE RGT

678TH HEAVY ART RGT

689TH ANTI-TANK ART RGT

76TH GUARDS MORTAR RGT

6TH ANTI-AIRCRAFT DIV, comprising
146th, 366th, 516th &
1062nd AA Rgts

377TH IND ENGINEER BTN

994TH LIGHT BOMBER RGT

FIFTH GUARDS TANK ARMY AT KURSK

VISUAL BATTLE GUIDE

FIFTH GUARDS TANK ARMY AT KURSK

12 JULY 1943

DAVID PORTER

amber
BOOKS

This edition first published in 2011

Published by
Amber Books Ltd
Bradley's Close
74–77 White Lion Street
London N1 9PF
United Kingdom
www.amberbooks.co.uk

ISBN: 978-1-907446-61-0

Project Editor: Michael Spilling
Design: Hawes Design
Picture Research: Terry Forshaw

Printed in China

PICTURE CREDITS:
Art-Tech/Aerospace: 8, 11, 146
Nik Cornish/STAVKA: 14, 34, 37, 94, 106, 130, 161, 166, 175, 178
Topfoto/RIA Novosti: 6
Ukrainian State Archive: 26, 32, 70, 82, 90, 102, 125, 128, 129, 153

All artworks © Art-Tech and Oliver Missing (www.05m6.de)
All maps © Amber Books

CONTENTS

Chapter 1
Trial and Error: Soviet Armour, 1918–42

During the 15 years following its victory in the Russian Civil War, the Red Army created the world's largest armoured force and highly sophisticated operational concepts including the theory of 'deep operations'. However, just as technological advances were on the point of making such futuristic military theories viable, Stalin's paranoia led him to inflict near fatal damage on the Red Army. His belief that senior officers, especially the brilliant Marshal Tukhachevsky, were planning a military *coup d'etat*, drove him to instigate the murderous purges of the late 1930s. Estimates vary wildly, but it is quite possible that 50 per cent of the Soviet officer corps was executed or imprisoned.

The brutal suppression of innovative military thought was an important factor in the disasters of the Winter War against Finland and its effects were still evident in 1941, when they brought the Red Army to the very brink of total defeat.

OPPOSITE: Raising the banner – a Soviet tank crewman raises a regimental flag on his KV-1 heavy tank during the defence of Moscow, 31 December 1941.

Forging and Destroying a Weapon, 1918–39

The Red Army was officially founded on 23 February 1918 and its initial organisation was largely the work of Leon Trotsky, the People's Commissar for War from 1918 to 1924.

Trotsky's ruthlessness mobilized a force which at one stage totalled 5.5 million men, although many of these had very little equipment or training and front line strength rarely exceeded 580,000. During the first four years of its existence, the Red Army was engaged in constant fighting, against both the White forces in the Civil War (1918–22) and the Polish Army in the Russo-Polish War (1919–21). Despite a humiliating defeat by Poland, victory in the Civil War ensured the survival of the Communist regime, but it had cost the Red Army an estimated one million casualties and had wrecked the economy.

Some of the war booty was particularly useful – small numbers of Medium Mark Vs, Whippets and Renault FTs had been supplied to the White forces during the Civil War. Many of these were captured and taken into service with the Red Army where they provided a small cadre of personnel with experience of operating armoured fighting vehicles (AFVs) until Soviet tank production began in the late 1920s.

In the aftermath of the Civil War, the newly created USSR forged a seemingly improbable military agreement with the German Weimar Republic. In a secret annex to the Treaty of Rapallo, signed in 1922, the Soviet government made extensive facilities available for the Germans to test weapons which were banned by the Treaty of Versailles. Soviet observers monitored all research and tests and from 1925 onwards Red Army officers attended German manoeuvres.

Russo-German military co-operation provided the Red Army with much-needed technical expertise, but not the industrial base to equip a modern military force.

As Stalin consolidated his power in the late 1920s, he became increasingly concerned at Soviet economic and military weakness compared to

Training shot: A BT-7 advances with infantry – the lack of any camouflage or extra kit stowed on the tank and the remarkably evenly spaced shell bursts would suggest that this is a pre-war exercise rather than a true combat photograph.

Western powers and instituted a series of Five Year Plans. These were ruthless programmes of industrialisation which marked the beginning of the process of transforming a largely peasant-based agrarian nation into an industrial superpower. By the early 1930s, massive industrial complexes had been completed, all of which were either built specifically for producing military equipment or could easily be switched to war production.

NEW MECHANIZED BRIGADES

The Five Year Plans provided the resources for modernising the Red Army, an achievement which was largely due to the remarkable ability of Mikhail Tukhachevsky who served as Chief of Staff of the Red Army (1925–1928) and as Deputy Commissar for Defence. He attempted to transform the ill-trained conscripts of the Red Army into a professional military force and to replace cavalry with powerful armoured forces. Such radical views aroused the enmity of traditionalists in the Soviet military establishment and his ideas were rejected by Stalin, leading to his removal from the Red Army staff and censure for encouraging Red militarism.

Despite this official hostility, an experimental Mechanized Brigade was formed during the summer of 1929 which demonstrated the potential of such formations and Tukhachevsky was given a chance to put his ideas into practice in 1931, following Stalin's grudging acceptance of the need for a modernized Red Army.

Although Tukhachevsky's theory of deep operations, using all-arms formations in strikes far behind enemy lines to destroy HQs and rear area services, were still opposed by conservative senior officers, they were largely adopted by the Red Army in the mid-1930s. The idea was steadily developed from 1929 and finally appeared in definitive form in the Provisional Field Regulations of 1936.

During this period annual tank production figures soared, allowing the creation of larger armoured units, the Mechanized Corps, which were in many respects the forerunners of the later Tank Armies. Each Mechanized Corps included two Mechanized Brigades totalling 430 tanks and 215 armoured cars plus a motorized infantry brigade and support units. This expansion allowed the new theories of warfare to be tested in ever-larger annual manoeuvres culminating in the huge 1935 exercises held in the Kiev Military District. Western observers at these manoeuvres were staggered to see hundreds of AFVs and a mock airborne assault by two battalions of paratroops. They would have been even more amazed had it been known that the Soviets had three full airborne brigades and more tank units (and indeed more AFVs) than the rest of the world's armies combined.

Just as it seemed that the Red Army was establishing an unassailable technological lead over other European armies that lead was swept away by Stalin's paranoia. Tukhachevsky's very ability proved to be fatal, as Stalin came to see him as a threat to his power. On 9 June 1937 Tukhachevsky and his most prominent supporters were suddenly arrested on treason charges, tried by a special military court on 11 June and shot at dawn the next day. Over the next year or so the total of those executed or imprisoned rose to three of the five Marshals of the Soviet Union plus 14 of the 16 army commanders, 60 of 67 corps commanders, 136 of 199 divisional commanders and 221 of 397 brigade commanders. Thousands of more junior officers were also shot or imprisoned and the wave of terror spread out to include the heads of the defence industries and even weapons design teams.

THE PURGES

Stalin's iron grip on the Red Army was emphasized by the re-introduction of Trotsky's system of dual command in May 1937 under which each unit had its commissar, a political officer whose effective rank was equal to that of its military commander and who had the authority to countermand his orders. The overall effect of the purges was to stifle innovation and professionalism throughout the Red Army as the survivors were thoroughly cowed and understandably terrified of the secret police, the NKVD.

Many key posts which fell vacant as a result of the blood-letting were filled by incompetents who were appointed more because they were politically 'safe' than for any military ability. Although large armoured formations remained, the traditionalists regained their former influence. Marshal Budenny ensured that his beloved cavalry remained a major component of the army and in 1938 it reached its greatest strength with an establishment of seven cavalry corps (over 32 divisions).

Development of the T-34

By the mid-1930s it was becoming clear that the majority of the Red Army's tanks were reaching the end of their development potential and that a new generation of AFVs was required. This was emphasized by the limitations of the tanks sent to Spain to aid the Republican forces in the Spanish Civil War.

Despite prolonged wrangling over the new designs and the disruption caused by Stalin's purges, the process resulted in the T-34, one of the greatest tanks of all time. The Spanish Civil War provided an invaluable opportunity to test Soviet military equipment in combat conditions and an estimated 600 aircraft, 350 tanks, 60 armoured cars, 1200 field guns and 350,000 rifles were supplied to the Republican forces from Red Army stocks. Roughly 700 Soviet military personnel – mainly aircrews and tank crewmen – were also sent to Spain under assumed foreign names as 'volunteers'.

General Pavlov commanded the sizeable Soviet armoured contingent operating in support of the Republicans which included 300 T-26s and 50 BT-5s. Whilst there were no large scale tank battles, a number of actions proved that these machines were technically far superior to the Panzer Is and Italian tankettes fielded by the Nationalist forces. Despite this technological superiority, there were worrying signs that all was not well with Soviet tank designs. The petrol engines of the T-26s and BT-5s were found to be a significant fire hazard when the Nationalist infantry began to use Molotov cocktail improvised incendiary grenades. There was even greater concern at the ease with which the Nationalists' German-supplied 37mm (1.45in) anti-tank guns could penetrate the tanks' thin armour.

DESIGN STUDIES

Reports from Spain helped to frame the requirements for the new tank designs – including the need for armour immune to 37mm (1.45in) anti-tank guns at point-blank range and to 76mm (3in) guns at ranges over 1000 metres (3280ft). The poor fuel-efficiency of contemporary petrol engines and their inherent fire risk led to the decision that diesel engines should be used if at all possible.

The first of the new types was the T-111, which began development in 1936/37. The prototype, which was tested in 1938, had exceptionally good

A-20 prototype

CREW

SPECIFICATIONS

Weight: 18 tonnes (17.7 tons)
Length: 5.7m (18ft 8in)
Width: 2.7m (8ft 10in)
Height: 2.4m (7ft 10in)
Engine: 335.56kW (450hp) V-2 diesel
Speed (road): 65km/h (40.4mph)
Range: n/k
Armament: 1 x 45mm (1.8in) Model 38 tank gun, plus 2 x 7.62mm (0.3in) DT machine guns

The A-20 marked the transition from the BT series fast tanks to the T-34 and its successors. Although it never went into production, it was a vital test-bed for many of the features later incorporated in the T-34.

armour protection of up to 60mm (2.3in), but was too slow. A much more promising programme began in 1937, when Mikhail Koshkin was assigned to lead a newly-formed team to design a replacement for the BT tanks at the KhPZ tank factory in Kharkov. The prototype, designated A-20, was developed to meet specifications set by General Pavlov commanding the Directorate of Armoured Forces (ABTU), including 20mm (0.8in) of armour, a 45mm (1.8in) gun, and the new V-2 diesel engine. It also featured an 8x6 convertible drive similar to the BT's 8x2, allowing it to run on wheels. This capability had greatly reduced the failure rates of the unreliable tank track of the early 1930s, and allowed tanks to achieve high road speeds whilst doing far less damage to the road surface than when moving on their tracks. However, removing and refitting the tracks was a time-consuming business which crews did their best to avoid and by the late 1930s, designers considered convertible drive a waste of space and weight. The A-20 also incorporated sloped armour first trialled in the experimental BT-IS and BT-SW-2 projects, which offered significantly better protection than the same thickness of vertical armour.

Koshkin was so concerned at the unexploited potential for developing the A-20 that he took the matter up with Stalin and convinced him to let him develop a second prototype, a more heavily armed and armoured 'universal tank' which could replace both the T-26 and the BT series tanks. The second prototype was initially designated A-30 (subsequently T-32). This had sloped armour up to 30mm (1.2in) thick, a 76.2mm (3in) L-11 gun and was powered by the V-2 diesel engine.

Prototypes of both the A-20 and the T-32 were sent for comparative field trials at Kubinka in 1939. The A-20 performed miserably when operating in the wheeled mode, whilst having a similar performance to the T-32 whilst running on its tracks. Both types were then included in a special display of new AFVs held for the senior officers of the Main Military Council (GVS), who were unable to agree on which should be selected for service. Although Koshkin argued that the T-32 could

replace the T-26, T-28 and BT series tanks, some members of the GVS were concerned that production costs of the T-32 were three times those of the T-26, whilst General Pavlov still supported the A-20.

Whilst the merits of the two types were still being debated, the Red Army's disastrous showing in the Winter War against Finland emphasised the vulnerability of current Soviet tanks to 37mm (1.45in) anti-tank guns and the inability of their 45mm (1.8in) guns to destroy Finnish field defences. This gave Koshkin the opportunity to press for the adoption of an up-armoured version of the T-32, which was authorized for production as the T-34.

Two prototypes of the T-34 were completed in February 1940 and were subjected to a gruelling winter test drive from Kharkov to Moscow where they were demonstrated to Stalin before continuing to Finland for trials against the Mannerheim Line defences and then returning to Kharkov via Minsk and Kiev. Some automotive shortcomings were

T-34 Model 1941 tanks with appliqué armour fitted to the hull front and driver's hatch in response to the threat posed by increasing numbers of German towed and SP 75mm (2.95in) anti-tank guns.

identified and corrected during this 2000-kilometre (1242-mile) run, which did much to overcome official resistance to the adoption of the design.

The stunning panzer victories in France in the summer of 1940 prompted a badly shaken Stalin to demand production of at least 600 T-34s by the end of the year. However, the type's complexity made it impossible to meet this schedule – the first production tanks were not completed until September 1940 and the programme was further disrupted by Koshkin's death towards the end of the month.

PRODUCTION

At the time of its introduction, the T-34 posed new challenges for Soviet industry. It had thicker armour than any previous medium tank and sub-assemblies were provided by several widely dispersed plants: Kharkov Diesel Factory No. 75 supplied the model V-2 engine, Leningrad Kirovsky Factory (the former Putilov works) made the original L-11 gun, and the Dinamo Factory in Moscow produced electrical components. The KhPZ factory simply did not have the capacity to produce all the T-34s required and in early 1941 production began at the Stalingrad Tractor Factory (STZ), followed by the Krasnoye Sormovo Factory No. 112 in Gorky in July 1941.

The new design suffered plenty of teething problems, including:
■ Defective armour plates
■ Weak transmission and clutch

T-34 Model 1940

■ CREW

■ SPECIFICATIONS

Weight: 26 tonnes (25.59 tons)
Length: 5.92m (19ft 5in)
Width: 3m (9ft 8in)
Height: 2.45m (8ft)
Engine: 335.56kW (450hp) V-2 diesel
Speed (road): 55km/h (34mph)
Range: 300km (186.4 miles)
Armament: 76.2mm (3in) L-11 tank gun, plus 2 x 7.62mm (0.3in) DT machine guns

ABOVE: The T-34 Model 1940 was plagued with the sort of teething problems such as unreliable transmissions which were to afflict many wartime tanks. Fortunately for the Red Army, the design was sufficiently robust to accept a succession of upgrades which ensured that it remained a viable battle tank throughout the war.

LEFT: Two types of turret were produced for the early T-34: a cast version (top), and a welded turret (left). The turret was small and only had room for two crew members: the loader and commander/gunner.

T-34 Model 1941

CREW

SPECIFICATIONS

Weight: 26.5 tonnes (26.08 tons)
Length: 6.68m (21ft 10in)
Width: 3m (9ft 8in)
Height: 2.45m (8ft)
Engine: 373kW (500hp) V-2 diesel
Speed (road): 53km/h (33mph)
Range: 400km (248.55 miles)
Armament: 76.2mm (3in) F-34 tank gun, plus 2 x 7.62mm (0.3in) DT machine guns

Combat experience during the early months of the German invasion showed that the armour of the Model 1940 could be penetrated by the German 50mm (1.97in) gun of the Panzer III (and its towed anti-tank version, the PaK 38) firing tungsten-cored APCR ammunition. The Model 1940's L-11 gun was also found to be only marginally effective against the newer German tanks and assault guns. The Model 1941 was accordingly up-armoured and fitted with the far more powerful 76.2mm (3in) F-34 tank gun.

■ Ineffective engine air filters
■ Poorly welded hull joints

Shortages of the V-2 diesel engine forced the Gorky factory to install the old M-17T petrol engine as used in the BT-7 in the first production batches of the T-34. These shortages were soon rectified, but the dire lack of radios was never completely overcome. At first there were only sufficient for company commander's tanks and, although the situation gradually improved, very few tank units were ever equipped on a scale approaching that of Western armoured forces.

The rapid German advances in the summer and autumn of 1941 badly disrupted production as factories were hastily evacuated to the safety of the Urals. KhPZ was re-established around the Dzherzhinski Ural Railcar Factory in Nizhny Tagil and the complex was renamed Stalin Ural Tank Factory No. 183. The Kirovsky Factory was evacuated a few weeks before Leningrad was surrounded, and moved with the Kharkov Diesel Factory to the Stalin Tractor Factory in Chelyabinsk. The city was soon dubbed Tankograd ('Tank City'). Voroshilov Tank Factory No. 174 from Leningrad was incorporated into the Ural Factory and the new Omsk Factory No. 174. The Ordzhonikidze Ural Heavy Machine Tool Works

(UZTM) in Sverdlovsk also absorbed several small factories. While these factories were being moved at frantic speed, the industrial complex surrounding the Stalingrad Tractor Factory produced 40 per cent of all T-34s. (Stalingrad maintained production until the factory was obliterated in the fierce fighting of September 1942.)

The mass evacuation of the tank factories meant that many planned improvements had to be delayed or abandoned altogether. The only changes allowed on the production lines were to make the tanks simpler and cheaper to produce. New techniques were developed for automated hardening and welding armour, whilst the number of components in the 76.2mm (3in) F-34 gun was reduced from 861 to 614. Production costs were dramatically reduced from 269,500 roubles in 1941, to 193,000 in 1942 and finally to 135,000 in 1943. Production time was halved by the end of 1942, even though most experienced factory workers had been conscripted and replaced by a workforce comprising 50 per cent women, 15 per cent boys and 15 per cent invalids and old men. During this period, T-34s, which had originally been described as '…beautifully crafted machines with excellent exterior finish' were much more roughly finished, although their mechanical reliability was not compromised.

Soviet Armoured Forces, 1939

By 1939, the Red Army's armoured forces were numerically impressive with a front-line peacetime strength of over 8000 tanks. However, with one notable exception, the malign influence of Stalin's purges crippled their combat effectiveness.

By the late 1930s, Japan had established control of Manchuria, which it transformed into the puppet state of Manchukuo. This brought it into conflict with the Soviet satellite state of Mongolia as the Japanese claimed that the Khalkhyn Gol (Khalkha River) formed the border between Manchukuo and Mongolia, whilst the Mongolians and Soviets maintained that it ran some 16 kilometres (10 miles) east of the river, just east of Nomonhan village.

The Kwantung Army formed the main Japanese force in Manchukuo which included some of the best Japanese units. On the other side of the frontier, the Red Army's 57th Special Corps, deployed from the Trans-Baikal Military District,

BT-7 tanks of 27th Armoured Brigade parade in Riga, Latvia, November 1940. To left and right in the front rank are 1937 production types with conical turrets, the central machine has a cylindrical turret produced from 1935.

was responsible for the defence of the border between Siberia and Manchuria.

Small border skirmishes in May 1939 gradually escalated, leading to the destruction of a regiment of the Kwantung Army's 64th Division at the end of the month. Large scale Japanese air attacks the following month raised the tension as the Kwantung Army prepared an offensive to 'expel the invaders'. This was to be a pincer movement by elements of the 23rd Division and the Yashuoka Detachment to encircle and destroy Soviet and Mongolian forces along the Khalkhyn Gol. (The Yasuoka Detachment was one of the few sizeable Japanese armoured formations with almost 100 AFVs.)

Whilst preparations for the offensive were under way, Georgi Zhukov, the most promising general to survive Stalin's purges, was appointed to command the Soviet forces. He quickly recognized the need for massive transport resources to support the

powerful armoured force which would be needed to inflict a decisive defeat on the Japanese – initially 1000 fuel tankers and over 1600 cargo trucks were deployed over the 750-kilometre (466-mile) route from his supply bases to the front line, later supplemented by a further 1625 vehicles from European Russia. This logistic support allowed him to assemble a striking force of as many as 550 tanks (mainly T-26s and BT-7s), plus 450 armoured cars.

When the Japanese offensive opened on 2 July, the Yasuoka Detachment lost over half its tanks to Soviet anti-tank guns, whilst perhaps 120 Soviet AFVs were destroyed (many by 37mm (1.45in) anti-tank guns and infantry with Molotov cocktails). Despite these losses, Zhukov still had overwhelming armoured strength – nearly 500 tanks and 350 armoured cars – to spearhead a devastating counter-offensive launched on 20 August. Within five days, this achieved a classic

double envelopment of the Japanese 23rd Division, which was effectively destroyed by 31 August.

Zhukov had proved himself as a capable commander of armoured forces. His victory ended the power of the 'Strike North' group within the Japanese High Command which sought to expand into Soviet Central Asia and Siberia. The balance of power swung to the 'Strike South' group who

Heavy Tank Brigade, 1939

UNIT	BA-20	BTS	T-28
Brigade HQ	–	–	2
HQ Company	5	–	–
Reconnaissance Company	10	6	–
Signal Platoon	2	3	–
Reconnaissance Platoon	3	–	–
Heavy Tank Company x 3	5	3	10

Heavy Tank Company, 1939

T-28 heavy tanks: 10
BT light tanks: 3
BA-20 armoured cars: 5

Three of these companies formed the main strike force of each heavy tank battalion. (Each heavy tank brigade had three such battalions.) Even by the standards of 1939, the T-28 was inadequately armoured for its role and proved to be vulnerable to Finnish 37mm (1.45in) anti-tank guns during the Winter War. A number of vehicles were rebuilt, with frontal armour increased from 30mm to 80mm (1.2in to 3.1in), but the extra weight impaired speed, range and agility.

COMPANY

SIGNALS PLATOON

favoured gaining control of the natural resources of South East Asia and the Pacific islands. In April 1941, the Soviet-Japanese Neutrality Pact removed the lingering threat to Stalin's eastern frontiers.

THE INVASION OF POLAND

The fighting in the Far East had barely ended when, on 17 September 1939, Soviet forces invaded Poland in accordance with the secret provisions of the Russo-German Non-Aggression Pact of August 1939. The Red Army deployed seven field armies totalling at least 450,000 men with over 3000 AFVs against Polish forces which were hopelessly outnumbered, but took unnecessary losses in a number of actions through over-confidence and tactical ineptitude.

At Grodno on 20 September, XV Tank Corps attempted a frontal assault on the city with minimal infantry support which was beaten off with the loss of 19 tanks and four armoured cars. On 28 September a scratch Polish force comprising elements of the Border Defence Corps and the Independent Operational Group Polesie near Szack ambushed the 52nd Rifle Division and its supporting T-26 brigade, inflicting roughly 2000 casualties and destroying or capturing 40 tanks.

These setbacks were no more than pin-pricks as Soviet forces were deployed in overwhelming

strength, but the warning signs were ignored by Stalin and his cronies. In November 1939 the four Tank Corps (which had replaced the former Mechanized Corps barely a year earlier) were broken up to form motorized divisions. These had roughly 275 tanks apiece and were intended to operate in conjunction with horsed cavalry. Independent tank brigades were to be more closely integrated with infantry and cavalry whilst it was planned to increase the armoured component of rifle divisions from a tank battalion to a tank brigade.

HUMILIATION IN FINLAND: THE WINTER WAR

The extent of the self-inflicted damage to the combat capability of the Red Army was shown in the bloody fiasco of the Soviet Union's Winter War against Finland which began on 30 November 1939. Before being overwhelmed by sheer weight of numbers, the Finns graphically demonstrated the often self-inflicted problems that bedevilled contemporary Soviet warfare.

One such problem was the fact that the majority of the Red Army's troops that fought in the Winter War were conscripts from the Ukraine as Stalin believed that troops from the areas bordering Finland could not be trusted to fight against the Finns. These conscripts with no experience of

BT-2 fast tank

CREW

SPECIFICATIONS

Weight: 10.2 tonnes (10 tons)
Length: 5.58m (18ft 3in)
Width: 2.23m (7ft 3in)
Height: 2.2m (7ft 2in)
Engine: 298kW (400hp) Liberty petrol
Speed: 100km/h (62mph)
Range: 300km (186 miles)
Armament: 1 x 37mm (1.45in) Model 31 tank gun, plus 1 x 7.62mm (0.3in) DT machine gun

The BT-2 was the first in a series of BT (Bystrokhodny Tank – Fast Tanks). These early BT tanks began life in 1932 as licensed copies of Walter Christie's M1930 tanks, but would ultimately lead to the development of the T-34.

Arctic winter conditions or training in forest survival skills stood little chance against the Finns who were experts in winter warfare and knew the land. Even the weather was against them as the winter of 1939/40 was one of the three worst winters in Finland in the twentieth century.

In Karelia, the initial Soviet assaults by the Seventh Army against the fortifications of the Mannerheim Line were repulsed with heavy losses, despite the support of the three tank brigades of X Tank Corps and four artillery regiments. At least 180,000 troops, 900 guns and 1400 AFVs were committed against roughly 133,000 Finnish defenders who were woefully short of artillery and armour – the most critical shortage being anti-tank guns, only 67 of which were available.

Staggering incompetence on the part of many Red Army officers and commissars helped even the odds – in the early stages of the war, camouflage was condemned as a sign of cowardice and units formed up for mass assaults in the open, in full view of Finnish machine guns and artillery observers who were able to inflict horrendous casualties.

There were reports of Soviet artillery opening fire without orders 'to help the infantry keep its spirits up' and causing mass panic amongst the infantry. The Red Army's tanks were frequently committed to assaults without adequate reconnaissance and with abysmal levels of artillery and infantry support. These failings made them horribly vulnerable to well camouflaged Finnish anti-tank guns and infantry anti-tank teams which scored numerous 'kills' with Molotov Cocktail incendiaries and demolition charges. Whilst most anti-tank guns opened fire at ranges of 400–600 metres (1300–2000ft), an unofficial record was set by a 37mm (1.45in) Bofors gun of the 7th Anti-Tank Detachment which destroyed a T-37 amphibious light tank on the ice of Lake Ladoga at a range of 1700 metres (5600ft).

It seems likely that as many as 6000 Soviet AFVs were deployed against Finland during the 3½ months of the war and that losses from all causes may have exceeded 3500 vehicles. (Finnish forces had captured or destroyed roughly 1600 of these, besides inflicting well over 250,000 casualties.) By the time of the armistice on 13 March 1940, the Finns had suffered 26,000 dead, 44,000 wounded and 450,000 homeless, a terrible price for a country of barely four million people.

T-28 Model 1938 medium tank

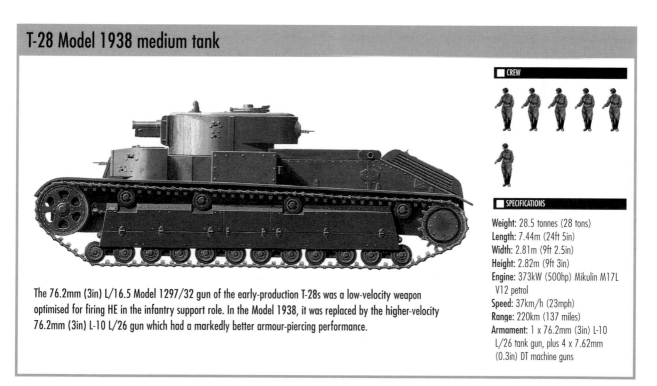

■ CREW

■ SPECIFICATIONS

Weight: 28.5 tonnes (28 tons)
Length: 7.44m (24ft 5in)
Width: 2.81m (9ft 2.5in)
Height: 2.82m (9ft 3in)
Engine: 373kW (500hp) Mikulin M17L V12 petrol
Speed: 37km/h (23mph)
Range: 220km (137 miles)
Armament: 1 x 76.2mm (3in) L-10 L/26 tank gun, plus 4 x 7.62mm (0.3in) DT machine guns

The 76.2mm (3in) L/16.5 Model 1297/32 gun of the early-production T-28s was a low-velocity weapon optimised for firing HE in the infantry support role. In the Model 1938, it was replaced by the higher-velocity 76.2mm (3in) L-10 L/26 gun which had a markedly better armour-piercing performance.

Facing Reality, 1940–41

Even before the end of the Winter War, senior Soviet officers were drawing lessons from their army's 'shambolic' performance against Finland's tiny forces.

One of the most perceptive analyses was prepared by the Ninth Army's Chief of Staff who believed that the Red Army had become too reliant on heavy equipment, but lacked the training to use it effectively, especially in the harsh conditions of a Finnish winter. His report concluded that: 'Our units, saturated by technology (especially artillery and transport vehicles) are incapable of manoeuvre and combat in this theatre: they are burdened and chained down by technology which can only go by road.'

The Supreme Military Soviet met in April 1940 to review the lessons of the Finnish campaign and recommend reforms. The power of units' political commissars was reduced and pre-revolutionary ranks and discipline were reintroduced. Clothing, equipment and tactics for winter operations were all improved. However, most of these reforms were still very much work in progress when the Germans launched Operation *Barbarossa* 15 months later.

Even Stalin was finally forced to face reality in the aftermath of the German victory in France and the Mechanized Corps began to be reformed from June 1940 onwards (by the time of the German invasion no less than 30 had been raised). The malign effect of Stalin's purges was again felt as it became clear that there were insufficient suitably qualified officers to command anything other than a small number of massive formations. As a result, the corps were huge – each had an official strength of 1031 tanks, 268 armoured cars, 358 guns and mortars, 5000 motor vehicles, 350 tractors and 1700 motorcycles.

Although frantic efforts were made, these corps were far from being effective combat formations when they were thrown into action in the summer of 1941, despite the massive numbers of AFVs then available which may well have totalled:
- 400 T-27 tankettes
- 1200 T-37 amphibious light tanks
- 1300 T-38 amphibious light tanks
- 222 T-40 amphibious light tanks
- 400 T-18 light tanks
- 11,000 T-26 light tanks
- 6000 BT fast tanks
- 500 T-28 medium tanks
- 967 T-34 medium tanks
- 40 T-35 heavy tanks
- 508 KV heavy tanks
- 4819 armoured cars

Even these holdings were inadequate to meet the needs of so many massive formations – over 6000 more tanks were required! The situation was even worse than the totals would suggest as there were far too few modern vehicles – 3000 more KVs and almost 11,000 more T-34s should have been available (see table below left). Equally seriously, the emphasis on producing new tanks rather than spare-parts led to appalling serviceability – it seems likely that only 27 per cent of Soviet tanks were fully operational at the time of the German invasion.

THE 'COUNTDOWN TO WAR'

The Russo-German Non-Aggression Pact of August 1939 shocked governments across the world who could not imagine such fierce enemies making a lasting treaty. Indeed, from the beginning, both Stalin and Hitler were trying to twist its provisions for their own advantage. In less than a year, Stalin seized a great arc of territory to protect his western frontiers, including eastern Poland (September 1939), eastern Finland (March 1940), the

Tank Strengths (June 1941)

TYPE	REQUIREMENT	ACTUAL
KV Heavy Tanks	3528	508
T-34 Medium Tanks	11,760	967
T-28 Tanks (obsolete)	–	500
BT Light Tanks	7840	6000
T-26 Light Tanks	5880	11,000
T-37/38/40 Scout Tanks	476	4222
Total Tanks	29,484	23,197
Armoured Cars	7448	4819

Rumanian provinces of Northern Bukhovina and Bessarabia (June 1940) and Lithuania, Latvia and Estonia (July 1940).

These annexations greatly strengthened the Soviet strategic position – in terms of defence, they provided a valuable buffer zone protecting the industrial and agricultural resources of Belorussia and the Ukraine. However, they also brought Soviet forces within easy striking distance of potential targets essential for the German war effort – the annexation of the Rumanian provinces was especially serious as it posed a direct threat to the vital Ploesti oilfields.

Hitler had, at least temporarily, removed any threat of a war on two fronts and was able to concentrate his forces for the campaigns in Norway and France, but he was understandably concerned by Stalin's moves. Perhaps significantly, it was in July 1940 that Hitler ordered the first studies for the invasion which finally evolved into Operation *Barbarossa*, which was intended to be launched by a total of 152 divisions on 15 May 1941.

After much debate, the key roles of the *Wehrmacht*'s three main army groups were finalised:

Soviet Ground Forces (May 1940)

UNIT	STRENGTH
Headquarters	
Rifle Corps	52
Cavalry Corps	5
Infantry	
Rifle Divisions (inc Mountain & Motorized)	161
Rifle Brigades	3
Cavalry	
Cavalry Divisions	24
Cavalry Brigades	2
Armour	
Armoured Car Brigades	3
Tank Brigades	38
Separate Tank Regiments	6
Separate Armoured Car and Motorcycle Battalions	3
Airborne	
Airborne Brigades	6
Artillery	
Separate Artillery Regiments	106
Separate Artillery Battalions	12

T-26 Model 1938 light tank

CREW

SPECIFICATIONS

Weight: 10.5 tonnes (10.33 tons)
Length: 4.88m (16ft)
Width: 2.39m (7ft 10in)
Height: 2.41m (7ft 11in)
Engine: 67.86kW (91hp) GAZ-202 6-cylinder petrol
Speed: 30km/h (18.64mph)
Range: 225km (139.8 miles)
Armament: 1 x 45mm (1.8in) Model 38 tank gun, plus 3 x 7.62mm (0.3in) DT machine guns

The T-26 formed the bulk of the Soviet tank fleet in June 1941, with an estimated 11,000 vehicles in service. Huge numbers were lost during the early stages of Operation *Barbarossa* and in the winter battles of 1941/42.

■ Army Group North was to advance from East Prussia through the Baltic states and join with the Finns to take Leningrad.

■ Army Group Centre's initial operations from its concentration areas around Warsaw were intended to clear the traditional invasion route to Moscow as far as Smolensk before swinging north to help the attack on Leningrad. After the city was taken, the advance on Moscow would be resumed.

■ Army Group South, including Rumanian and Hungarian divisions, was tasked with taking the rich agricultural lands of the Ukraine and clearing the Black Sea coast.

LAYING A TRAP

The overall objective was to trap and destroy the bulk of the Red Army in a series of encirclements in western Russia before finally securing a line from Archangel to Astrakhan. The invasion's chances of success depended on the 19 Panzer divisions concentrated in four *Panzergruppen* which also incorporated the 14 motorized divisions. These were to form the cutting edge of the German offensive and had the daunting task of cutting through the massive forces that the Red Army could deploy in European Russia which totalled perhaps 170 divisions, including up to 60 tank divisions and at least 13 motorized divisions.

Most of these units were deployed close to the frontier and the accepted explanation for this has been Stalin's obsession with securing his newly conquered territories. German wartime claims that they invaded to pre-empt a Soviet attack have almost always been dismissed as crude propaganda, but this view has been challenged as new material has emerged from Soviet archives. One of the most significant of these documents is the plan formulated by Zhukov in May 1941 within a few months of his appointment as Chief of the Soviet General Staff. The introduction to the draft plan stated:

'In view of the fact that Germany at present keeps its army fully mobilized with its rear services deployed, it has the capacity of deploying ahead of us and striking a sudden blow. To prevent this I consider it important not to leave the operational initiative to the German command in any circumstances, but to anticipate the enemy and attack the German army at the moment when it is in the process of deploying and before it has time to organize its front and the coordination of its various arms'.

This proposed a pre-emptive strike by 152 Red Army divisions (including 76 tank divisions and 44 mechanized divisions) against the Axis forces assembling in German-occupied Poland. Whilst this may have been no more than a contingency plan, it is at least possible that Stalin really was intending to make just such an attack. Certainly the first months of 1941 saw frantic activity as 500,000 Red Army reservists were mobilized in March, followed by a further 300,000 a few days later. In the same

Tank Division Equipment (June 1941)

UNIT	ARM CAR	T-26	T-34	T-40	KV	37MM AA	122MM HOW	152MM HOW	FLAME THROW	50MM MORT	82MM MORT	76MM INF GUN	45MM AT	AAMG	MG	LMG
Divisional HQ	–	–	–	–	–	–	–	–	–	–	–	–	–	–	–	–
Signal Battalion	–	–	–	–	–	–	–	–	–	–	–	–	–	–	–	–
Recon Battalion	15	–	–	17	–	–	–	–	–	3	–	–	–	–	–	12
2 x Tank Rgt, each	13	–	1	–	–	–	–	–	–	–	–	–	–	3	–	–
Heavy Tank Btn	3	–	–	–	31	–	–	–	–	–	–	–	–	–	–	–
2 x Med Btns, each	3	–	52	–	–	–	–	–	–	–	–	–	–	–	–	–
Flamethrower Btn	3	10	–	–	–	–	–	–	27	–	–	–	–	–	–	–
Motor Infantry Rgt	10	–	–	–	–	–	–	–	–	27	6	4	6	6	18	108
Artillery Regiment	–	–	–	–	1	–	12	12	–	–	–	–	–	3	–	12
Anti-Aircraft Btn	–	–	–	–	–	12	–	–	–	–	–	–	–	–	–	–
Pioneer Battalion	–	–	–	–	–	–	–	–	–	–	–	–	–	–	–	–

month, Stalin ordered the formation of a total of 20 new Mechanized Corps and 106 new Air Regiments, only a small fraction of which were anything like combat-ready at the time of the German invasion. (This lack of combat readiness does not necessarily rule out the possibility that Stalin was planning a prc-cmptive attack – in the aftermath of the purges it is entirely possible that no one dared to tell him about the true condition of these formations.)

Heavy Tank Battalion (1941)

KV-1 heavy tanks: 31
BA armoured cars: 3

When fully up to strength, the heavy tank battalions were the world's most powerful armoured units of their size in 1941. However, only a small number of these battalions were fully operational at the time of the German invasion, as the Red Army had only 508 of the 3528 KVs it required to equip all its units.

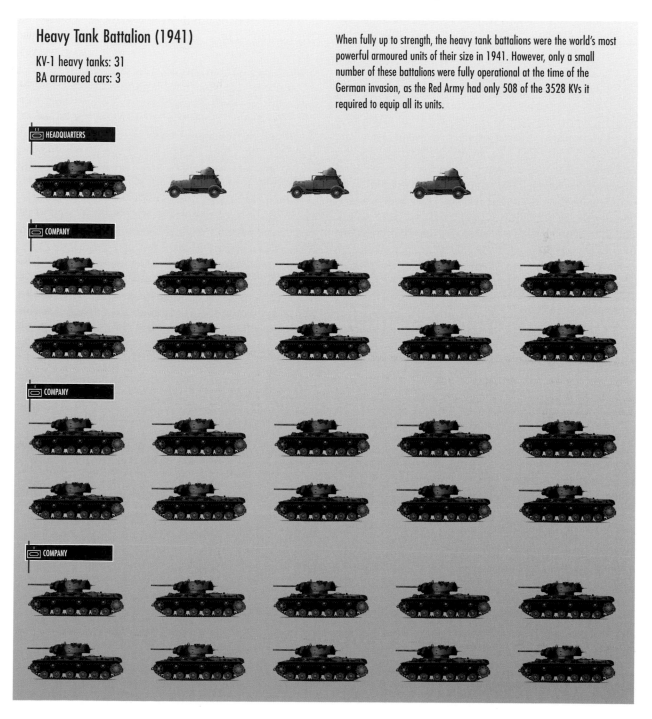

Operation *Barbarossa*

The German offensive achieved almost complete surprise when it opened on 22 June 1941. The *panzergruppen* quickly broke through the Russian lines; General Hoepner's *Panzergruppe* IV destroyed the Soviet III and XII Mechanized Corps before driving through the Baltic states as the spearhead of Army Group North's advance on Leningrad, which was besieged by 8 September.

*P*anzergruppen II (Guderian) and III (Hoth) leading Army Group Centre's advance pulled off a spectacular encirclement east of Minsk which trapped about 30 Soviet divisions (including six Mechanized Corps) barely a week after the invasion began. These units were destroyed by the following German infantry divisions over the next three weeks whilst Guderian and Hoth raced on to trap a further 21 Red Army divisions around Smolensk in mid-July. Far away to the south, Kleist's *Panzergruppe* I attached to Army Group South thrust deep into the Ukraine, advancing to within 20 kilometres (12 miles) of Kiev by 11 July after decimating counter-attacks by the Mechanized Corps of the Kiev Special Military District.

Evidence of the Red Army's staggering ineptitude was to be seen everywhere during the first months of the German offensive. Poorly trained Russian radio operators used simple codes which were easily broken by German monitoring stations. (It was not uncommon for German commanders to receive intercepted Red Army orders before situation reports from their own troops.) Sometimes desperate Soviet signals officers resorted to sending messages in clear – as one lieutenant remarked 'What else are we supposed to do when they want everything sent without delay?'

The most glaring contrasts between the two sides lay in their basic methods of operation – German forces were supremely professional, working on the basis of *Auftragstaktik*, which today has been widely adopted by the world's leading armies under the title of 'Mission Command'. Detailed written orders were largely abolished and replaced by general directives – for example a unit might be told to take a village, in which case the unit commander was free to use whatever tactics were appropriate in the circumstances and was expected to take full

KV-1 Model 1941

Although Soviet tank production dramatically increased in the first half of 1942, this was not matched by comparable improvements in strategic or tactical skill. A high proportion of the new Red Army armoured formations were destroyed in Timoshenko's over-ambitious Kharkov offensive in May 1942.

CREW

SPECIFICATIONS

Weight: 45 tonnes (44.3 tons)
Length: 6.75m (22ft 2in)
Width: 3.32m (10ft 10in)
Height: 2.71m (8ft 9in)
Engine: 450kW (600hp) 12-cylinder V-2 diesel
Speed: 35km/h (22mph)
Range: 335km (208 miles)
Radio: None
Armament: 1 x 76mm (3in) F-32 tank gun; 3 x 7.62mm (0.3in) DT MGs

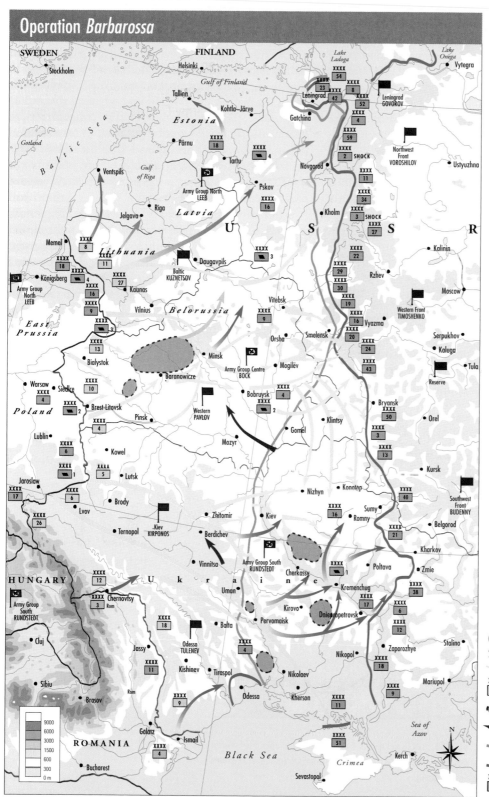

Operation *Barbarossa*

22 JUNE – EARLY OCTOBER 1941
The German plan involved three army groups (North, South and Centre), with the bulk of the forces concentrated in Army Groups North and Centre. Army Group Centre, which contained around half the German armour, was to shatter Soviet forces in Belorussia before turning to assist Army Group North in the drive on Leningrad. Army Group South, meanwhile, was to deal with Soviet forces in the Ukraine. At 3.05 a.m. on 22 June, Army Group North began the drive to Leningrad. By the evening of the first day, the leading panzers were 60km (37 miles) into Lithuania. By the end of the second day, only the wrecks of 140 Soviet tanks lay between the Panzer divisions and Pskov. But the *Panzergruppe*'s infantry could not keep up. The terrain encountered on the Soviet side of the border was so marshy and impenetrable that even the motorized infantry were reduced to the pace of the marching columns.

Operation Barbarossa
22 June – early October 1941

- German attack
- Soviet positions, 22 June
- Soviet units encircled
- Soviet counter-attacks
- German front line, end of August
- German front line, early October
- Soviet positions, early October

advantage of any unexpected opportunities. On the other side of the front line, Soviet commanders simply did not know what to do in the absence of detailed orders – one of the most telling episodes on the first day of the war was the German interception of a mass of frantic signals from Soviet units to their HQs all plaintively asking the same question: 'We're being fired on – what shall we do?'

THE TECHNICAL BALANCE

By mid-July, Soviet losses were staggering, totalling perhaps 5700 AFVs, 4500 guns and 610,000 prisoners whilst the Soviet Air Force had been virtually wiped out, losing almost 6000 aircraft. Complete German air superiority allowed the *Luftwaffe* to mount unopposed reconnaissance and bombing sorties which disrupted many of these counter-attacks before they got under way. Those that survived the air attacks were usually badly mishandled, often being delivered by armour without any proper infantry or artillery support. In most cases, Russian armour was shot to pieces by the German anti-tank units screening the flanks of the advance before the remnants were mopped up by the panzers.

On the technical level, the majority of Russian AFVs were far outclassed by their German counterparts – very few Red Army vehicles had radios which reinforced their tendency to stick rigidly to detailed orders regardless of rapidly changing battlefield conditions, whereas the radio-controlled panzers could rapidly concentrate to defeat the clumsy counter-attacks. (Hapless Red Army tank crews soon found that the signal flags on which they were supposed to rely were almost impossible to read accurately under combat conditions.)

The thinly-armoured BTs and T-26s which formed such a high proportion of the total Soviet tank strength at the beginning of the campaign were vulnerable to almost all German tank and anti-tank guns at normal battle ranges. In contrast, the Soviet 45mm (1.8in) in both its anti-tank and tank gun versions could only penetrate the up-armoured Panzer IIIH/J and Panzer IVE/F at point-blank range. The three-man turrets of the Panzer III and Panzer IV which allowed the commander to concentrate on command duties also gave them a distinct edge in tank versus tank actions against most Red Army AFVs with their two-man turrets in

BT-7A artillery tank

CREW

SPECIFICATIONS

Weight: 14.5 tonnes (14.27 tons)
Length: 5.66m (18ft 6.8in)
Width: 2.29m (7ft 6in)
Height: 2.52m (8ft 3in)
Engine: 372.85kW (500hp) M-17T V12 petrol
Speed: 86km/h (53.44mph)
Range: 250km (155.34 miles)
Armament: 1 x 76.2mm (3in) Model 27/32 tank howitzer, plus 3 x 7.62mm (0.3in) DT machine guns

This variant of the BT-7 was armed with a 76.2mm (3in) howitzer for the close support role. The howitzer's HE shell was far more effective against anti-tank guns or field defences than the equivalent rounds fired by the 45mm (1.8in) tank guns of the standard BT tanks.

which the commander was distracted by having to act as gunner or loader.

LENINGRAD AND BELORUSSIA

This picture of panzer superiority was only marred by the relatively few encounters with T34s and KVs, both of which were formidable opponents. Apart from the few Panzer IIIs armed with the 50mm (1.97in) L/60 gun, the T-34's sloped armour was almost invulnerable to all German AFV weapons except at point-blank range, whilst the KVs could only be effectively countered by 88mm (3.5in) Flak guns or medium artillery.

The KVs had the greatest psychological impact as even single vehicles could impose significant delays on the German advance. On 23/24 June, a single KV-2 of III Mechanized Corps cut the supply route to 6th Panzer Division's bridgeheads across the Dubissa River in Lithuania for over 24 hours. It proved invulnerable to fire from German tanks and was only destroyed by an '88' brought up to close range whilst a panzer platoon acted as a decoy.

Such isolated examples of skill and courage could do little more than harass Army Group North's advance on Leningrad. By mid-July, the North Western Front had sustained 75,000 casualties, besides losing 2500 AFVs, 3600 guns and at least 1000 aircraft. In little more than 10 weeks, Lithuania, Latvia and Estonia were overrun and German artillery was shelling Leningrad.

On paper, General Pavlov's Western Front was a match for Army Group Centre as it had 700,000 men, over 2000 tanks (including 383 T-34s and KVs) plus 1900 aircraft, but events were to turn out very differently.

Army Group Centre's initial offensive into Belorussia achieved almost complete surprise. Its progress was greatly assisted by *Luftflotte* II's thousand or so aircraft which effectively destroyed the VVS (Red Air Force) units assigned to the Western Front within a matter of days. Pavlov's initial reaction was to order an immediate counter-attack by Tenth Army which was concentrated around Bialystok – this failed and simply ensured

KV-2 heavy artillery tank

CREW

SPECIFICATIONS

Weight: 52 tonnes (51.1 tons)
Length: 6.79m (22ft 3in)
Width: 3.32m (10ft 10in)
Height: 3.65m (12ft)
Engine: 410kW (550hp) V2K V12 diesel
Speed: 26km/h (16mph)
Range: 150km (93 miles)
Armament: 1 x 152mm (5.9in) M-10T howitzer, plus 3 x 7.62mm (0.3in) machine guns

Even the most heavily-armed Soviet tanks proved to be ineffective against well-constructed Finnish defences during the Winter War. The KV-2 was designed in early 1940 as the 'assault gun' counterpart of the KV-1 heavy tank and the prototypes carried out firing trials against captured Finnish bunkers with devastating results. The type was far less successful when committed to action in the summer of 1941 – whilst its armour and firepower were impressive, it was prone to frequent breakdowns. (The experience of 41st Tank Division was typical – it quickly lost 22 of its 33 KV-2s, five to enemy action and 17 to a depressingly wide variety of mechanical failures.) Production of the type ended in October 1941 after a total of 334 vehicles had been completed.

that Tenth Army would be the first major Soviet formation to be encircled and destroyed when the Germans sealed off the Bialystok pocket on 25 June. A further counter-attack by VI and XI Mechanized Corps, plus VI Cavalry Corps, was ordered against the flank of *Panzergruppe* III which was making rapid progress towards Vilnius. The operation was harried by constant air attacks and finally collapsed when the Soviet forces hit a strong German anti-tank screen supported by infantry.

On 28 June, *Panzergruppen* II and III linked up east of Minsk, the Belorussian capital, which was captured 24 hours later. In six days, they had advanced over 320 kilometres (200 miles), covering a third of the distance to Moscow. When the remnants of the Soviet Third, Fourth, Tenth and Thirteenth Armies finally surrendered, the Red Army had lost roughly 420,000 men (including 290,000 prisoners) plus 2500 tanks and 1500 guns. However, the panzers had far out-run their supporting infantry divisions which were essential for effectively sealing the pocket and as many as 250,000 Soviet troops were able to break out after abandoning their heavy equipment.

STALIN'S RESPONSE

The run of German victories provoked characteristically drastic action from Stalin who in early July had General Pavlov, the commander of the Western Front facing Army Group Centre, arrested and shot, together with his Chief of Staff and chief signals officer. This warning was reinforced in the next few weeks by the restoration of the dual command principle (abolished in 1940) under which each unit's political commissar shared authority with its CO. All too often the effect was simply to saddle hard-pressed COs with political officers whose fanaticism was only matched by their military incompetence. At times it must have been hard for senior officers to decide if the Germans or the commissars posed the greater threat – Corps Commissar Vashugin commanding a counter-attack by a reinforced tank division from IV Mechanized Corps directed it into a swamp, losing the entire formation in the fiasco.

DISASTER AT KIEV

Operation *Barbarossa*'s most demanding tasks were assigned to Field Marshal von Rundstedt's Army Group South. He only had Kleist's *Panzergruppe* I to provide the armoured punch for a motley collection of forces, including ill-equipped Rumanian, Hungarian and Italian formations.

These faced General Kirponos' Southwestern Front, the best-equipped Soviet Front which included a total of eight mechanized corps fielding a total of 4800 AFVs. The initial Soviet response to the invasion was to activate the Zhukov pre-emptive

A column of T-34 Model 1941 tanks waits in a holding area somewhere in the Crimea in October 1941. The driver's large hatch offered a quick escape route if the tank was hit and the driver could not escape through the main turret.

strike plan. All eight mechanized corps were ordered to destroy *Panzergruppe* I before launching an offensive across the frontier into German-occupied Poland to seize Lublin. Unfortunately for Kirponos, some of his forces had to cover roughly 400 kilometres (250 miles) to intercept Kleist, which was a recipe for disaster given *Luftwaffe* air superiority.

Kirponos planned to destroy *Panzergruppe* I with flank attacks by six mechanized corps – a total of 3700 tanks. The corps' concentration was chaotic – air attacks and mechanical breakdowns took a steady toll of tanks and support vehicles long before they encountered Kleist's panzers. On 26 June the counter-attack was made in the Brony-Dubno area. Elements of VIII, IX, XV and XIX Mechanized Corps were sent against Kleist's flanks, with the aim of cutting the *panzergruppe* in two. Although 16th Panzer Division took significant casualties and the *panzergruppe*'s advance was delayed for several days, by the beginning of July all four mechanized corps had been comprehensively defeated. Southwestern Front had sustained over 173,000 casualties, besides losing an estimated 4381 tanks and 1218 aircraft.

As Army Group Centre's advance approached Smolensk in mid-July, Hitler became increasingly concerned at the potential threat to its southern flank posed by the substantial Soviet forces in the Ukraine. By late August, he was convinced that Army Group South needed reinforcement to eliminate this threat and ordered Guderian's *Panzergruppe* II into the Ukraine. Guderian made rapid progress, linking up with Kleist on 16 September and trapping the South-Western Front in the vast Kiev pocket, which surrendered ten days later, with the loss of approximately 665,000 men, 900 tanks and 3700 guns.

OPERATION TYPHOON

As it became clear that the Kiev pocket was doomed, Hitler ordered that Leningrad was to be blockaded and starved into surrender in order to free resources for a renewed attack on Moscow. To give the new offensive a reasonable chance of success before it became bogged down by the autumn rains, both Army Group North and Army Group South were stripped of most of their panzer units. Guderian's command was re-designated Second Panzer Army and launched the drive on

Moscow (code-named Operation Typhoon) on 30 September whilst the other two *panzergruppen* began their attacks two days later.

Both sides were now feeling the effects of three months of combat – the Red Army's massive losses forced the disbandment of the Mechanized Corps in mid-July and in August most of the surviving armour was concentrated in tank brigades with a nominal strength of 93 tanks in a single tank regiment plus a motor rifle battalion. The tank regiment had a heavy company with KVs, a company of T-34s and a third company equipped with whatever light tanks were available. By September, combat casualties had forced a reduction in the paper strength of these units to 67 tanks, although very few had that many.

On the other side of the lines, the panzer divisions were in better shape, but their tanks and other vehicles were in need of major overhauls after covering thousands of kilometres across country or over appalling dirt roads. The infantry divisions (which had virtually no motor vehicles) were exhausted by the epic marches needed to keep up with the rapidly advancing panzers, but all were buoyed up by the scale of their victories and the thought that Moscow was now within reach. The *panzergruppen* quickly broke through the Soviet

Tank Brigade, December 1941

UNIT	MANPOWER	EQUIPMENT
Brigade Headquarters	22	
Headquarters Company	170	2 light MGs
2 Tank Battalions, each		
Battalion HQ	20	
Light Tank Company	17	8 T-60
Medium Tank Company	43	10 T-34
Heavy Tank Company	27	5 KV-1
Trains Platoon	40	
Motorized Rifle Battalion		407
Battalion HQ		
2 Rifle Companies, each	108	9 light MGs, 2 MGs, 3 anti-tank rifles
Submachine Gun Company	79	
Mortar Company	42	6 82mm
Trains		
Anti-Aircraft Battery	47	3 Heavy MGs, 4 37mm
Trains & Medical	206	

lines and by 9 October had pulled off two more major encirclements, one between Smolensk and Vyazma and the other around Bryansk, netting a total of 657,000 prisoners, 1241 AFVs plus 5396 guns. On 6 October the first snows fell and rapidly melted, turning the roads to thick, clinging mud which slowed the German advance and increased the already alarming rate of breakdowns.

Despite this, Hoth's *Panzergruppe* IV captured Kalinin on 14 October, cutting the Moscow-Leningrad highway and the main north-south railway, sparking off a temporary panic in the capital. By mid-November, sharp frosts had frozen the mud and restored the panzers' mobility which allowed a renewed drive on Moscow. During the next two weeks, the Germans came tantalisingly close to taking the city and by 4 December, leading German units were within 45 kilometres (28 miles)

of Moscow when plummeting temperatures finally brought the advance to a halt. It was so cold that guns could not be fired because oiled parts froze solid and fires had to be lit under vehicles at night to prevent their engines freezing. Very few German units had proper winter clothing and cases of severe frostbite soared, rapidly exceeding the number of battlefield casualties.

Red Army equipment was far less severely affected by the intense cold and deep snow – the T-34 was fitted with a compressed-air starting system which could operate even in the temperatures of -28°C (-18°F) which were not uncommon that winter. The wide tracks of the KV-1 and T-34 resulted in low ground pressure, which allowed them to operate far more easily in deep snow than German AFVs with their narrower tracks and higher ground pressure.

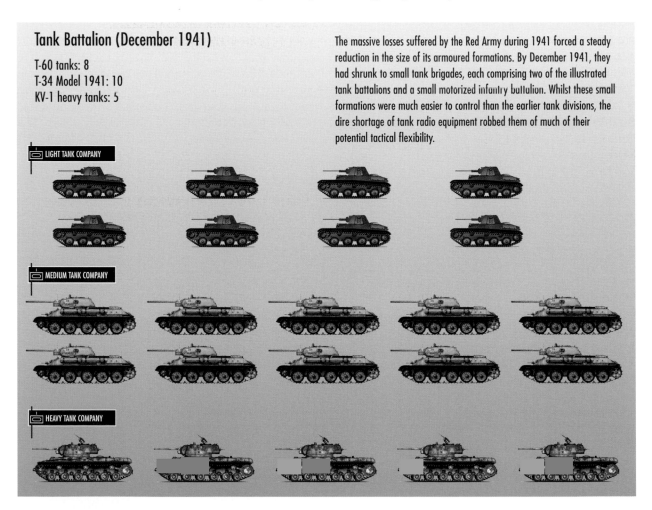

Tank Battalion (December 1941)

T-60 tanks: 8
T-34 Model 1941: 10
KV-1 heavy tanks: 5

The massive losses suffered by the Red Army during 1941 forced a steady reduction in the size of its armoured formations. By December 1941, they had shrunk to small tank brigades, each comprising two of the illustrated tank battalions and a small motorized infantry battalion. Whilst these small formations were much easier to control than the earlier tank divisions, the dire shortage of tank radio equipment robbed them of much of their potential tactical flexibility.

LIGHT TANK COMPANY

MEDIUM TANK COMPANY

HEAVY TANK COMPANY

Ebb and Flow of Battle: Dec 1941 – Nov 1942

As the German advance ground to a halt in early December, the Soviet war machine was showing signs of recovery. Despite the loss of 200 divisions and 4.3 million casualties, a ruthless mobilisation programme had brought the Red Army's strength up to 4.196 million men.

However, this was at the expense of a further reduction in industrial manpower which had already been hit by the loss of population (35 million) in territories overrun by Axis forces. Coupled with the disruption caused by the evacuation of war industries, this meant that the newly raised and sketchily trained forces suffered from a dire shortage of all types of weaponry from tanks to small arms.

In this crisis, there was no chance to rebuild the grandiose mechanized corps with their official tank strengths of over 1000 tanks apiece – the tanks simply did not exist and most surviving commanders were too inexperienced to cope with anything other than the simplest units. The small tank brigades which had replaced all larger formations in August 1941 shrank steadily – in December they were reduced to 46 tanks apiece, with a further reduction to 42 in January 1942 and a final cut to 27 tanks in February 1942. (These were all 'official strengths' – in practice, many brigades were significantly weaker.)

By 5 December 1941, average temperatures around Moscow had dropped to -12°C (10°F) and the *Wehrmacht* lay horribly exposed at the end of tenuous supply lines, with frostbite casualties climbing to 100,000 during the month. It was the ideal time for a Soviet counter-attack which was launched by a force totalling eight tank brigades, 15 rifle divisions and three cavalry divisions, many of which had been transferred from the Far East.

Shortages of tanks and artillery, combined with sheer inexperience led to heavy Soviet casualties, but the initial counter-attacks succeeded in pushing back Army Group Centre and eliminating the immediate threat to Moscow. Buoyed by this success, Stalin became over-confident, ordering a succession of further attacks.

On 5 January he announced to a horrified meeting of Stavka that the current operations were to be supplemented by a general offensive from the Baltic to the Black Sea to defeat Army Group North, destroy Army Group Centre and recapture the Donbass and the Crimea.

None of the objectives were attained, although the general offensive was maintained for almost two months at the cost of appalling casualties, which were worsened by continuing acute shortages of the most basic weapons and ammunition. Nonetheless, Axis forces were pushed back between 80 and 300 kilometres (50 and 186 miles), and Red Army morale was boosted by the arrival of Lend-Lease equipment including the first Matilda and Valentine infantry tanks.

DISASTERS – KHARKOV AND THE CRIMEA

In the spring of 1942, Stalin became convinced of the need for a major operation in the Ukraine to pre-empt an anticipated German offensive. Marshal Timoshenko was given the objective of recapturing Kharkov, but expanded the scope of the operation to include the recapture of a great swathe of territory as far west as the Dnieper – a total advance of roughly 250 kilometres (155 miles). Stavka's planning staff were concerned that this was dangerously over-ambitious, but Stalin angrily dismissed such reservations, asking 'Are we supposed to sit in defence, idling away our time and wait for the Germans to attack first?'

The operation began on 12 May, with a thrust by Southwestern Front from Volchansk to the north of Kharkov, whilst the Southern Front attacked from the Barvenkovo Salient to the south of the city. The offensive was spearheaded by 15 of the Red Army's 20 operational tank brigades whose initial objective was to envelop Kharkov before driving westwards to the Dnieper. Timoshenko achieved initial successes by sheer weight of numbers, but he was unable to maintain the tempo of the offensive in the face of constant German counter-attacks.

Nonetheless, Soviet forces were still advancing on 17 May when Kleist's Army Group A (First

Panzer Army and Seventeenth Army) launched a devastating counter-offensive against the southern flank of the Barvenkovo Salient. Stalin rejected increasingly urgent requests from Timoshenko to call off the offensive and a bizarre situation developed as Soviet armour continued to advance westwards whilst Kleist's panzers were cutting through the neck of the salient. By the time that Stalin authorized a retreat, it was too late – the salient was sealed off on 23 May and during the next six days the trapped units were virtually wiped out. Red Army losses probably totalled 208,000 men – 22 rifle divisions, seven cavalry divisions and 15 tank brigades were destroyed. Equipment losses were equally severe – 1200 tanks, 1600 guns, 3200 mortars and 540 aircraft.

The disaster at Kharkov vividly demonstrated the fragility of the Red Army at this stage of the war. Its ranks were full of barely-trained conscripts and the officer corps, emasculated by Stalin's purges, was struggling to learn the basics of armoured warfare in the midst of campaigning against a sophisticated enemy.

All ranks went in fear of the NKVD – whose malign influence was personified by Lev Mekhlis,

the Stavka representative to the Crimean Front, who was also Head of the Main Political Administration of the Red Army. He was an arrogant bully who quarrelled with General Kozlov, the Front commander, and engineered the dismissal of his highly competent chief of staff, the future Marshal Tolbukhin.

Mekhlis was largely responsible for failing to effectively attack von Manstein's force besieging Sevastopol when it was at its most vulnerable in early 1942 and, when the Germans counter-attacked on 8 May, his incompetence contributed to the destruction of the Crimean Front in barely 10 days. As at Kharkov, there was little co-ordination between the Soviet tank brigades whose 350 AFVs were committed to action piecemeal, negating their numerical superiority over the sole German armoured formation, the under-strength 22nd Panzer Division, which was largely equipped with obsolescent Panzer 38(t)s.

Once again, Soviet losses were staggering – three armies totalling 21 divisions had been broken and von Manstein's forces had taken more than 170,000 prisoners, besides capturing 258 tanks and over 1100 guns.

Infantry Tank Mark III, Valentine Mark II

CREW

SPECIFICATIONS

Weight: 17.27 tonnes (17 tons)
Length: 5.89m (19ft 4in)
Width: 2.64m (8ft 8in)
Height: 2.29m (7ft 6in)
Engine: 97.73kW (131hp) AEC A190
    6-cylinder diesel
Speed: 24km/h (14.9mph)
Range: 145km (90 miles)
Armament: 1 x 40mm (1.57in) OQF 2
    pounder gun, plus 1 x 7.92mm (0.31in)
    Besa machine gun

The Valentine was regarded by the Red Army as the best British tank supplied under Lend-Lease. (Its popularity was such that the type was kept in production throughout 1944 purely to meet Soviet requirements.) A total of 3782 Valentines of all Marks were shipped to Russia between 1941 and 1945, of which 320 were lost en route.

Defending Stalingrad and the Caucasus

In April 1942, Hitler chose to make his main effort for that year at the southern end of the vast front with the aim of taking Stalingrad and driving into the Caucasus to seize the oilfields of Maikop, Grozny and Baku (Plan Blue).

Timoshenko's offensive at Kharkov had disrupted preparations for the offensive, but the magnitude of that disaster (almost 75 per cent of the Red Army's tanks were destroyed) meant that there was very little left to oppose the panzers as they struck deep into southern Russia on 28 June. By 5 July, Hoth's Fourth Panzer Army had taken Voronezh, reinforcing Stalin's instinctive belief that Moscow was still the primary German objective. Whilst Stavka concentrated on directing reserves to counter the illusory threat to Moscow, Paulus' Sixth Army was making for Stalingrad and Kleist's First Panzer Army was well on its way to the oilfields of the Caucasus. Both the Stalingrad Front and the Southern Front temporarily collapsed, with the loss of 350,000 men and over 2000 AFVs.

SLOW PROGRESS

In a matter of weeks, Kleist's First Panzer Army took Maikop, whilst Hoth's Fourth Panzer Army led the drive on Stalingrad. The sheer scale of the advance soon began to cause problems as the panzers outran their overstretched supply lines, allowing the Russians just enough time to reinforce the city's garrison with the Sixty-second Army before the Germans arrived in August. Thus instead of taking a largely undefended city, more and more German forces were sucked in to fierce street fighting in which their rate of advance slowed to no more than a few hundred metres a day.

As Sixth Army and Fourth Panzer Army became ever more deeply committed to fighting in Stalingrad itself, responsibility for protection of their long, vulnerable flanks had to be assigned to comparatively weak and ill-equipped satellite armies. Eighth Italian Army and Third Rumanian Army held a long sector of front north-west of the city, whilst Fourth Rumanian Army held the line south of Stalingrad.

At first, Kleist's drive into the Caucasus achieved spectacular results – First Panzer Army took the oilfields at Maikop on 9 August and pushed on towards Grozny and Baku. However, the dire over-stretch caused by Hitler's decision to take Stalingrad and the Caucasus simultaneously, rather than consecutively, rapidly became apparent.

Ultimately, so many resources were diverted to the interminable battle of attrition in Stalingrad that Kleist was robbed of any chance of taking the remaining oilfields and was left stranded deep in the Caucasus in a dangerously exposed salient.

OPERATION URANUS

In September 1942, Stalin approved plans for Operation Uranus, an ambitious counter-offensive intended to punch through the Third and Fourth Rumanian armies, before enveloping Sixth Army and Fourth Panzer Army. Throughout the autumn of 1942, the Red Army built up reserves around

Tank Corps Weapons Strength, 1942

WEAPON	STRENGTH
HQ:	
Medium tank	3
Tank Brigade x 3:	
Light tank	21
Medium tank	32
LMG	18
MG	4
ATR	6
82mm (3.2in) mortar	6
76mm (3in) guns	4
Motorized Rifle Brigade:	
LMG	110
MG	18
HMG	3
ATR	54
82mm (3.2in) mortar	30
120mm (4.7in) mortar	4
45mm (1.8in) AT	12
37mm (1.45in) AA	12
76mm (3in) guns	12
Reconnaissance Battalion:	
Armoured car	20
Rocket Launcher Battalion:	
Rocket launcher	8

Stalingrad whilst feeding in just enough reinforcements to prevent any decisive German breakthrough. General Chuikov's Sixty-Second Army held the city itself, steadily wearing down Sixth Army and Fourth Panzer Army. At the same time, Zhukov steadily assembled his forces, including 894 tanks and 13,500 guns to strike at the Rumanian forces on either side of Stalingrad.

When the Southwestern Front launched its attack on Third Rumanian Army on 19 November, the 80 minute Soviet barrage by at least 3000 guns could be heard 50 kilometres (31 miles) away. A 12-kilometre (7.5-mile) gap was ripped in the Rumanian defences, which was rapidly exploited by Fifth Tank Army. Twenty-four hours later, the Stalingrad Front's offensive hit Fourth Rumanian Army, tearing a 30-kilometre (18-mile) hole in its line before launching IV Mechanized and IV Cavalry Corps into the breach.

Most German planners had simply not believed that the Red Army had the resources or the skill to conduct an offensive on this scale and Soviet armour was now being employed far more effectively than even a few months earlier. In contrast, the German response was clumsy and ineffective. XXXXVIII Panzer Corps had been assigned to act as an armoured reserve for Third Rumanian Army, but it was an exceptionally weak

formation, comprising 22nd Panzer Division with only 45 operational tanks and 1st Rumanian Tank Division with 40 R-2 tanks (obsolete Panzer 35(t)s). Despite being massively outnumbered by Soviet armour, these two divisions managed to break out to the West.

The under-strength elements of Fourth Panzer Army which attempted to block Fifth Tank Army's advance at the Don crossings near Kalach were not so fortunate. They were inadequately briefed and committed to an understandably rushed deployment with low stocks of fuel and ammunition. Although they reached Kalach just ahead of the Soviets, their small ad hoc combat teams lacked infantry support to hold vital ground and were quickly overrun by Soviet armour operating en masse.

On 23 November, the Red Army pincers closed at Sovietskiy, 20 kilometres (12 miles) southeast of Kalach, trapping an estimated 300,000 Axis troops in Stalingrad. The tables had been decisively turned.

Infantry of the Southwestern Front's Twenty-First Army advance past a knocked-out T-70 light tank on the banks of the Don at Kalach, November 1942. It was here that the Fifth Tank Army broke through the Fourth Panzer Army's defences to link up with the Fourth Mechanized Corps and trap the Sixth Army in Stalingrad. (The transport and spectators on the bridge make it highly likely that this is a staged propaganda photograph.)

Tank Brigade, November 1942

T-34 Model 1943: 32
T-70 light tank: 21

By late 1942, tank brigades were receiving more T-34s, although there were still too few to dispense with the light tanks. However, more and more of these light tanks were T-70s, which were far better armed than the earlier T-60s. The tactical flexibility of tank formations was still hampered since only the company and platoon HQ vehicles were fitted with radios.

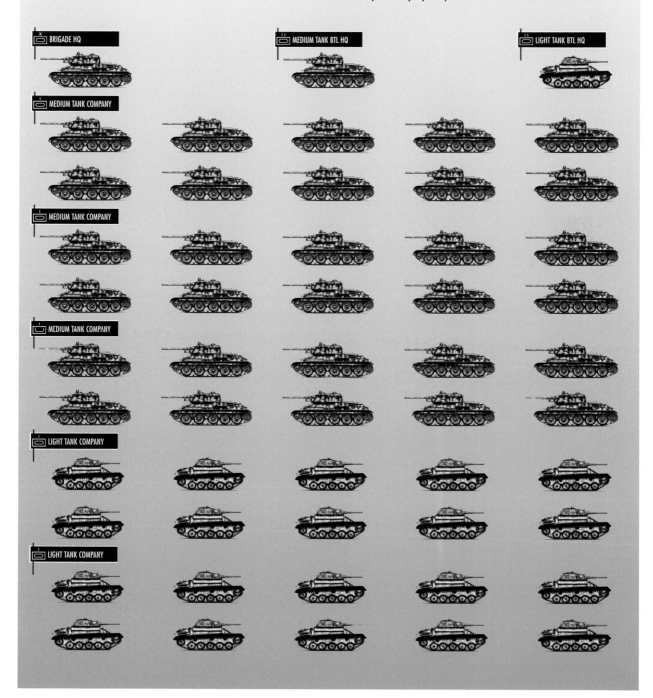

BRIGADE HQ

MEDIUM TANK BTL HQ

LIGHT TANK BTL HQ

MEDIUM TANK COMPANY

MEDIUM TANK COMPANY

MEDIUM TANK COMPANY

LIGHT TANK COMPANY

LIGHT TANK COMPANY

Chapter 2

Building an Elite:
Fifth Guards
Tank Army

Stalin is supposed to have remarked that, 'Quantity has a quality
all of its own.' However, a succession of Soviet disasters in the early stages of
Operation *Barbarossa* showed that the Red Army's sheer numerical superiority would
count for nothing unless it could be effectively deployed. The vast pre-war mechanized
corps, each theoretically comprising well over 1000 AFVs, were totally unmanageable
by the largely ill-trained and demoralized commanders who had
survived Stalin's purges.

It took much costly, bloody trial and error before the Red Army could
nurture the officers needed to develop and command tank armies – large, resilient
armoured formations which could absorb the worst attacks that the veterans of the
Panzerwaffe could throw at them. Moreover, these formations were then to prove
capable of spearheading strategic offensives which would ultimately carry them
on to Berlin, despite the most desperate and
skilful German resistance.

OPPOSITE: Soviet infantry file past a disabled German Panzer V Panther from an unidentified unit that has been wrecked by
its crew. Demolition charges have blown off the turret and it has been purposely driven off its tracks. Mechanical failure
dogged the Panther's effectiveness at Kursk.

Tank Armies

The tank armies which evolved from 1942–1945 were a uniquely Soviet solution to the problem of creating large armoured formations capable of sustaining major offensive operations, whilst retaining a high degree of centralized control.

Few Soviet commanders at any level had the ability to successfully practise the *Wehrmacht*'s system of *Auftragstaktik* – mission command – under which a formation or unit was assigned a particular mission and it was then left up to the commander to decide how to carry out the task.

The Soviet system was what the Germans termed *Befehlstatik* – order command – which required detailed centralized planning and the issue of equally detailed orders which had to be followed to the letter. In the early stages of the war, with the Red Army suffering a steady succession of disastrous defeats, any failure or deviation from written orders could quite literally be fatal.

The paranoia and suspicion of the time led Stalin to consider every higher military HQ to be a potential hotbed of plots and treachery – he had General Pavlov, the commander of the Western Front, and his senior staff shot for their part in an imaginary conspiracy after their failure to halt the first devastating German offensives in the summer of 1941. (Even normal staff duties could be hazardous – shortly before his own arrest, Pavlov sent two officers to HQ Tenth Army to pass on Stalin's orders for counter-attacks when both radio and telephone links were cut. No one recognized or believed them and they were shot as German spies.)

RECKLESS OPERATIONS

Stalin slowly came to recognize that pure terror would not create a Red Army capable of defeating the highly professional *Wehrmacht* and gradually began to listen to his ablest generals, but it was a slow process. Such commanders as Zhukov and Rokossovsky proved that they were capable of defeating the German drive on Moscow, but were overruled when they protested at the over-ambitious counter-offensives which Stalin ordered in the winter of 1941/42.

These operations certainly were reckless – the Red Army's losses of manpower could be largely replaced, but the thousands of AFVs destroyed in the summer of 1941 meant that there was no immediate hope of recreating the massed armoured formations of the pre-war period. All that could be done was to form small tank brigades and even their official strengths dropped steadily from 67 tanks each in September 1941 to a mere 27 in February 1942 as the Red Army battered itself against strengthening German defences.

PRODUCTIVITY

However, the situation slowly improved from this point onwards. The flow of Lend-Lease equipment was really beginning to take effect and the tank factories which had been hastily evacuated beyond the Urals to escape the German advance were able to resume mass production.

This allowed the formation of the first new tank corps in April 1942 which were in fact the equivalent of weak armoured divisions with no more than 100 tanks apiece. Stalin was still insisting on major offensives and the few tank corps which had formed in time were committed to Timoshenko's offensive to recapture Kharkov which was launched on 11 May. The attack included the great bulk of the painfully rebuilt Red Army's armoured force – probably in the region of 1200 AFVs. Almost all of these were caught up in the disaster which occurred when the *Wehrmacht* counter-attacked and shredded Timoshenko's force. Quite possibly no more than 100 or so survived – an incredible loss for the Red Army to suffer.

Kharkov confirmed the suspicions of Soviet analysts that the existing tank corps were simply too small to remain effective combat formations for more than a few days, given the level of losses which could be expected in action. (At this time the situation was worsened by the poor equipment and

Lt Gen P.A. Rotmistrov

Rotmistrov joined the Red Army in April 1919, serving in the Russian Civil War, and the Russo-Polish War before entering the Smolensk Infantry School. He was amongst the School's students who were mobilized to suppress the Kronstadt Rebellion of March 1921. He was wounded in the assault on the fortress and was subsequently awarded the Order of the Red Banner. In the autumn of 1922, Rotmistrov resumed his officer training and was commissioned in 1924.

He initially commanded a platoon and later a rifle company in the 11th Rifle Division's 31st Rifle Regiment. His academic ability led to his selection in 1928 for a place at the prestigious Frunze Military Academy. After graduating in May 1931, he was appointed Chief of Staff of the 36th Transbaikal Rifle Division and in 1935 he was promoted to command the armoured forces of the Special Red Banner Far Eastern Army. Between 1937 and 1940 Rotmistrov served as an instructor at the Moscow Motorized and Mechanized Military Academy, specialising in armoured warfare studies and was fortunate to survive Stalin's savage purges of the Red Army. He was equally lucky to survive the disastrous Winter War against Finland in which he temporarily commanded a tank battalion and was awarded the Order of the Red Star. As one of the few officers to have gained a reputation for professionalism in the Winter War, Rotmistrov's articles in Soviet military journals influenced the development of the Red Army's future armoured warfare doctrine.

In the debacle of the German invasion, Rotmistrov helped salvage a cadre of the surrounded III Mechanized Corps in an epic eight week breakout operation. Turning down the offer of promotion to Chief of Staff of the Red Army's Armoured Forces, he took command of the 8th Tank Brigade which had just been formed from the remnants of the 2nd Tank Division and led the formation throughout the fierce winter fighting of 1941/42 in the defence of Moscow and the Soviet winter offensive. In the spring of 1942, Rotmistrov was designated as commander of the newly formed VII Tank Corps which fought in support of the defence of Stalingrad. Its outstanding performance brought his promotion to Lieutenant General and the formation's redesignation as III Guards Tank Corps.

In February 1943, Stalin appointed him as commander of the new Fifth Guards Tank Army, which, as it completed its build-up that spring, was assigned to the Steppe Front. The Front was effectively Stavka's strategic reserve. In the event, the unexpected progress of II SS Panzer Corps forced the early deployment of Fifth Guards Tank Army to prevent a major German breakthrough and the Rotmistrov's heavy losses at Prokhorovka prevented him from immediately following up the German withdrawal from the Kursk salient.

Throughout the late summer and autumn of 1943, Fifth Guards Tank Army was heavily committed to the various Soviet offensives in the Ukraine leading to the recapture of Kharkov and in early 1944, it played a key role in the reduction of the Korsun-Cherkassy Pocket. Rotmistrov's last great battle came in June 1944 when he commanded the formation in Operation *Bagration*, which destroyed the Wehrmacht's Army Group Centre. However, his reputation suffered as a result of the heavy losses which his command suffered in fierce actions with 5th Panzer Division during the offensive. In August 1944, Rotmistrov was ordered to relinquish command and take up a new post as Deputy Commander of Red Army Armoured and Mechanized Forces, which he retained for the remainder of the war.

ORBAT: Fifth Guards Tank Army, July 1943

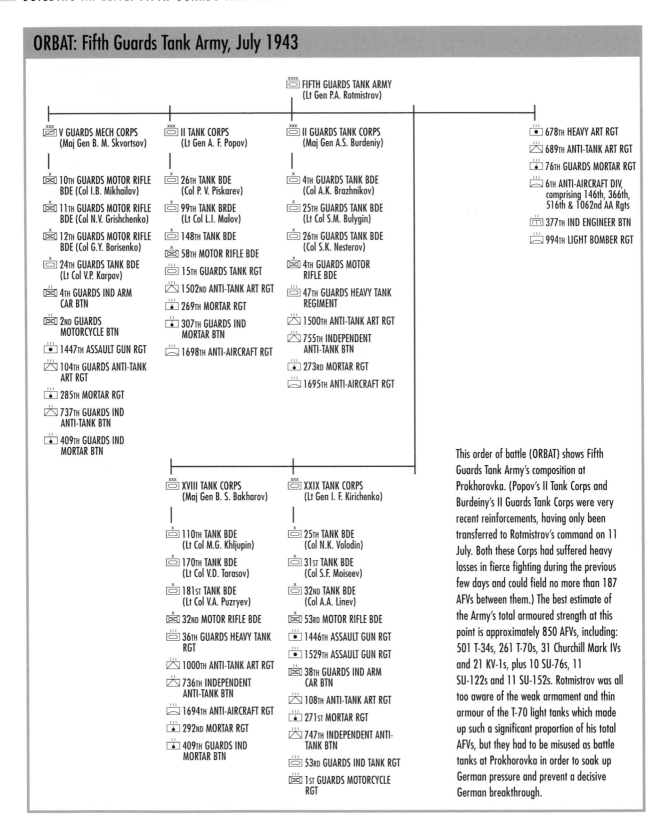

xxxx
FIFTH GUARDS TANK ARMY
(Lt Gen P.A. Rotmistrov)

xxx
V GUARDS MECH CORPS
(Maj Gen B. M. Skvortsov)

x
10TH GUARDS MOTOR RIFLE BDE (Col I.B. Mikhailov)

x
11TH GUARDS MOTOR RIFLE BDE (Col N.V. Grishchenko)

x
12TH GUARDS MOTOR RIFLE BDE (Col G.Y. Borisenko)

24TH GUARDS TANK BDE (Lt Col V.P. Karpov)

4TH GUARDS IND ARM CAR BTN

2ND GUARDS MOTORCYCLE BTN

1447TH ASSAULT GUN RGT

104TH GUARDS ANTI-TANK ART RGT

285TH MORTAR RGT

737TH GUARDS IND ANTI-TANK BTN

409TH GUARDS IND MORTAR BTN

xxx
II TANK CORPS
(Lt Gen A. F. Popov)

26TH TANK BDE
(Col P. V. Piskarev)

99TH TANK BRDE
(Lt Col L.I. Malov)

148TH TANK BDE

58TH MOTOR RIFLE BDE

15TH GUARDS TANK RGT

1502ND ANTI-TANK ART RGT

269TH MORTAR RGT

307TH GUARDS IND MORTAR BTN

1698TH ANTI-AIRCRAFT RGT

xxx
II GUARDS TANK CORPS
(Maj Gen A.S. Burdeniy)

x
4TH GUARDS TANK BDE
(Col A.K. Brazhnikov)

25TH GUARDS TANK BDE
(Lt Col S.M. Bulygin)

26TH GUARDS TANK BDE
(Col S.K. Nesterov)

4TH GUARDS MOTOR RIFLE BDE

47TH GUARDS HEAVY TANK REGIMENT

1500TH ANTI-TANK ART RGT

755TH INDEPENDENT ANTI-TANK BTN

273RD MORTAR RGT

1695TH ANTI-AIRCRAFT RGT

678TH HEAVY ART RGT

689TH ANTI-TANK ART RGT

76TH GUARDS MORTAR RGT

6TH ANTI-AIRCRAFT DIV, comprising 146th, 366th, 516th & 1062nd AA Rgts

377TH IND ENGINEER BTN

994TH LIGHT BOMBER RGT

xxx
XVIII TANK CORPS
(Maj Gen B. S. Bakharov)

x
110TH TANK BDE
(Lt Col M.G. Khljupin)

170TH TANK BDE
(Lt Col V.D. Tarasov)

181ST TANK BDE
(Lt Col V.A. Puzryev)

32ND MOTOR RIFLE BDE

36TH GUARDS HEAVY TANK RGT

1000TH ANTI-TANK ART RGT

736TH INDEPENDENT ANTI-TANK BTN

1694TH ANTI-AIRCRAFT RGT

292ND MORTAR RGT

409TH GUARDS IND MORTAR BTN

xxx
XXIX TANK CORPS
(Lt Gen I. F. Kirichenko)

x
25TH TANK BDE
(Col N.K. Volodin)

31ST TANK BDE
(Col S.F. Moiseev)

32ND TANK BDE
(Col A.A. Linev)

53RD MOTOR RIFLE BDE

1446TH ASSAULT GUN RGT

1529TH ASSAULT GUN RGT

38TH GUARDS IND ARM CAR BTN

108TH ANTI-TANK ART RGT

271ST MORTAR RGT

747TH INDEPENDENT ANTI-TANK BTN

53RD GUARDS IND TANK RGT

1ST GUARDS MOTORCYCLE RGT

This order of battle (ORBAT) shows Fifth Guards Tank Army's composition at Prokhorovka. (Popov's II Tank Corps and Burdeiny's II Guards Tank Corps were very recent reinforcements, having only been transferred to Rotmistrov's command on 11 July. Both these Corps had suffered heavy losses in fierce fighting during the previous few days and could field no more than 187 AFVs between them.) The best estimate of the Army's total armoured strength at this point is approximately 850 AFVs, including: 501 T-34s, 261 T-70s, 31 Churchill Mark IVs and 21 KV-1s, plus 10 SU-76s, 11 SU-122s and 11 SU-152s. Rotmistrov was all too aware of the weak armament and thin armour of the T-70 light tanks which made up such a significant proportion of his total AFVs, but they had to be misused as battle tanks at Prokhorovka in order to soak up German pressure and prevent a decisive German breakthrough.

training of the Red Army's tank repair and recovery units.) The solutions adopted were a steady strengthening of the corps and their grouping in tank armies.

THE FIRST TANK ARMIES

The first two tank armies (the Third and Fifth) were formed in May/June 1942. Within the next month or so the First and Fourth Tank Armies were formed under the command of the Stalingrad Front and were assigned to the Thirty-Eighth and Twenty-Eighth Armies, respectively. However they were disbanded a month later.

A special meeting of the State Committee for Defence (GKO) was held in January 1943 to develop guidelines for the organisation of the tank armies, but it took time to resolve some contentious points. (The principle that tank armies should not include any non-motorized rifle formations was only finally accepted the following month after Rotmistrov personally briefed Stalin on the subject.) Although in general each tank army was built around two tank and one mechanized corps, this was by no means an invariable rule. (In 32 out of 64 offensive operations tank armies only fielded two rather than three corps. Only one (Third Guards Tank Army) had three corps throughout the course of the war.

Whilst 'fine-tuning' the structure of tank armies was important, they could be destroyed as easily as the enormous Soviet Mechanized Corps had been in the summer of 1941 if they were incorrectly deployed. (Manstein's annihilation of Popov's Mobile Group and mauling of Third Tank Army in his 'backhand offensive' of February/March 1943 gave a stark warning of the danger of under-estimating German capabilities.)

FIFTH GUARDS TANK ARMY

Even as Manstein's forces began their advance to recapture Kharkov and Belgorod, Stalin ordered the formation of Fifth Guards Tank Army. Rotmistrov's recent briefing on the future structure of tank armies had impressed Stalin who appointed him to command the new formation. (This was despite strong pressure from the influential General Fedorenko, the Commander of Red Army Armoured and Mechanized Forces, who wanted Rotmistrov to become his deputy.) Throughout

February and March 1943 Rotmistrov put in long hours with his able Chief of Staff, Colonel Baskakov, to supervise the formation of his new command. Initially, it was one of the smaller tank armies, built around XXIX Tank Corps and V Guards Mechanized Corps. During the formation process, the army's concentration area was at Millerovo, 400 kilometres (250 miles) southeast of Kursk.

Whilst this work was in hand, Stalin kept Stavka's planning staff equally busy with the preparation of a series of studies of the Red Army's operational options for the coming campaign season. As always,

Guards Units of the Red Army

The Guards badge was formally introduced in May 1942 and comprised a gold wreath, surrounding a red enamel star on a white background. The badge was topped by a red enamel banner bearing the title 'Guards' in gold.

The Guards title was introduced on 18 September 1941 by Order No. 308 of the People's Commissar of Defence in recognition of distinguished service during the Yelnya Offensive. The 100th, 127th, 153rd and 161st Rifle Divisions were renamed as the 1st, 2nd, 3rd and 4th Guards Divisions, respectively. They were the first of many formations and units to be awarded Guards status throughout the war.

Eventually Guards units received special banners and badges in line with the steady re-introduction of traditional Soviet military symbols. As a part of this process, Red Army officers' uniforms were redesigned in early 1943 to incorporate *pogony* – shoulder boards – remarkably similar to those of the old Imperial Russian Army. (There is an apocryphal story that Stalin asked the British government to include a million metres of gold braid for senior officers' full dress uniforms in Lend-Lease shipments.)

What probably mattered more to the officers and men of Guards units were more practical advantages – privates and junior NCOs received double pay, whilst sergeants and officers were entitled to 50 per cent more pay than their line counterparts. Guards units also tended to have priority in the issue of new equipment and better rations.

his instinct was to launch a major offensive to pre-empt any further German attacks. (At the very time when Manstein's forces were on the point of recapturing Kharkov, he overruled Rokossovsky's professional judgement and insisted on a rushed offensive to encircle the reinforced German formations holding Orel which was defeated with heavy losses.)

This was probably very much in Stalin's mind when he agreed with Zhukov's proposals of 8 April that no pre-emptive Soviet offensive should be launched that summer and that: 'It would be better for us to wear down the enemy on our defences and

destroy his tanks. Subsequently, by committing fresh reserves we should finish off his main grouping with a general offensive.'

RESERVE ROLE

Fifth Guards Tank Army was earmarked as a key part of this reserve – initially coming under command of the Reserve Front, which became the Steppe Military District with effect from 15 April. (At about this time, the army was moved to Ostrogozhsk, 250 kilometres (155 miles) southeast of Kursk, to bring it closer to its anticipated area of operations.) Rotmistrov was

M3A1 Scout Car, Voronezh Front/HQ Fifth Guards Tank Army

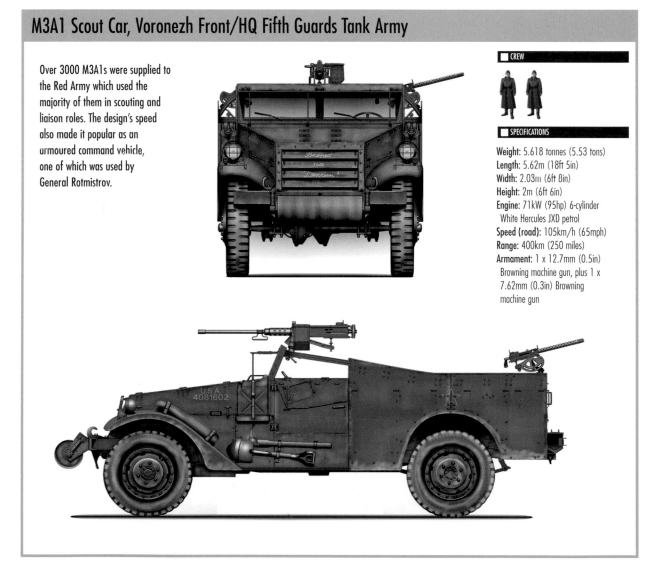

Over 3000 M3A1s were supplied to the Red Army which used the majority of them in scouting and liaison roles. The design's speed also made it popular as an armoured command vehicle, one of which was used by General Rotmistrov.

CREW

SPECIFICATIONS

Weight: 5.618 tonnes (5.53 tons)
Length: 5.62m (18ft 5in)
Width: 2.03m (6ft 8in)
Height: 2m (6ft 6in)
Engine: 71kW (95hp) 6-cylinder
    White Hercules JXD petrol
Speed (road): 105km/h (65mph)
Range: 400km (250 miles)
Armament: 1 x 12.7mm (0.5in)
    Browning machine gun, plus 1 x
    7.62mm (0.3in) Browning
    machine gun

fortunate to have been given his command at a time when a new sense of professionalism was stirring throughout the Red Army. The powers of the *politruks* (political officers) had been drastically curbed, so that senior army officers were far freer to take decisions based on military judgement without constantly worrying about how to justify their actions to political appointees, most of whom had very limited military training.

As a result of these changes, Rotmistrov was able to concentrate on training his officers and men rather than their political indoctrination. He paid particular attention to command, control and communications which were frequently 'problem areas' in the Red Army. (This was partly due to the endemic shortage of radios which reinforced the Soviet preference for rigid centralized operational planning. Such rigidity increased the chances of

spectacular failures when commanders 'on the spot' were unable to cope with rapidly changing situations on the battlefield.)

It was not just a matter of training his own command. Rotmistrov was acutely aware of the difficulties in achieving coordination with neighbouring formations – the boundary between two armies has always been a weak point, eagerly sought by every enemy attack. He was equally keen to do everything possible to improve the procedures governing close air support as the cumbersome Soviet communications systems made 'friendly fire' incidents all too common.

Events would prove that Zhukov's confidence of April was justified – the tank armies defending the Kursk salient itself and those held in reserve with the Steppe Military District would indeed 'do the job', albeit at a terrible cost.

ZiS-6 4-Ton 6 x 4 Truck

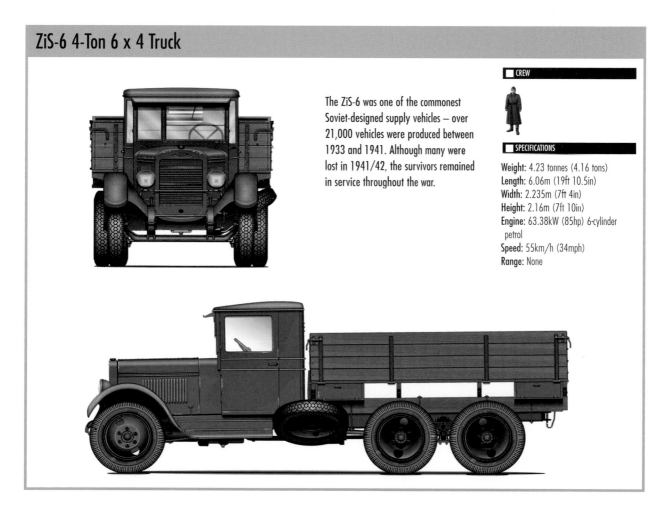

The ZiS-6 was one of the commonest Soviet-designed supply vehicles – over 21,000 vehicles were produced between 1933 and 1941. Although many were lost in 1941/42, the survivors remained in service throughout the war.

■ CREW

■ SPECIFICATIONS

Weight: 4.23 tonnes (4.16 tons)
Length: 6.06m (19ft 10.5in)
Width: 2.235m (7ft 4in)
Height: 2.16m (7ft 10in)
Engine: 63.38kW (85hp) 6-cylinder petrol
Speed: 55km/h (34mph)
Range: None

II Guards Tank Corps

II Guards Tank Corps began its existence in April 1942 as XXIV Tank Corps. It was initially assigned to Sixth Army, and was heavily engaged in the Stalingrad defensive operation on the Don during July 1942, where it lost almost two-thirds of its armoured strength.

Following reconstruction, it was transferred to Third Guards Army in December 1942 to participate in Operation *Little Saturn*, which was intended to trap Manstein's forces as they attempted to break through to relieve Stalingrad.

The corps' role in this operation is an important example of the evolving Soviet doctrine of armoured warfare in 1942/43. Lieutenant General Badanov's XXIV Tank Corps was designated as Third Guards Army's exploitation force, in line with

ORBAT: II Guards Tank Corps

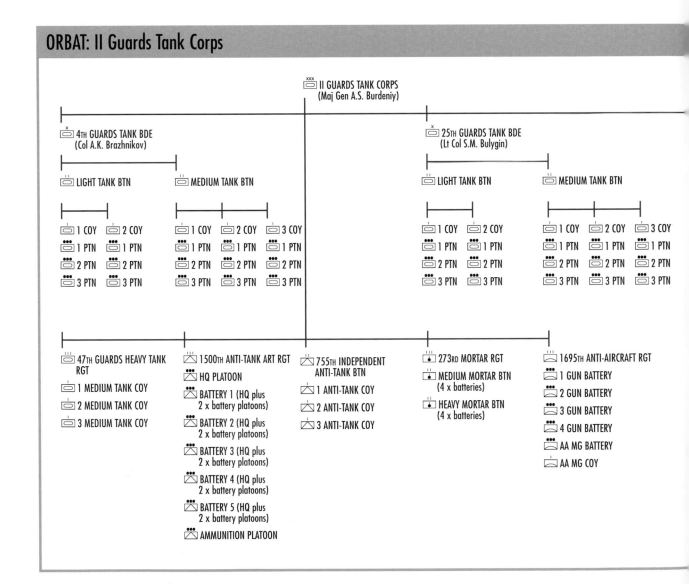

the doctrine of Deep Battle originally proposed by Tukhachevsky and now belatedly recognized as a potentially war-winning concept. It was therefore to be held in reserve until the Axis defences had been breached, after which it was to attack the airfields at Tatsinskaya, the principal bases for the *Luftwaffe*'s transport aircraft committed to the increasingly desperate attempts to resupply Paulus' Sixth Army trapped in Stalingrad.

ASSAULT

The assault by General Lelyushenko's Third Guards Army began on the morning of 16 December 1942. In order to achieve a swift breakthrough of the Axis defences, he committed his other two armoured formations (XVII and XXV Tank Corps) during the initial phase of the battle. XXIV Tank Corps was held back until 11:30 on 17 December by which time XVII and XXV Tank Corps were in the process of encircling the Italian Eighth Army and engaging the forces of Army Detachment Hollidt.

By the early hours of 24 December, Badanov's reconnaissance units had approached their objective and selected brigade attack positions around Tatsinskaya, which the tank brigades

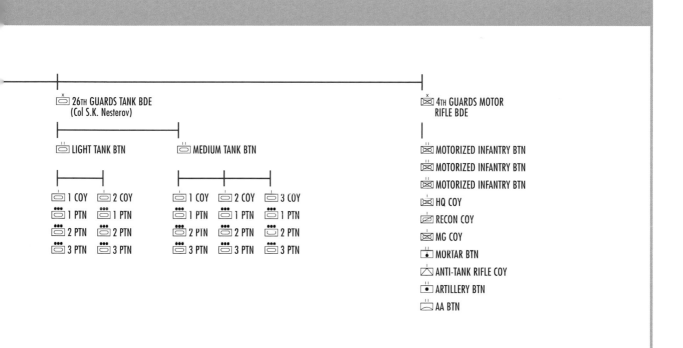

The II Guards Tank Corps was assigned to Voronezh Front reserves in the spring of 1943 in anticipation of the German offensive against the Kursk salient. Within a matter of hours of the start of this much-delayed operation, the Front commander, General Vatutin, ordered it forward in an attempt to halt the alarming advance of II SS Panzer Corps. Over the next few days the Corps fought a series of fierce actions in which it sustained heavy losses. It also had the dubious distinction of being the first victim of the Fw-190 fighter-bombers and Hs 129 'tank busters' of the *Luftwaffe*'s *Panzerjagdkommando Weiss*, which subjected it to a series of particularly prolonged and damaging attacks on 8 July. Unsurprisingly, it was much reduced in strength (to fewer than 160 AFVs) by the time that it was transferred to Fifth Guards Tank Army on 11 July in preparation for the counter-attack at Prokhorovka.

occupied at 07:00. A blanket of dense morning fog covered their deployment and allowed them to surprise the German garrison. At 07:30, after a salvo from Badanov's multiple rocket launchers struck German positions, the tank brigades attacked the town. The 54th Tank Brigade seized the airfield south of town while the 130th Tank Brigade passed through the town and attacked the other airfield from the east.

After advancing 240 kilometres (150 miles) in five days of combat, XXIV Tank Corps had little ammunition left and resorted to ramming the German planes on the ground. The 54th Tank Brigade's 1st Battalion commanded by Captain S. Strelkov and the 2nd Battalion of the 130th Tank Brigade commanded by Captain M. Nechaiev claimed the destruction of a total of nearly 300 aircraft (including 72 of the invaluable Ju-52 transports) on the airfields.

As the initial surprise wore off, German forces sealed off the area before making a succession of probing attacks. Badanov's supplies were rapidly dwindling and his tank units, originally totalling 159 vehicles, were reduced to a total of 58 tanks (39 x T-34 and 19 x T-26). Captured stocks of aviation fuel and lubricants were mixed to provide a rough and ready substitute tank fuel to keep the remaining armour more or less mobile, whilst the rest of the force dug in and waited for a relief force to arrive.

PARTIAL VICTORY

It rapidly became clear that any relief force was going to face strong opposition. Manstein had ordered XLVIII Panzer Corps to counter-attack. Its 6th and 11th Panzer Divisions tightened the noose around Badanov's force in conjunction with a variety of other units, including four armoured trains. Stavka ordered a 'maximum effort' to break through to XXIV Tank Corps, but the resources simply weren't available.

The badly battered XXV Tank Corps, which was down to 25 serviceable tanks and the equally exhausted I Guards Mechanized Corps were reinforced and unsuccessfully attempted to cut through the German forces. At this point, even Stavka realized that 'the game was up' and authorized Badanov to break out on 28 December. He and a number of his men escaped, although almost all his tanks and artillery were lost. The

Soviet propaganda machine played up the raid for all it was worth, claiming the destruction of 300 aircraft, 84 tanks and 106 guns. Axis casualties were claimed by the Soviets to total 12,000 dead and 5000 captured.

The reality was almost certainly less spectacular, but much had been achieved – the raid had badly disrupted the Stalingrad airlift and the destruction of a high proportion of the *Luftwaffe*'s serviceable transport aircraft in the area would badly restrict the future quantity of supplies which could be flown in.

DIVERSION

Equally seriously, elite panzer formations spearheading Manstein's drive to break through to Stalingrad had to be diverted to deal with the threat posed by XXIV Tank Corps. Whilst it is probably an exaggeration to claim that the raid decided the outcome of the Battle of Stalingrad, it certainly hastened the Soviet victory. XXIV Tank Corps operated up to 240 kilometres (150 miles) from its supply base, and had to rely on captured supplies to remain operational. Crucially, the supporting rifle units did not have sufficient mobility to keep pace with the tanks. This allowed the Germans to isolate the raiding force from its base, and ultimately defeat the operational intent of cutting off a large part of the German forces in the region.

Despite this, the raid was the first time that a corps-sized armoured formation had penetrated deep into the German rear, forcing the German command to adapt its operational plans. Previous raids had been carried out by much weaker cavalry or airborne forces operating with partisans which had not been able to inflict as much damage.

LEARNING CURVE

The raid provided much data for planning future operations and the development of Soviet armoured forces. It was probably instrumental in the flurry of measures taken in early 1943 to strengthen tank corps with additional mortars, assault guns and anti-tank units.

The operation emphasized the need to deploy more powerful forces in future missions of this type. (Even the more powerful tank corps of 1945 lacked the resilience for sustained offensive operations – in the last months of the war, one corps lost 90 per cent of its tanks in just three days of attacks on German field fortifications.) Tank armies were seen as the solution to this problem, but the problems experienced with infantry support during the raid were an important factor in the decision to make them fully motorized formations.

POSTSCRIPT

Stavka was quick in recognising the exceptional achievement of XXIV Tank Corps, which was renamed II Guards Tank Corps and given the honorific title Tatsinskaya. Major General Badanov became the first recipient of the newly created Order of Suvorov for this operation, and quickly went on to command Fourth Guards Tank Army, which he led in Operation *Kutuzov* in July 1943. From 1944 onwards, he commanded the Red Army's Armoured School, and ultimately rose to the rank of Lieutenant General.

Following the Tatsinskaya operation, the corps was so badly mauled that it was incapable of further combat. It was initially assigned to Stavka reserves where it provided cadres to help form Fourth Guards Tank Army in February 1943. After the corps had been slowly rebuilt during the spring, it was transferred to Voronezh Front reserves in anticipation of the German offensive against the Kursk salient.

Within a matter of hours of the start of this much-delayed operation, it was ordered forward by the Front commander, General Vatutin, in an attempt to halt the alarming advance of II SS Panzer Corps. Over the next few days it suffered heavy losses in a series of fierce actions, primarily against *Totenkopf*. (It was also subjected to a series of particularly prolonged and damaging attacks by Fw-190 fighter-bombers and the Hs 129 'tank busters' of the *Luftwaffe*'s *Panzerjagdkommando Weiss*. Unsurprisingly, it was much reduced in strength by the time that it was transferred to Fifth Guards Tank Army on 11 July in preparation for the counter-attack at Prokhorovka.)

Although there were probably very few veterans of Tatsinskaya in the ranks of II Guards Tank Corps at Prokhorovka, the confidence instilled by the raid would be an important element in its ultimate success against II SS Panzer Corps.

II Guards Tank Corps: AFVs 11 July 1943

UNIT	VEHICLE	STRENGTH
4th Guards Tank Brigade	T-34	28
	T-70	19
25th Guards Tank Brigade	T-34	28
	T-70	19
26th Guards Tank Brigade	T-34	30
	T-70	14
47th Heavy Guards Tank Regiment	KV-1	21

Tank Corps, early 1943: Typical personnel and small arms strength

UNIT	OFFICERS	NCOS	OTHER	SMGS	RIFLES
HQ	56	38	36	5	27
1st Tank Brigade	229	423	464	490	225
2nd Tank Brigade	229	423	464	490	225
3rd Tank Brigade	229	423	464	490	225
Motor Rifle Battalion	390	1187	1960	1364	1396
Reconnaissance Battalion	41	146	21	50	56
Rocket Launcher Battalion	30	56	164	5	104
Pioneer Mine Company	9	20	77	36	60
Fuel Transport Company	8	9	58	0	51
1st Maintenance Company	9	13	53	10	20
2nd Maintenance Company	9	13	53	10	20
NKVD Section	11	6	32	10	20
Total	1250	2757	3846	2960	2429

T-34 Model 1942

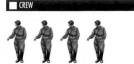

SPECIFICATIONS

Weight: 28.5 tonnes (28.05 tons)
Length: 6.68m (21ft 10in)
Width: 3m (9ft 8in)
Height: 2.45m (8ft)
Engine: V-2 diesel delivering 373kW (500hp)
Speed: 55km/h (34.18mph)
Range (Road): 400km (248 miles), **(Cross-Country):** 260km (161 miles)
Radio: 9R (when fitted – even by 1945, not all Soviet AFVs had radios)
Armament:
 Main: 76.2mm (3in) F-34 gun
 Secondary: 2 x 7.62mm (0.3in) DT machine guns

The oldest T-34 sub-type to remain in widespread service in 1943 was the Model 1942. This was essentially the same as the Model 1941, but incorporated numerous small changes to simplify its production.

4th Guards Tank Brigade

At the time of the Kursk offensive, 4th Guards Tank Brigade was organized in accordance with the 1942 establishment (as were the other tank brigades in Fifth Guards Tank Army). The next reorganisation of tank brigades did not take place until November 1943.

Tank brigades were the basic 'building blocks' of Soviet armoured formations, in fact at the most critical period of the war, they were the only Red Army tank units of any size. The tank brigades' ancestor was an experimental 'Mechanized Brigade' which was formed in the summer of 1929 at Naro Fominsk near Moscow. In modern terms, it was a true combined arms team comprising a tank regiment, a motor rifle regiment, an artillery battalion and support elements. The brigade's equipment included 60 tanks, 32 'tankettes' (tracked machine gun carriers), 17 armoured cars, 12 tractors and 264 trucks. This represented a significant proportion of the Red Army's total armoured strength and of the output of the fledgling Soviet tank and automotive industry.

The brigade took part in the 1930 Belorussian and Moscow Military District manoeuvres and those held the following year in the Ukrainian Military District. However, the dire problems experienced with Soviet tank designs delayed the formation of further brigades until the situation began to improve with the introduction of the T-26 and BT series in the early 1930s. In the summer of 1931, as annual Soviet tank production reached 1000 vehicles, the Kalinovsky Mechanized Regiment was expanded to include:
■ A Scout Group of two tankette battalions, an armoured car detachment, a motorized machine gun battalion and an artillery battery.
■ An Attack Group comprising two tank battalions and two batteries of SU-12 self-propelled guns.
■ A Support Group (a single motor rifle battalion).
■ An Artillery Group with three batteries (76mm and 122mm – 3in and 4.8in) plus an AA battery.

The unit totalled 4700 men with 119 tanks, 100 tankettes and 15 armoured cars, a brigade in fact, if not in name. Three more similarly structured regiments were formed in 1932, before the emphasis shifted to divisional-sized armoured formations dubbed Mechanized Corps, although independent brigades continued to be formed.

The Mechanized Corps had evolved into large formations with over 600 AFVs and 118 guns apiece by 1938 when they were redesignated as Tank Corps. This was the era of Stalin's purges of the Red Army and significantly, no more corps were

4th Guards Tank Brigade: Strength

UNIT	STRENGTH
Troops	1038
T-70 tanks	21
T-34/76	32
BA-64 armoured cars	3
Lorries	110
Staff cars or jeeps	3
Motorcycles	12
Tractors	5
76mm (3in) ZiS-3 AT-guns	4
AT-rifles	6
82mm (3.2in) mortars	6

4th Guards Tank Brigade: Manpower

UNIT	STRENGTH
Brigade HQ and HQ Company	147
Medium Tank Battalion	
1st Tank Company	44
2nd Tank Company	44
3rd Tank Company	44
Supply & Trains Group	39
Motor Rifle Battalion	
1st Rifle Company	112
2nd Rifle Company	112
Submachine Gun Company	79
Mortar Company	43
Anti-tank Battery	52
Trains Company	101

ORBAT: 4th Guards Tank Brigade

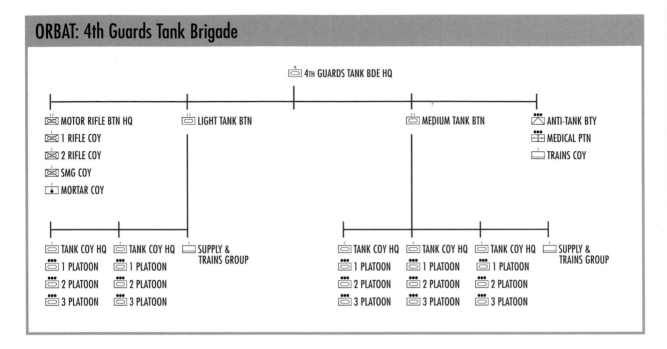

⊠ 4TH GUARDS TANK BDE HQ

⊠ MOTOR RIFLE BTN HQ
⊠ 1 RIFLE COY
⊠ 2 RIFLE COY
⊠ SMG COY
⊡ MORTAR COY

⊟ LIGHT TANK BTN

⊟ MEDIUM TANK BTN

△ ANTI-TANK BTY
⊞ MEDICAL PTN
⊟ TRAINS COY

⊟ TANK COY HQ
⊟ 1 PLATOON
⊟ 2 PLATOON
⊟ 3 PLATOON

⊟ TANK COY HQ
⊟ 1 PLATOON
⊟ 2 PLATOON
⊟ 3 PLATOON

⊟ SUPPLY & TRAINS GROUP

⊟ TANK COY HQ
⊟ 1 PLATOON
⊟ 2 PLATOON
⊟ 3 PLATOON

⊟ TANK COY HQ
⊟ 1 PLATOON
⊟ 2 PLATOON
⊟ 3 PLATOON

⊟ TANK COY HQ
⊟ 1 PLATOON
⊟ 2 PLATOON
⊟ 3 PLATOON

⊟ SUPPLY & TRAINS GROUP

formed, as the more conservative senior officers who survived favoured independent tank brigades and smaller units whose role would be restricted to providing close support for infantry and cavalry divisions. (Independent tank brigades had 145 tanks, 56 artillery (close support)/flamethrower tanks and 28 armoured cars.)

The purges, coupled with a misinterpretation of the lessons of the Spanish Civil War, caused catastrophic disruption throughout the Red Army – in November 1939 the high incidence of breakdowns suffered by the XV and XX Tank Corps in the invasion of Poland was seized upon as a pretext for disbanding all four corps. They were replaced by four motorized divisions each of which fielded 275 tanks, but which were supposedly confined to operating as part of horse-mechanized groups. The independent tank brigades were ordered to become more closely integrated with rifle and cavalry divisions, whilst plans were drawn up to increase the armoured component of each rifle division to a full brigade.

This attempt to completely subordinate armoured units to the cavalry and infantry coincided with the outbreak of the Winter War against Finland. Instead of the anticipated easy victory, the war turned into a humiliating fiasco for the Red Army which may well have lost a total of

1200 AFVs plus over 250,000 casualties. The stunning panzer victories in the summer of 1940 finally discredited the military conservatives and there was a panic-stricken rush to re-establish tank and motorized divisions concentrated in a planned total of 30 enormous Mechanized Corps, each of which fielded 1031 tanks and 268 armoured cars.

BARBAROSSA SHOCK

Many of these Mechanized Corps were little more than paper formations when Operation *Barbarossa* was launched in June 1941 and all suffered horrendous casualties before being disbanded within a month of the German invasion. Their surviving tank divisions were allocated to infantry support duties and were quickly destroyed in the *Wehrmacht*'s seemingly unstoppable advances of the summer and autumn of 1941.

Incredibly, the crisis of July 1941 which led to the disbandment of the Mechanized Corps was seen by Marshal Voroshilov as a vindication of his opposition to the mechanisation of the Red Army's cavalry, but fortunately, his incompetence as a commander was so blatant that Stalin ignored his views and began a pragmatic reorganisation of what was left of the Soviet armoured forces. In August 1941, Stavka abandoned any thought of raising new divisional-sized armoured formations and concentrated its efforts on the creation of small tank brigades.

These brigades had a nominal total strength of 93 tanks in three battalions, plus a motor rifle battalion and support units. In theory, there were 7 x KV-1, 22 x T-34, 64 x T-40 (or whatever other light tanks were available) and 10 armoured cars. In recognition of the threat posed by the Panzers, the motor rifle battalion included an anti-tank company with 8 x 45mm (1.8in) guns, plus a tank-destroyer company armed solely with a variety of improvized anti-tank weapons including grenades, demolition charges, Molotov cocktails and flamethrowers. In an attempt to give some degree of protection from the *Luftwaffe*'s devastating attacks, the brigade incorporated an AA battalion which fielded 8 x 37mm (1.45in) AA guns and 6 x machine guns.

The chaotic state of the Red Army as it was pushed back throughout the summer and autumn of 1941 meant that the vast majority of the tank brigades bore only a vague resemblance to the official establishment tables. Despite the dire shortages of equipment and massive losses sustained by these formations, they had a number of key advantages:

■ They were small enough to be handled with some chance of success by inexperienced officers trying to learn the practicalities of armoured warfare in the middle of a campaign.

■ They could be formed quickly – many were assembled from existing tank units in just a few short weeks.

■ Enough of them could be formed that everybody could have some armoured support, even if it was only to a very limited extent.

■ Although it was a small formation, the brigade provided at least some degree of infantry and AA protection for the tanks.

DEVASTATING LOSSES

As the Germans overran Belorussia and the Ukraine, the horrendous scale of the Red Army's tank losses forced a steady reduction in the official strengths of the tank brigades. In September, they were cut to a total of 67 tanks apiece (7 x KV-1, 22 x T-34 and 38 light tanks) with a further cut to 46 in December (10 x KV-1, 16 x T-34 and 20 light tanks). The final reduction came in February 1942 when each brigade was supposed to field a mere 27 tanks

4th Guards Tank Brigade: Equipment

UNIT	VEHICLE	STRENGTH
Brigade HQ & HQ Company	T-34	1
	Motorcycles	12
	Radio vehicles	3
	Cargo trucks	8
	Field Cars/Staff Cars	2
Medium Tank Battalion HQ	T-34/76	1
1st Tank Company HQ	T-34/76	1
Platoons x3	T-34/76	3
2nd Tank Company HQ	T-34/76	1
Platoons x3	T-34/76	3
3rd Tank Company HQ	T-34/76	1
Platoons x3	T-34/76	3
Supply & Trains Group	radio vehicle	1
	cargo trucks	10
	workshop vehicles	5
	tractors	3
Light Tank Battalion HQ	T-70	1
1st Tank Company HQ	T-70	1
Platoons x3	T-70	3
2nd Tank Company HQ	T-70	1
Platoons x3	T-70	3
Supply & Trains Group	radio vehicle	1
	cargo trucks	4
	workshop vehicles	3
	tractors	2
Motor Rifle Battalion HQ	Field Car/Staff Car	1
	BA-64 armoured cars	3
	radio vehicle	1
	cargo trucks	5
1st Rifle Company	light machine guns	9
	medium machine guns	2
	anti-tank rifles	3
2nd Rifle Company	light machine guns	9
	medium machine guns	2
	anti-tank rifles	3
Submachine Gun Company		
Mortar Company	82mm mortars	6
	trucks	4
Anti-tank Battery	76.2mm towed guns	4
	trucks	4
Medical Platoon	trucks/ambulances	3
Trains Company	workshop vehicles	8
	fuel tankers	10
	recovery vehicles	4
	cargo trucks	36

(10 x KV-1 and 17 x T-34) – not much more than half the strength of most Western tank battalions.

This whittling away of the tank brigades emphasised a lack of resilience. A tank brigade could lose all its tanks in just a few days of heavy fighting. Later in the war, when the brigades' parent tank and mechanized corps had their own repair bases, spare tanks, and even reserve tank crews, the problem became less acute. In 1941, individual tank brigades operating under army HQs with no dedicated repair organisation and few supporting units quickly shrank to a point at which they became ineffective. By December 1941, the average combat strength of tank brigades in the Battle of Moscow was no more than 12 tanks each – less than that of a pre-war tank company!

TRANSITION
By the end of 1941, the Red Army fielded 76 tank brigades and 100 independent tank battalions, plus seven remaining tank divisions. (Four of these divisions were stationed in Manchuria, where they provided some of the 3000 AFVs protecting the vulnerable frontier with the Japanese puppet state of Manchukuo.) In the Spring of 1942, tank factories evacuated to the Urals resumed production. Their output, together with the first Lend-Lease AFVs, allowed the tank brigades to be restored to their December 1941 strengths of 46 tanks each.

The fighting of early 1942 highlighted the incompatibility of the heterogeneous tank brigades. The future Marshal Rotmistrov, who would head the Soviet armoured force after the war, candidly explained this to Stavka: 'The difficulty is that while there isn't much difference in speed between the light (T-60) tank and the medium (T-34) tank on the roads, when moving across country, the light tanks are quickly left behind. The heavy (KV) tank is already behind and often crushes bridges, which cuts off units behind it. Under battlefield conditions, this has meant that too often only the T-34s arrived; the light tanks had difficulty fighting

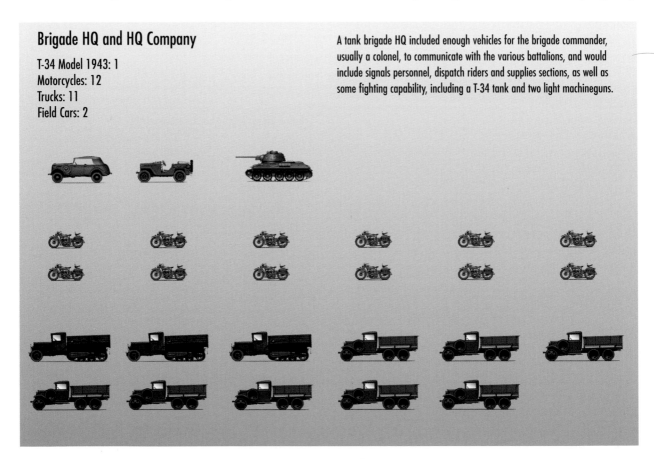

Brigade HQ and HQ Company

T-34 Model 1943: 1
Motorcycles: 12
Trucks: 11
Field Cars: 2

A tank brigade HQ included enough vehicles for the brigade commander, usually a colonel, to communicate with the various battalions, and would include signals personnel, dispatch riders and supplies sections, as well as some fighting capability, including a T-34 tank and two light machineguns.

Harley-Davidson 42WLA

CREW

SPECIFICATIONS

Weight: 245kg (540lb)
Length: 2.24m (7ft 4in)
Width: 1.04m (3ft 5in)
Height: n/k
Engine: 17kW (23hp) V-2 air-cooled petrol
Speed: 105km/h (65.2mph)
Range: 161km (100 miles)

The Red Army greatly appreciated the reliability of the 25,000 WLA motorcycles shipped under Lend-Lease by 1945.

GAZ-61-40 staff car

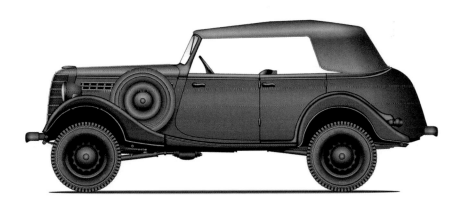

CREW

SPECIFICATIONS

Weight: 1.54 tonnes (1.52 tons)
Length: 4.67m (15ft 3in)
Width: 1.75m (5ft 9in)
Height: 1.9m (6ft 3in)
Engine: 63kW (85hp) 6-cylinder
Speed: 100km/h (62.1mph)
Range: n/k

The GAZ-61-40 was the first Soviet 4x4 staff car to enter service, proving far more versatile than earlier 4x2 vehicles.

the German tanks anyway, and the KVs were delayed in the rear. It was also difficult to command these companies because…they were equipped with different types of radios or none at all.'

Rotmistrov's comments summarised the frustrations of many officers as they struggled to cope with the logistical problems of keeping at least three different tank types serviceable. (In some brigades the situation was even worse – a substantial number of T-26s still survived, together with T-37 and T-40 amphibious light tanks and more modern T-60s. Although it is improbable that any one unit was unlucky enough to be saddled with all four types, bizarre mixtures of light tanks were not uncommon.) The lack of organisational standardisation worsened the problem – tank brigades in service in the first half of 1942 could be organized on any one of three establishment tables. In May the situation was further complicated by the formation of a number of tank corps each of which included a brigade primarily equipped with KV-1s.

REORGANISATION: JULY 1942 ESTABLISHMENT

These problems were partially rectified at the end of in July 1942, when the next major reorganisation of the tank brigade structure took place. The most important single measure was the removal of powerful KV-1s from the brigade to form separate Guards Heavy Breakthrough Tank Regiments with a total of 21 tanks each. The brigade's tanks were

now concentrated in two battalions, one with 31 x T-34 and the other with 21 x T-60 or T-70. All tank brigades were directed to adopt this organisation, but it inevitably took a significant time to fully implement this change.

The July 1942 establishment was subjected to fine tuning throughout early 1943, but provided the basis for the organisation of 4th Guards Tank Brigade and the other tank brigades of Fifth Guards Tank Army.

Whilst the new establishment tables solved some problems, many more remained. They could do nothing to rectify the almost complete lack of armoured personnel carriers (APCs) which

ZiS-42M 2.5 Ton Halftrack

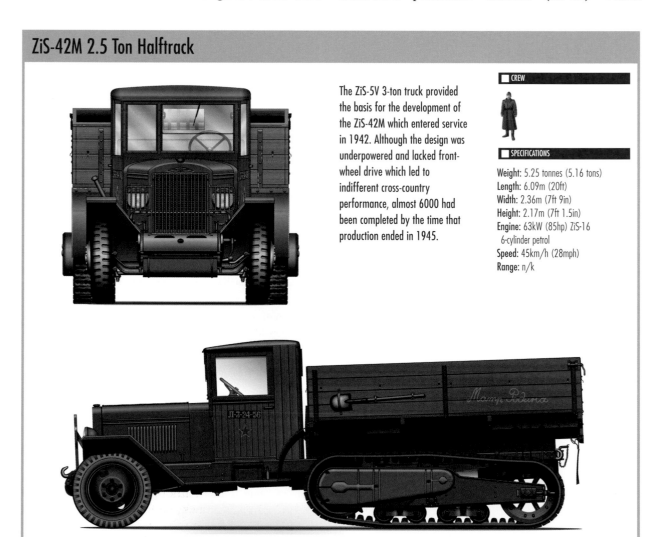

The ZiS-5V 3-ton truck provided the basis for the development of the ZiS-42M which entered service in 1942. Although the design was underpowered and lacked front-wheel drive which led to indifferent cross-country performance, almost 6000 had been completed by the time that production ended in 1945.

■ CREW

■ SPECIFICATIONS

Weight: 5.25 tonnes (5.16 tons)
Length: 6.09m (20ft)
Width: 2.36m (7ft 9in)
Height: 2.17m (7ft 1.5in)
Engine: 63kW (85hp) ZiS-16
  6-cylinder petrol
Speed: 45km/h (28mph)
Range: n/k

Willys MB 'Jeep'

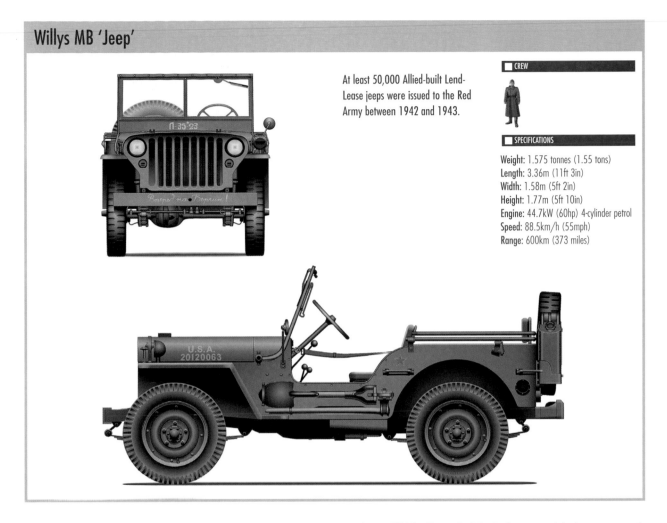

At least 50,000 Allied-built Lend-Lease jeeps were issued to the Red Army between 1942 and 1943.

CREW

SPECIFICATIONS

Weight: 1.575 tonnes (1.55 tons)
Length: 3.36m (11ft 3in)
Width: 1.58m (5ft 2in)
Height: 1.77m (5ft 10in)
Engine: 44.7kW (60hp) 4-cylinder petrol
Speed: 88.5km/h (55mph)
Range: 600km (373 miles)

bedevilled the Red Army throughout the war. (Only a handful of formations managed to acquire sufficient US Lend-Lease halftracks or captured SdKfz 250/251 APCs to carry a significant proportion of their infantry.) In the vast majority of cases, the motor rifle units' mobility depended on a mixture of trucks and the tanks themselves. Trucks, when available in sufficient numbers, could give the infantry reasonable mobility when outside the combat zone, but they lacked the protection (and often the cross-country performance) to operate in the front line.

A further serious tactical weakness was the lack of radios that was endemic throughout the Red Army. This was particularly serious for its mobile forces, which had to operate with weaker communications than any of their Western or Axis counterparts. Even in 1944, an elite formation

such as Fifth Guards Tank Army, with its two tank and one mechanized corps, had a mere 254 radios, less than the total held by a single US armoured division at that time. The effect at brigade level and below was particularly serious, as it degraded the tactical handling of armoured forces, slowing their response to enemy movements and leading to increased casualties.

Such weak radio communications also reinforced by default the doctrine of decentralisation of tank forces in the pursuit, as there was simply no way to guarantee that higher commanders could maintain contact with the tank armies and their subordinate units in combat. Even more seriously, the critical shortage of radio sets hampered air to ground communications, weakening the effectiveness of Soviet close air support operations throughout the war.

Medium Tank Battalion, 4th Guards Tank Brigade

By 1943, the vast majority of medium tank battalions were equipped with the T-34. The Model 1940 entered production at the KhPZ factory in Kharkov in September 1940 and the final variant, the T-34/85, was produced under licence in Czechoslovakia until 1958. It is likely that over 84,000 were completed as tanks, in addition to more than 13,000 self-propelled guns based on the hull of the T-34.

The first Soviet tank crews to take the T-34 Model 1940 into action in the summer of 1941 found that they had a weapon which was immune to most German tank and anti-tank guns at normal battle ranges. The type's only major drawbacks were its main armament (the low-velocity 76.2mm (3in) L11 gun) and mechanical unreliability which led to such desperate measures as crews going into action with spare transmission units lashed to their engine decks.

The solution to the armament problem was already in existence thanks to the initiative shown by the Grabin design bureau at Gorky Factory No. 92 which had designed the far better F-34 76.2mm (3in) gun. No bureaucrat would approve production, but Gorky and KhPZ started manufacturing the gun unofficially – an incredibly brave decision in the paranoid atmosphere of the time. (Whole tank design teams had been shot in the purges of the late 1930s.) The F-34 was installed in the new up-armoured T-34 Model 1941 which entered production just before the German invasion, but official authorisation was only received from Stalin's State Defence Committee after the firepower of the few examples of the Model 1941 to reach the front was praised in a flood of enthusiastic reports.

FIRST COMBAT

The T-34s which went into action in the opening stages of Operation Barbarossa were terrifying to German units which were shaken by their firepower, cross-country mobility and their apparent invulnerability to the majority of German AFV guns and anti-tank weapons. This was especially apparent in the case of the German standard anti-tank gun of 1941, the 37mm (1.45in) PaK 36. Combat reports included that from a particularly determined (and lucky!) crew of a PaK 36 who fired 23 rounds at a single T-34 and only succeeded in jamming the turret. Whilst this highlights the effectiveness of the T-34's armour on the 1941 battlefield, it also emphasises the tank's abysmal fire control system which allowed the gunners to fire 23 rounds and survive without taking a single hit or damaging near miss in return.

Several factors contributed to this situation, including:

■ The two-man turret of the T-34, in which the grossly over-worked tank commander also acted as the gunner. If he was also a platoon or company commander, he had the additional daunting task of controlling several other tanks.

■ The poor quality of the tank's sighting and observation equipment. There was no commander's cupola and he had to rely on a single periscopic sight for observation when the tank was operating 'closed down'. (Soviet periscopic and telescopic sights were markedly inferior to their

Medium Tank Battalion: Typical AFV strength

UNIT	VEHICLE	STRENGTH
Battalion HQ and HQ Platoon	T-34/76	1
1st Tank Company HQ	T-34/76	1
1st Platoon	T-34/76	3
2nd Platoon	T-34/76	3
3rd Platoon	T-34/76	3
2nd Tank Company HQ	T-34/76	1
1st Platoon	T-34/76	3
2nd Platoon	T-34/76	3
3rd Platoon	T-34/76	3
3rd Tank Company HQ	T-34/76	1
1st Platoon	T-34/76	3
2nd Platoon	T-34/76	3
3rd Platoon	T-34/76	3
Supply & Trains Group	radio vehicle	1
	cargo trucks	10
	workshop vehicles	5
	tractors	3

Medium Tank Battalion

Combat vehicles:
T-34 Model 1943: 31

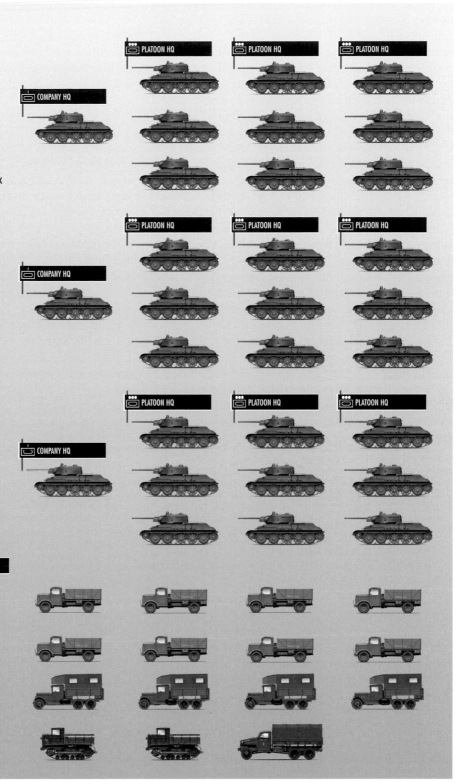

The medium tank battalions were the basic building block of Fifth Guards Tank Army's striking force at Prokhorovka. Lack of tactical training led to heavy losses as crews tried to learn basic skills on the battlefield itself. Even in mid-1943, at least a third of all the Red Army's tanks still lacked radios, which all too often meant that unit command and control was little more than a matter of everyone following the company commander, which frequently had dire results if his tank was knocked out. More experienced crews might be able to operate a 'two up, one back' company battle drill with two platoons deployed in line abreast whilst the third followed ready to engage any enemy which fired on the leading platoons. Even if this drill was adopted, it was rarely developed to include 'overwatch' tactics in which the platoons covered each other's movements.

German counterparts, whilst the armoured glass blocks used in vision ports were often cloudy and full of bubbles.)

■ Any attempt by the commander to overcome this problem by operating with the turret open was hindered by the design of the hatch. This was a single large forward-opening hatch covering almost the entire rear half of the turret. Its weight and awkwardness were hated by Soviet tank crews who dubbed it *pirozhok* (stuffed bun) after its characteristic shape. When opened, it stood almost upright and blocked the commander's forward vision, forcing him to lean out to one side to get a clear view. If it jammed, the turret crew were trapped, with only a slim chance of being able to escape through the driver's hatch. Tank commander Nikolai Evdokimovich Glukhov remembered that it was: 'A big hatch – very inconvenient, very heavy.' The flood of complaints from tank crews finally led to its replacement with twin hatches in the Model 1943 turret.

■ Up to and including the Model 1942, the turret was very cramped and so low that the maximum depression of the 76.2mm (3in) and co-axial machine gun was restricted to only 3°. This severely limited the tank's ability to take up hull-down firing positions on reverse slopes and to fire on close-range targets.

Even in 1941, when they were theoretically markedly superior in firepower and protection to any German AFV, T-34s suffered horrendous losses. In part, this was due to the factors already mentioned, but the sheer lack of training and inexperience of Red Army tank crews was also responsible for many losses.

NEW ARMOURED TACTICS

There were also dire problems with Soviet armoured doctrine which was still fixated on the idea of unsophisticated all-out offensive operations. The limitations of this approach had become bloodily apparent and at the end of June 1942, General Fedorenko, the Commander of Red Army Armoured and Mechanized Forces, issued a directive on the principles for its future employment. Whilst hardly original, they represented a willingness to learn from German practice, calling for the use of armour en masse against strategic targets. There was new emphasis

on the importance of surprise, the exploitation of favourable terrain and a call for logistic support capable of sustaining prolonged advances. For the time being, these were little more than hopes for the future – the pressing issue was whether the Red Army could survive long enough to put them into practice.

As the Germans advanced during the summer of 1942, a few of the Soviet tank units fought effective delaying actions in accordance with the principles laid down by General Fedorenko, such as that at the River Resseta in July, where 11th and 19th Panzer Divisions had to tackle well dug-in anti-tank guns whilst fending off repeated counter-attacks directed against their flanks by small groups of T-34s. However, across most of the vast front, the impression was one of the Red Army almost on the point of collapse.

The first signs that the new doctrine was really taking effect were observed during Operation Uranus, an ambitious counter-offensive intended to punch through the Third and Fourth Rumanian armies, before enveloping the German Sixth Army and Fourth Panzer Army around Stalingrad. In this case Soviet armour was employed and most effectively – in accordance with the principles laid down by General Fedorenko earlier in the year. In contrast, the German response was clumsy and ineffective. The under-strength elements of Fourth Panzer Army which attempted to block Fifth Tank Army's advance at the Don crossings near Kalach were inadequately briefed and committed to an understandably rushed deployment with low stocks of fuel and ammunition.

Although they reached Kalach just ahead of Soviet forces, their small ad hoc combat teams lacked infantry support to hold vital ground and were quickly overrun by Soviet armour operating en masse. On 23 November, the Russian pincers closed at Sovietskiy, 20 kilometres (12 miles) southeast of Kalach, trapping an estimated 300,000 Axis troops in Stalingrad. The tables had been decisively turned.

FALSE DAWN

The final German surrender at Stalingrad on 1 February 1943 seemed to presage a catastrophic collapse of the entire line as the Red Army winter offensive gained momentum, but General Erich von

T-34 Model 1943

Weight: 30.9 tonnes (30.41 tons)
Length: 6.75m (22ft 1in)
Width: 3m (9ft 8in)
Height: 2.45m (8ft)
Engine: V-2 diesel delivering 373kW (500hp)
Speed: 55km/h (34.2mph)
Range (Road): 465km (289 miles)
 (Cross-Country): 365km (227 miles)
Radio: 9R (When fitted – even by 1945, not all Soviet AFVs had radios.)
Armament:
 Main: 76.2mm (3in) F-34 tank gun
 Secondary: 2 x 7.62mm (0.3in) DT MGs

ABOVE: Despite its designation, the T-34 Model 1943 actually entered service in 1942. The most obvious change from earlier versions was the enlarged turret, which gave welcome extra space for the crew. This T-34 has all-metal road wheels, a result of the dire shortage of rubber which affected Soviet war industries for much of 1942/43.

LEFT: The use of all-metal road wheels was soon found to create harmonic vibrations when the T-34 was running at high speed which loosened components throughout the tank and caused engine damage. Rubber-rimmed road wheels had to be re-instated in the first and fifth positions to partially solve the problem.

RIGHT: Rubber supplies gradually improved during 1943, largely due to Lend-Lease shipments, allowing the re-introduction of rubber rims on all road wheels in later production vehicles.

Manstein showed that the commanders of Soviet armoured formations still had much to learn. By getting a shaken Hitler to authorise withdrawals, he was able to shorten his front and concentrate the panzers to take advantage of Soviet overconfidence.

This overconfidence was understandable – by mid-February 1943, Soviet armour had advanced as much as 300 kilometres (200 miles) in a month, taken Kursk and Kharkov and seemed poised to re-conquer the entire Ukraine. Such spectacular successes brought their own problems as logistic systems became dangerously over-stretched – the tanks outran their supply lines and had to struggle forward with totally inadequate reserves of fuel and ammunition. On 20 February, Manstein unleashed four panzer corps which cut off the Soviet spearheads and regained much of the lost territory (except for the Kursk Salient) before the mud of the thaw put an end to further operations.

TRAINING

Manstein's offensive emphasised the continuing weaknesses in Soviet training at all levels. As late as 1943, it was not unusual for other ranks to spend no more than four to eight weeks undergoing basic training in a tank training battalion. There were separate battalions for training drivers, hull gunners/radio operators and loaders all of whom were solely trained to carry out their own duties with no cross-training to allow them to take over from other crew members. After completing their basic training, the crewmen would be sent to one of the training regiments, each processing 2000 men at a time, which were based near the principal tank factories.

Officers' training was little better than that of their men, generally comprising three to four months' instruction at a tank school after which they would also be posted to a training regiment where they would form their tank crews. The process was supposed to be completed in a month or so, but could stretch out for up to a year as officers and men were frequently drafted into the tank factories for varying periods to ease their perennial labour shortages.

This did nothing to help the poor standard of training – officers might well only have the chance to conduct a single simple tactical exercise and many were unable to read a map. Gunnery training was equally basic, often no more than firing three 76.2mm (3in) rounds and a single drum of machine gun ammunition at static targets.

Regardless of the accuracy of this perfunctory target practice, the crews were then considered to be combat-ready and were posted to their battalion. On arrival at their unit, there was frequently little if any gunnery or manoeuvre training – even in the weeks immediately before Kursk many tank crews were sent to work on local farms as food shortages were considered more serious than the imminent battle.

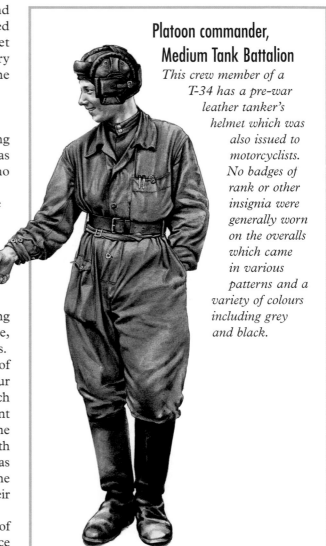

Platoon commander, Medium Tank Battalion

This crew member of a T-34 has a pre-war leather tanker's helmet which was also issued to motorcyclists. No badges of rank or other insignia were generally worn on the overalls which came in various patterns and a variety of colours including grey and black.

T-34 Model 1943 (with commander's copula)

■ SPECIFICATIONS

Weight: 30.9 tonnes (30.41 tons)
Length: 6.75m (22ft 1in)
Width: 3m (9ft 8in)
Height: 2.16m (7ft 1in)
Engine: V-2 diesel delivering 373kW (500hp)
Speed: 55km/h (34.2mph)
Range (Road): 465km (289 miles), **(Cross-Country):** 365km (227 miles)
Radio: 9R (When fitted – even by 1945, not all Soviet AFVs had radios.)
Armament:
  Main: 76.2mm (3in) F-34 tank gun
  Secondary: 2 x 7.62mm (0.3in) DT machine guns

This T-34 Model 1943 incorporates the final updates applied to the type, notably the commander's 360 degree vision cupola and 'drum type' long-range fuel tanks.

THE LESSONS OF COMBAT

The firepower and agility of the Models 1941 and 1942 were impressive, but they were not easy tanks to operate effectively. Apart from the problems inherent in any two-man turret, the ruthless elimination of all non-essential fittings certainly degraded crew performance. The loader had a particularly demanding time in action as only nine of the 77 x 76.2mm (3in) rounds carried were stowed in readily accessible racks. There was no turret basket and the remainder of the main armament ammunition was stowed in bins covered by neoprene mats. In combat, the floor soon became a mess of open bins and matting as ammunition was removed, whilst every time the

76.2mm (3in) fired, a very hot cartridge case was ejected, adding to the loader's hazards.

The crews were soon aware of the dangers inherent in the T-34's design. It was hard enough to acquire targets such as tanks and anti-tank guns, but infantry were particularly difficult to spot. The Red Army's generally poor standard of tank/infantry co-operation was rapidly exploited by German infantry who soon became adept at stalking T-34s, especially in close terrain or built-up areas. Although they were immune to many German anti-tank weapons of 1941/42, T-34s prior to the Model 1943 all had turrets with a large rear 'overhang'. The gap between this overhang and the engine deck was not only a 'shot trap', but an ideal point for

Zis-6 with PARM-1 Type B field workshop body

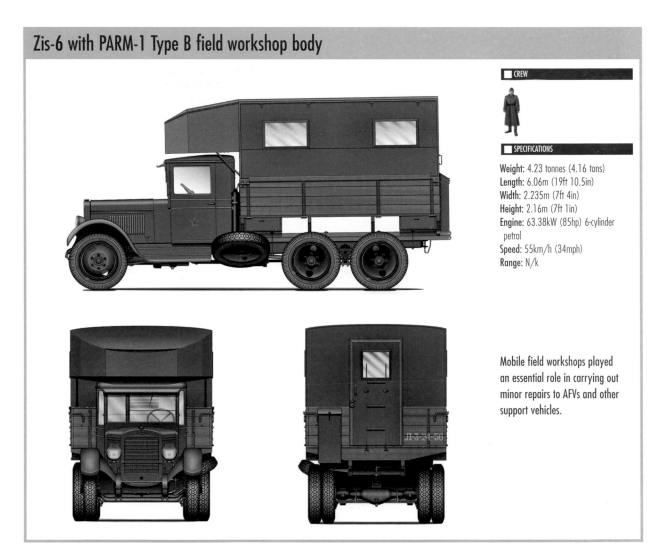

CREW

SPECIFICATIONS

Weight: 4.23 tonnes (4.16 tons)
Length: 6.06m (19ft 10.5in)
Width: 2.235m (7ft 4in)
Height: 2.16m (7ft 1in)
Engine: 63.38kW (85hp) 6-cylinder petrol
Speed: 55km/h (34mph)
Range: N/k

Mobile field workshops played an essential role in carrying out minor repairs to AFVs and other support vehicles.

German infantrymen to wedge demolition charges or time-fused anti-tank mines, which were easily capable of blowing off the entire turret.

A series of modifications partially rectified some of these problems. The two-man turret would only be replaced with a three-man design in the T-34/85 which entered service in 1944, but other improvements could be made more easily. One of the first was the fitting of a bin below the breach of the 76.2mm (3in) gun to collect ejected cartridge cases, a modification probably made as early as 1942.

The threat from steadily improving German tank and anti-tank guns was countered by modestly increased armour protection, including the fitting of appliqué armour on older vehicles. (However, it was never possible to incorporate protection capable of stopping 88mm (3.5in) armour-piercing rounds.)

The T-34 Model 1943 was the ultimate 76.2mm (3in) armed variant – crews welcomed the modestly enlarged cast hexagonal turret which gave a small degree of extra working space (although priority was given to increasing main armament ammunition stowage from 77 to 100 rounds) and especially the twin forward-opening circular turret hatches. Whilst these hatches improved crew access (and most importantly their chances of escape if the tank was knocked out) commanders were still handicapped by their poor field of vision when operating closed down. This was belatedly rectified in later production Model 1943 tanks which incorporated a 360° degree vision commander's cupola fitted with split hatches.

ASSESSMENTS

The T-34 was far from perfect, but its balance of protection, mobility and firepower greatly impressed its opponents. Field Marshal von Kleist called it 'The finest tank in the world.' The Panther was rushed into production specifically to counter it (and might have been far more reliable had the diesel-powered Daimler-Benz design been adopted). This was a 'near copy' of the T-34 which was in many respects more promising than the complex MAN-designed version which finally went into service). Although the Panther did indeed out-class the T-34 of 1943, it was far less robust and much less suited to wartime mass-production – monthly Panther production never exceeded 380, whereas Tankograd alone churned out almost 2000 T-34s each month. As Stalin commented: 'Quantity has a quality all of its own.' However, qualitative factors were never completely ignored and the Soviet design was capable of being readily upgraded to produce the T-34/85 which remained a viable battle tank until well after 1945.

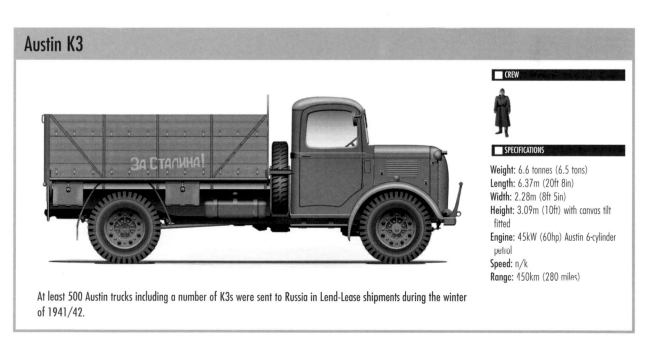

Austin K3

CREW

SPECIFICATIONS

Weight: 6.6 tonnes (6.5 tons)
Length: 6.37m (20ft 8in)
Width: 2.28m (8ft 5in)
Height: 3.09m (10ft) with canvas tilt fitted
Engine: 45kW (60hp) Austin 6-cylinder petrol
Speed: n/k
Range: 450km (280 miles)

At least 500 Austin trucks including a number of K3s were sent to Russia in Lend-Lease shipments during the winter of 1941/42.

Light Tank Battalion, 4th Guards Tank Brigade

Light tanks were regarded as a 'necessary evil' by the Red Army as early as 1942. They were too thinly armoured to stand much chance of survival against most German AFVs and anti-tank guns, whilst their weak armament further limited the scope for their battlefield deployment.

However, they remained in service to make up numbers in tank units as they could be easily produced in small factories which lacked the facilities to build T-34s.

The variety of light tanks with which the Red Army began the war had been considerably reduced by 1943. The pre-war T-37, T-38 and T-40 amphibious light tanks which survived the first months of combat were largely relegated to training duties as the T-60 entered service in late 1941. By the standards of the time, the T-60 was a reasonable light tank, superior to the Panzer I and roughly equal to the Panzer II, which made up a significant proportion of the German tank force in the opening

Light Tank Battalion

T-70M light tank: 21   Tractors: 2
Radio Vehicle: 1
Cargo Trucks: 4
Workshop Vehicles: 3

By mid-1943, the light tank battalions had long been recognized as a liability to the tank brigades, but had to be retained as there were still insufficient T-34s to fully equip these formations. (Brigade commanders hated them as they were slower than the T-34, had poorer cross-country capabilities and were so vulnerable in action. There was also the considerable problem of supplying and maintaining two different tank types in every brigade.) Although the T-70M was the best wartime Soviet-designed light tank to see service in any numbers, it was out-classed by virtually every German tank at Prokhorovka. Ideally, the type should have been restricted to reconnaissance, command and liaison duties, but as the light tank battalions represented a significant proportion of the armoured strength of each tank brigade, they often had to be thrown into action as 'substitute battle tanks' and suffered accordingly.

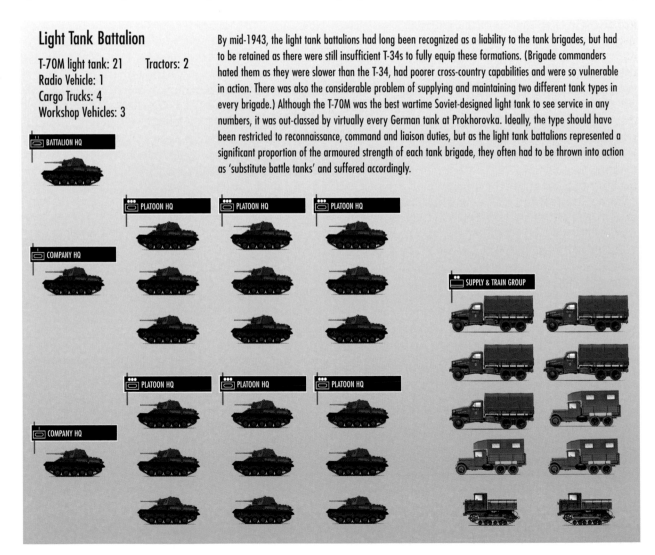

BATTALION HQ

PLATOON HQ   PLATOON HQ   PLATOON HQ

COMPANY HQ

SUPPLY & TRAIN GROUP

PLATOON HQ   PLATOON HQ   PLATOON HQ

COMPANY HQ

stages of Operation Barbarossa. The massive losses of 1941 virtually destroyed the pre-war Soviet tank fleet which, coupled with the disruption caused by the evacuation of tank factories, created a desperate need for tanks of any sort to provide even a limited level of armoured support for the hard-pressed Red Army. The T-60 provided an ideal interim solution to the problem – it utilized the readily-available GAZ-202 truck engine and its relatively small, flat armour plates were far easier to produce than the massive castings and welded components of the KV-1 and T-34.

RELIABLE AND TOUGH

The type was reliable enough, but it had a poor cross-country performance due largely to its low ground clearance and narrow tracks. Its battlefield use was limited by its two-man crew, thin armour and weak armament. Its 20mm (0.79in) TNSh cannon had a similar theoretical performance to the German KwK 38 gun of the Panzer II, but in practice its muzzle velocity turned out to be poor due to the widespread use of cartridge cases loaded with the propellant charge of the 12.7mm (0.5in) machine gun. When using full-charge armour-piecing ammunition, the gun's anti-tank performance was quite good for its calibre (up to 35mm at 50 metres – 1.4in at 165ft) but it took a skilful crew to be survive long enough to close in to that sort of range.

Moreover, the behind-armour effects of the armour-piercing incendiary (API) rounds were poor unless they hit the crew, fuel or ammunition. To make matters worse, although the belt-fed gun had a high practical rate of fire (200rpm), its effectiveness against infantry and other 'soft' targets was compromised by the poor fragmentation characteristics of its HE ammunition.

The T-60 was unpopular with its crews due to its weak armament and thin armour. It was widely referred to as the 'BM-2' or *Bratskaya Mogila na dvoikh* (a grave for two brothers). Attempts were made to up-gun the design and improve its armour, but the turret ring was too small to take any worthwhile increase in armament and only modest thickening of the armour could be carried out without overloading the suspension. Despite these drawbacks, the type was manufactured in quantity – well over 6000 were completed when production

Light Tank Battalion: Typical AFV strength

UNIT	VEHICLE	STRENGTH
Battalion HQ and HQ Platoon	T-70	1
1st Tank Company HQ	T-70	1
1st Platoon	T-70	3
2nd Platoon	T-70	3
3rd Platoon	T-70	3
2nd Tank Company HQ	T-70	1
1st Platoon	T-70	3
2nd Platoon	T-70	3
3rd Platoon	T-70	3
Supply & Trains Group	radio vehicle	1
	cargo trucks	4
	workshop vehicles	3
	tractors	2

ended in September 1942 and they remained in service in steadily declining numbers until the end of the war. Throughout 1943 the type still frequently equipped light tank battalions and it was fielded by some armoured units at Kursk, although it seems unlikely that any served with Fifth Guards Tank Army.

T-70

The need to replace the T-60 with a more capable light tank became apparent within a few months of the German invasion and Nicholas Astrov's design team at Factory No. 38 in Kirov began design studies of the future T-70 in late 1941.

The team's priorities were to:
■ Work in frontal armour of at least 45mm (1.8in) to offer a reasonable degree of protection from 37mm (1.45in) armour piercing rounds.
■ Incorporate a 45mm (1.8in) gun to give the type at least a limited anti-tank capability.

Surprisingly, despite the emphasis given to improving firepower, the T-70 retained a one-man turret which drastically reduced its effectiveness in both its reconnaissance and combat roles. (This decision ignored the experience of the 1930s when a two-man turret had been considered essential for the BA-6 and BA-10 heavy armoured cars, both of which were also armed with a 45mm (1.8in) gun.)

The automotive design was also peculiar – two GAZ-202 truck engines were fitted, one on each side of the hull. Each engine powered one track via separate, unsynchronised transmissions, an arrangement which caused endless mechanical problems. A few production vehicles were completed with this layout, but it was clearly impractical for front-line service and a redesign was hastily undertaken resulting in what was officially designated the T-70M, although it was more usually simply referred to as the T-70. The two engines were repositioned in-line to the right of the hull with a conventional transmission and differential. In order to simplify production, the original conical turret was replaced with an hexagonal design on all but a few of the earliest vehicles.

The T-70 entered production in March 1942 at Zavod No. 37, and was also built alongside the T-60 at GAZ and Zavod No. 38. Later vehicles, sometimes referred to as the T-70A, had more powerful GAZ-203 engines and a range of minor improvements, including the replacement of the driver's vision slit by a traversable MK-4 periscope. Over 8200 were completed by the time that production ended in October 1943 and the type remained in service until 1948.

The all too obvious shortcomings of the T-70's one-man turret prompted a series of design studies in 1942 for a version mounting a more practical two-man turret. This entered production in 1943 as the T-80 and was little more than a slightly enlarged and up-armoured T-70. Its two-man turret made it far more effective than its predecessor, but its armament was unchanged. No more than 120 were completed before it was decided to terminate production as its roles could be equally well fulfilled by Lend-Lease light tanks such as the M3 Stuart.

PROJECTS

The T-60 and T-70 formed the basis of several projects, including the bizarre Antonov A-40 *Krylya Tanka* ('Winged Tank') glider. This was a T-60 mounted on a detachable cradle which was fitted with biplane wings and a twin fin and rudder assembly. The theory was that the contraption could be towed to the drop zone behind a Pe-8 or TB-3 bomber/transport, jettison its wings and tail immediately after landing and be combat-ready within a few minutes. It soon became clear that the A-40 was too heavy – as an emergency measure the tank was stripped of all armament and ammunition and drained of most of its fuel. Even in its lightened

state, the sole test flight in September 1942 was cut short when the elderly TB-3 towing aircraft had to jettison the glider to avoid crashing. Surprisingly, the A-40 glided smoothly, landed in open country and drove back to the airfield under its own power. The project was quickly abandoned as it was realised that none of the readily available aircraft had sufficient power to tow the high-drag glider under operational conditions.

The T-90 AA tank was a far more practical project which originated with the devastation caused by *Luftwaffe* ground attack aircraft in 1941/42. This highlighted the vulnerability of truck-based self-propelled AA guns and in 1942 an open-topped turret armed with twin 12.7mm (0.5in) DShK machine guns was designed for the T-60. The turret was then redesigned to fit the T-70 and at least one vehicle was completed as the prototype T-90. However, the type never went into production, possibly due to doubts about the effectiveness of machine gun fire against the Germans' increasingly heavily armoured ground attack aircraft.

LIMITED USE

By 1943 it was universally recognized that light tanks were virtual death traps in view of the improvements in German AFV armament and anti-tank weapons. The T-70M's gun at least stood some chance of penetrating the Panzer III and Panzer IV at short range – always assuming that it survived long enough to close in! However, this was always a dubious proposition as the T-70M was less well protected and slower than contemporary T-34s, whilst its petrol engines made the type prone to catching fire if the fuel tanks or engine compartment were penetrated.

Despite these hazards, the T-70M did have some advantages – it was significantly smaller than a T-34 and its petrol engines had a much less conspicuous 'signature' than the diesel of the T-34 which emitted clouds of exhaust fumes. The type had the potential to be useful as a reconnaissance vehicle (even allowing for the limitations imposed by its two-man crew) if used with intelligence and a degree of tactical flair. In practice, as the T-70M-equipped light tank battalions represented a significant proportion of the armoured strength of each tank brigade, they tended to be thrown into action as 'substitute battle tanks' and suffered accordingly.

T-70M light tank

■ CREW

■ SPECIFICATIONS

Weight: 9.2 tonnes (9 tons)
Length: 4.29m (14ft 1in)
Width: 2.32m (7ft 7in)
Height: 2.04m (6ft 7in)
Engine: 2 x GAZ-202 totalling 104kW (140hp)
Speed: 45km/h (28mph)
Range: 360km (224 miles)
Radio: 9R (When fitted — even by 1945, not all Soviet AFVs had radios.)
Armament:
  Main: 1 x 45mm (1.8in) Model 38
  Secondary: 1 x 7.62mm (0.3in) DT machine gun

The T-70M was the final Soviet light tank to enter service in quantity during the war. Whilst the 45mm (1.8in) gun and thicker armour were welcome improvements to earlier designs, the retention of a one-man turret severely limited the type's battlefield performance.

Motor Rifle Battalion, 4th Guards Tank Brigade

During the pre-war period, the proponents of armoured warfare tended to under-rate the importance of mechanized infantry as part of armoured formations. Combat experience would show that whether they were termed panzer grenadiers, armoured infantry or motor riflemen, they were all vital to the efficiency of their parent formations.

The Red Army of the mid 1930s was arguably the most innovative army of its era. Marshal Tukhachevsky had formulated the theory of deep operations in conjunction with Vladimir Triandafillov, the Deputy Chief of the Soviet General Staff and was intent on producing the equipment to transform the theory into reality. (Deep operations were intended to break through the enemy's forward defences, after which fresh mobile operational reserves would exploit by penetrating deep into his rear areas. The objective of a deep operation was to inflict a decisive strategic defeat on the enemy, but unlike most other doctrines, deep battle theory stressed combined arms cooperation at all levels: strategic, operational and tactical.)

ORBAT: Motor Rifle Battalion, early 1943

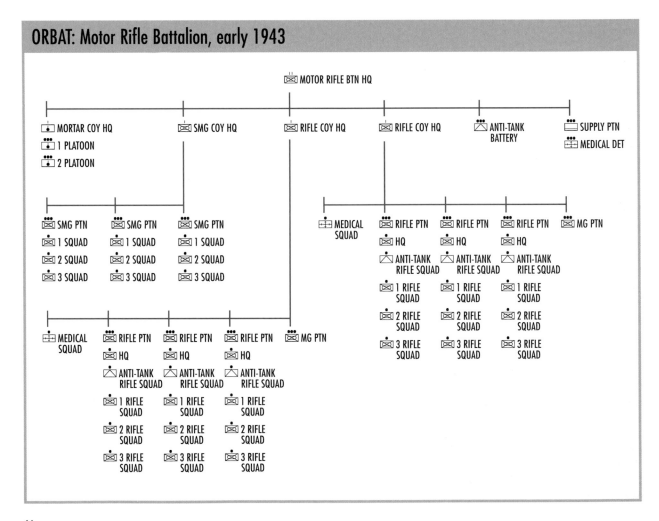

Tukhachevsky's drive and energy were not confined to overseeing the development of 'glamorous' weapons systems such as tanks and close-support aircraft. He ensured that attention was also given to the plethora of specialist vehicles required by the infantry and support units which would form a key part of future armoured formations. The need for fully tracked armoured personnel carriers (APCs) was recognized as one of the most urgent requirements and several prototypes were produced based on the T-26 light tank, including the TR-26 of 1932 which could carry up to eight infantry in addition to its two-man crew and the larger TR-4 with a maximum capacity of 15 fully-equipped troops.

REPRESSION AND INCOMPETENCE

The savage bloodbath of Stalin's purges brought an abrupt end to the era of free-ranging experimentation and tactical trials. Tukhachevsky himself was one of the earliest victims and his writings were immediately banned. By the time that the worst of the purges of the Red Army ended in late 1938, all those most closely associated with Tukhachevsky and his theories were either dead or imprisoned. The surviving members of the officer corps were understandably thoroughly cowed and unwilling to do anything other than slavishly follow the official Party line on military matters.

The official emphasis was now firmly on the traditional primacy of the cavalry and infantry – the senior officers most likely to have survived the purges were the politically 'safe' veterans of Budenny's First Cavalry Army of the Russian Civil War. One of these officers, Marshal Grigory Kulik, exercised a particularly baleful influence on the Red Army's motor rifle units – he scorned the German adoption of the MP38/40 submachine guns as a 'bourgeois fascist affectation', condemning such weapons on the grounds that they encouraged inaccurate firing and excessive ammunition consumption. He prevented issue of the PPD-40 to infantry units, stating it was only fit to be a 'pure police weapon'.

It was not until 1941, after a flood of demands for a weapon to match the MP38/40 overruled Kulik's prejudices, that an updated version of the PPD-40, the PPSh-41 was approved for infantry use. It proved to be one of the most widely

Motor Rifle Battalion: Personnel and Weapons

UNIT	VEHICLE	STRENGTH
Battalion HQ	Field Car	1
and HQ Platoon	BA-64 Armoured Car	3
(Manpower: 43 all ranks)	Radio Vehicle	1
	Cargo Truck	5
1st Rifle Company	Light MG	9
(Manpower: 112 all ranks)	Medium MG	2
	Anti-tank Rifle	3
2nd Rifle Company	Light MG	9
(Manpower: 112 all ranks)	Medium MG	2
	Anti-tank Rifle	3
Submachine Gun Company		
(Manpower: 79 all ranks)		
Mortar Company	82mm Mortars	6
(Manpower: 43 all ranks)	Trucks	4
Anti-tank Battery	76.2mm towed guns	4
(Manpower: 52 all ranks)	Trucks	4
Medical Platoon	Trucks/ambulances	3
(Manpower: 14 all ranks)		

produced, inexpensive and effective small arms of the war, with captured examples eagerly used by many German infantrymen who considered it to be superior to the MP38/40.

He also disparaged anti-tank and anti-personnel mines as 'a weapon of the weak' and incompatible with a properly aggressive strategy. As a result, Soviet wartime mines were hastily produced, crude designs which could be almost as dangerous to their users as the enemy. (Captured stocks of German mines were highly prized for their reliability.)

A FIRST HARD LESSON

The incompetence of commanders such as Kulik was dramatically illustrated in the Winter War against Finland. When the initial, wildly over-confident assumptions that the Red Army would quickly crush the Finns by sheer weight of numbers were proved wrong, many of Stalin's cronies simply did not know what to do. The Soviet infantry and motor rifle units suffered particularly badly – many were conscripts from the Ukraine who lacked even basic cold weather clothing and were not acclimatised to the extreme conditions of a Finnish winter. To add to their misery, the ramshackle supply system quickly broke down, and men went without hot food for days at a time.

Unsurprisingly, many Red Army casualties (possibly as many as 60,000) were due to hypothermia and disease. The small, but highly motivated Finnish army also inflicted massive casualties totalling almost 85,000 dead and over 186,000 wounded whilst losing no more than 26,000 dead and 44,000 wounded. Many of the Red Army's combat casualties were due to the Communist Party dogma which had largely replaced tactical training since the purges – some senior officers even banned any use of camouflage, as it was '…a sign of cowardice'.

Whilst the Winter War provided the necessary shock to begin the process of rebuilding an effective Red Army, so much damage had been done by the purges that the work was still far from complete at the time of the German invasion. Whilst all arms of service had severe problems, the infantry were arguably in the worst position. The Soviet system of conscription certainly did nothing to help matters – the most intelligent and best-educated conscripts tended to be assigned to the NKVD's internal security forces or technical arms of service such as the engineers, leaving the infantry with a high proportion of illiterate or semi-literate peasants and unskilled workers.

The grandiose plans for a massive expansion of Red Army's armoured forces in the aftermath of the

spectacular panzer victories of 1940 placed phenomenal demands on Soviet tank factories. Now there was no question of producing any APCs for motor rifle units, indeed there was real doubt whether there would be anything like enough trucks to transport them. In addition, Kulik's malign influence was still strong, so badly hindering attempts to re-equip the infantry with weapons suitable for modern warfare that many units faced the German invasion with rifles and machine guns which had first seen service in the Tsar's army of 1914.

TO THE BRINK OF DISASTER, 1941–42

The vast majority of the motor rifle formations which were caught up in the early German offensives were woefully ill-trained and often simply did not know how to work effectively with tanks. Their experienced opponents generally had little difficulty in pinning them down with well-directed artillery and mortar fire, so that the unsupported Soviet armour was frequently massacred by anti-tank guns and panzers.

Motor transport columns suffered particularly heavy losses from air attack, as the *Luftwaffe* concentrated its efforts on close air support after effectively neutralising the Red Air Force in the first few days of Operation Barbarossa. These losses had a severe impact on motor rifle units which had been short of transport even before the campaign began. (Attempts to deal with such problems were hindered by a long-standing Soviet trend to fake

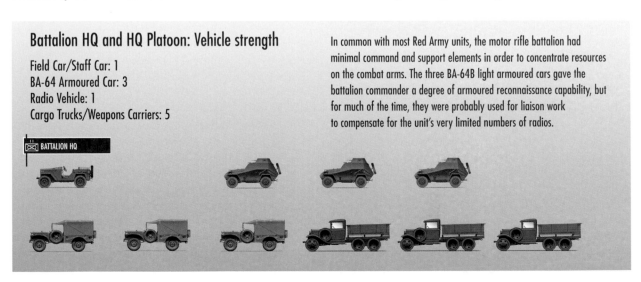

Battalion HQ and HQ Platoon: Vehicle strength

Field Car/Staff Car: 1
BA-64 Armoured Car: 3
Radio Vehicle: 1
Cargo Trucks/Weapons Carriers: 5

In common with most Red Army units, the motor rifle battalion had minimal command and support elements in order to concentrate resources on the combat arms. The three BA-64B light armoured cars gave the battalion commander a degree of armoured reconnaissance capability, but for much of the time, they were probably used for liaison work to compensate for the unit's very limited numbers of radios.

BATTALION HQ

BA-64B Model 1943 light armoured car

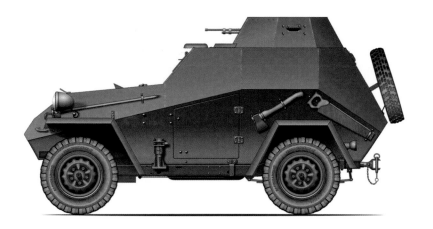

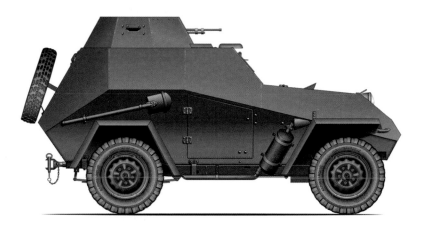

Weight: 2.36 tonnes (2.3 tons)
Length: 3.67m (12ft 4in)
Width: 1.53m (5ft)
Height: 1.9m (6ft 3in)
Engine: 40kW (54hp) 4-cylinder GAZ MM petrol
Speed: 80km/h (50mph)
Range: 560km (350 miles)
Armament: 1 x 7.62mm (0.3in) DT machine gun

The BA-64B gradually replaced pre-war types of armoured cars in reconnaissance units from 1943 onwards.

statistics – as factory managers and unit commanders could well be shot for failing to meet production or serviceability targets, they frequently falsified reports to give the impression that all was going according to plan.)

'TANK RIDERS' (*TANKODESANTNIKI*)

The lack of trucks forced motor rifle units to deploy most of their men as tank riders. The practice may well have originated in the Spanish Civil War with the Republican International Tank Regiment which was equipped with 48 of the BT-5s shipped to Spain in August 1937. Besides a cadre of Russian 'volunteers', their crews included Spaniards and International Brigade personnel who had trained at the Red Army's Gorky Tank School. On 13 October 1937, the unit was committed to an attack on the town of Fuentes de Ebro, which was intended to open the road to Zaragossa.

The attack was scheduled for noon on the 13th, but the tank crews only received their orders at 23:00 the previous day and then had a 50-kilometre (30-mile) road march to the assembly area.

'War-weary' T-34 Model 1942 tanks wait for the last of their 'tank riders' (*tankodesantniki*) to scramble aboard. Shortages of trucks with adequate cross-country performance and an almost total lack of armoured personnel carriers forced the Red Army to adopt the practice of carrying assault infantry on tanks, where they formed a concentrated target for MG and artillery fire.

Barely two hours before the attack was due to start, the unit was told that it would be carrying infantry from the 15th International Brigade into action on its tanks, despite the fact that neither unit had any training for this role. The crews were then told that there was no time to carry out any reconnaissance and that the Republican commanders could not give any information about the terrain or enemy anti-tank defences, which they regarded as trivial matters!

It was hardly surprising that things went wrong from the beginning of the operation – the BTs fired a single salvo before racing off with the infantry clinging to their decks. Many fell off as the tanks charged across country, whilst others became casualties when startled front-line Republican infantry (who hadn't been warned of the attack), opened fire as the BTs came roaring over their positions. The attackers then found that the plain in front of the Nationalist defences consisted mainly of sugar cane fields, criss-crossed with irrigation ditches. As the tanks attempted to force their way through, they came under fire from enemy artillery and anti-tank guns hidden in farm buildings. The handful of infantry who remained with the tanks were too few to neutralise the Nationalist guns or hold the ground which had been gained and the attack was abandoned with the loss of 19 tanks. This fiasco was a grim foretaste of the sort of actions

Motor Rifle Battalion, Rifle Company, early 1943

Officers: 5
Men: 103

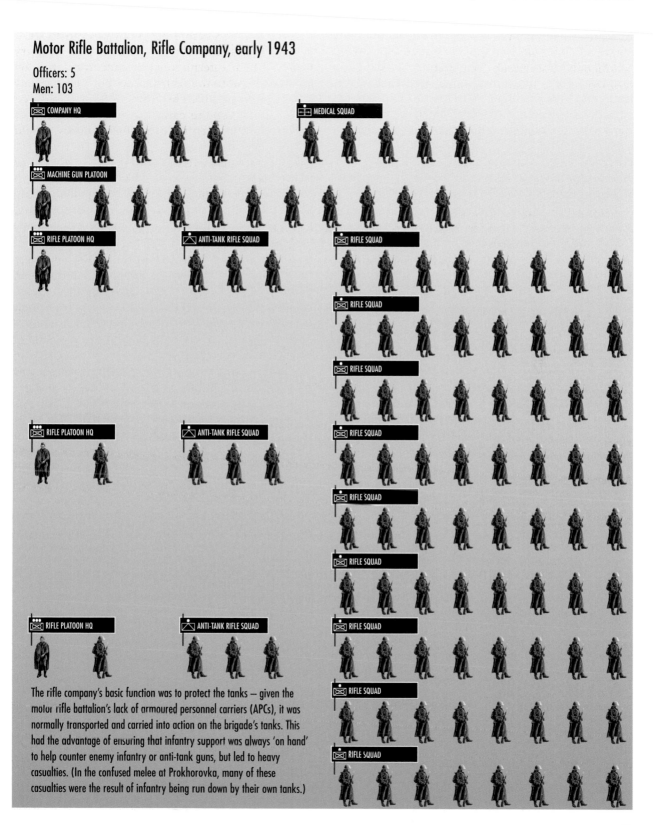

The rifle company's basic function was to protect the tanks – given the motor rifle battalion's lack of armoured personnel carriers (APCs), it was normally transported and carried into action on the brigade's tanks. This had the advantage of ensuring that infantry support was always 'on hand' to help counter enemy infantry or anti-tank guns, but led to heavy casualties. (In the confused melee at Prokhorovka, many of these casualties were the result of infantry being run down by their own tanks.)

fought by hapless Soviet tank riders in the early stages of the war. Initially there was little or no special provision for carrying infantry on the tanks – at best, rope 'grab lines' might be lashed to the hull and turret. This added to the already considerable risks run by the riflemen crowded onto the tanks' decks. The official carrying capacity of each class of tank was:

■ Heavy tanks: 10–12 men
■ Medium tanks: 8–10 men
■ Light tanks: 5–6 men

In practice, tanks frequently went into action seriously overloaded – a T-34 might well have up to 15 infantry desperately clinging to its hull and turret.

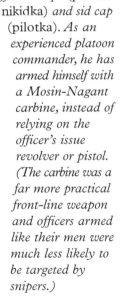

Lieutenant, Motor Rifle Battalion

This Lieutenant is in typical 'wet weather kit' – the officer's cape (plasch nikidka) *and sid cap* (pilotka). *As an experienced platoon commander, he has armed himself with a Mosin-Nagant carbine, instead of relying on the officer's issue revolver or pistol. (The carbine was a far more practical front-line weapon and officers armed like their men were much less likely to be targeted by snipers.)*

Later production examples of most Soviet tanks and assault guns were fitted with handrails to make life very slightly less hazardous for their passengers and occasionally logs would be lashed along the sides and rear of tanks' hulls to provide makeshift platforms.

Bitterly-won experience gradually led to greater professionalism, but even in the autumn of 1942, general standards were very low. This led Stalin to issue Order No. 325 in October 1942 which combined a scathing critique of shortcomings with basic tactical instructions. The following extracts give a vivid indication of the state of tank/motor rifle unit co-operation at the time:

■ Our tanks when attacking enemy defences separate from the infantry and lose contact with them. Infantry, cut off from tanks by enemy fire, cannot support our tanks with their fire. Tanks, having lost contact with the infantry, face enemy artillery, tanks and infantry unsupported, suffering heavy losses as a result.

■ Tanks operating with infantry have the destruction of enemy infantry as their primary mission and must not be separated from the infantry by more than 200 – 400 metres. In combat the tank unit commander must maintain observation of his infantry's combat formation. If the infantry goes to ground and fails to advance behind the tanks, the tank unit commander will designate some of his tanks to destroy the firing positions that hinder the advance of our infantry.

■ Infantry supporting tank operations must concentrate their fire and that of their accompanying guns on the enemy's anti-tank weapons, must locate and clear minefields, assist tanks in overcoming anti-tank obstacles and swampy terrain, fight German tanks, determinedly follow behind the tanks in the attack, quickly consolidate lines seized by them and help to evacuate damaged tanks from the battlefield.

■ This order is to be issued to tank and mechanized forces down to platoon commander, to rifle and artillery units down to company and battery commander and it is to be executed quickly and precisely.

The instructions placed exceptionally heavy demands on the infantry and, in practice, commanders would try to assign some of the more specialised tasks such as mine clearance to engineer detachments. (However, this was by no means always the case in the Red Army, as Zhukov remarked to Eisenhower: 'If we come to a minefield, our infantry attacks exactly as if it were not there.')

GREATER PROFESSIONALISM

By 1943, a greater degree of professionalism was beginning to be apparent throughout the Red Army, but this was not always apparent in the motor rifle and other infantry units. This was largely due to the horrendous casualties that they suffered – in the conditions of the Eastern Front, infantry on both sides almost invariably sustained far heavier losses than armoured or artillery units. The problem was compounded by the lack of long-service, professional NCOs; as a result, junior officers were burdened with basic training and administrative work, which corporals and sergeants would have dealt with in most Western armies. This left them over-worked, with little time for combat training.

Harassed junior officers soon encountered further problems as the conscription system was steadily expanded to include groups previously considered too politically unreliable for military service, such as 130,000 convicts from the Gulag. The system also swept in an increasing proportion of recruits from the Central Asian republics, many

Dodge WC51 4x4 weapons carrier

CREW

SPECIFICATIONS

Weight: 3.3 tonnes (3.25 tons)
Length: 4.47m (14ft 8in)
Width: 2.1m (6ft 11in)
Height: 2.15m (7ft 1in)
Engine 68.54kW (92hp) Dodge T214 6-cylinder petrol
Speed: n/k
Range: 384km (240 miles)

Almost 25,000 WC series vehicles were supplied to the Red Army between 1943 and 1945.

of whom could not speak any Russian and required a quick (and often brutal) course of language training so that they could understand basic instruction and battlefield commands.

Although there was a feeling in the Red Army that ultimate victory was a real possibility after the German defeat at Stalingrad, there were still plenty of men who were sufficiently disaffected to desert to the Germans. The number of desertions actually increased throughout the first half of 1943. One motor rifle unit lost seven deserters in a three-day period at the end of May. German intelligence reports recorded the following totals:

■ February – just over 1000
■ April – 1964
■ May – 2424
■ June – 2555

The vast majority of these deserters became volunteers ('Hiwis') serving with German units in a wide range of roles including drivers, cooks, hospital attendants and ammunition carriers. By 1943 the official establishment of each German infantry division in Russia included no less than 2000 Hiwis.

WEAPONS OF THE MOTOR RIFLE BATTALION

By 1943, motor rifle battalions fielded a variety of robust and effective weapons, with the only real weakness being the lack of modern infantry anti-tank equipment. At a time when US forces were receiving large numbers of bazookas, the Red Army was reliant on grenades and anti-tank rifles and surprisingly failed to adopt a shoulder-fired anti-tank rocket launcher until the RPG-2 entered service in 1949. (Ironically, 8500 Lend-Lease bazookas were sent to Russia in 1942 where a number were captured and subsequently used by the Germans.)

RIFLES & CARBINES

The Red Army's standard rifle, the Mosin-Nagant M1891/30, was a sturdy, if rather heavy and clumsy weapon. Its worst feature was an awkward safety mechanism which was operated by rotating a knob at the rear of the bolt. This was prone to freezing solid and troops were taught to urinate on it in an emergency for an immediate thaw-out. A further problem was that the rifle was intended to be used with the reversible bayonet permanently attached. This increased the length of an already long rifle to

Rations

Official Red Army rations were far better than those of the vast majority of civilians, but troops would be very lucky to receive anything like their full entitlement of:

■ Black bread – almost 907g (2lb) in winter, 795g (1.75lb) in summer
■ Wheat flour 20g (0.7oz)
■ Grits about 142g (5oz)
■ Macaroni, or egg noodles 150g (1oz) (quite popular with the troops)
■ Meat 150g (5.25oz) (either fresh or preserved)
■ Fish 100g (3.5oz) (either fresh or preserved)
■ Soy flour 14g (0.5oz)
■ Fats – lard, chicken fat or bacon grease – about 28g (1oz)
■ Vegetable oil 20g (0.7oz)
■ Sugar 35g (1.22oz)
■ Tea 1g (0.035oz)
■ Salt 30g (1.05oz)
■ Vegetables 360g (12.7oz), or 163g (5.74oz) of additional grits for ease of transport
■ Tomato paste 6g (0.21oz)

■ Spices 0.28g (0.01oz)
■ Tobacco 20g (0.7oz)
In addition, emergency rations were supposed to be carried comprising:
■ Biscuits (tinned or sealed cardboard/paper wrapper) 496g (17.5oz)
■ Concentrated food — First Course 75g (2.6oz) of instant soup or enriched biscuits
■ Concentrated food — Second Course 200g (7oz) – More of the same. (Where available after late 1942, Lend-Lease tinned food or even some pre-packaged ration items, such as British biscuits or dripping spread)
■ Smoked Sausages 100g (3.5oz) — sometimes replaced by lard, tinned fish or bacon
■ Sugar 35g (1.2oz)
■ Tea 2g (0.07oz)
■ Salt 10g (0.35oz)

In practice, many front line units had to manage on a diet largely made up of *shchi* (cabbage soup) and *kashka* (buckwheat porridge). The one universally popular ration item was the daily tot of 100g (3.5oz) of vodka.

Universal Carrier Mark I

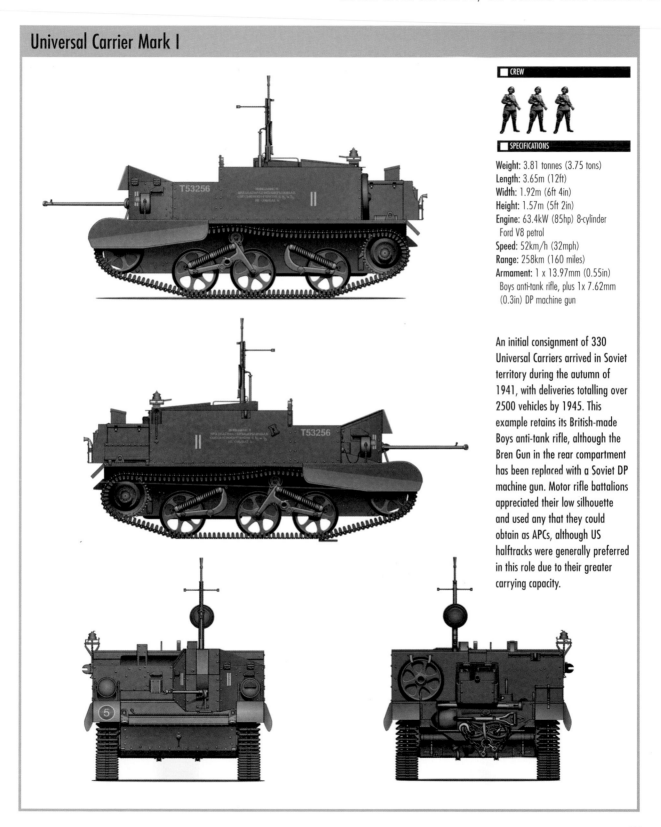

CREW

SPECIFICATIONS

Weight: 3.81 tonnes (3.75 tons)
Length: 3.65m (12ft)
Width: 1.92m (6ft 4in)
Height: 1.57m (5ft 2in)
Engine: 63.4kW (85hp) 8-cylinder Ford V8 petrol
Speed: 52km/h (32mph)
Range: 258km (160 miles)
Armament: 1 x 13.97mm (0.55in) Boys anti-tank rifle, plus 1x 7.62mm (0.3in) DP machine gun

An initial consignment of 330 Universal Carriers arrived in Soviet territory during the autumn of 1941, with deliveries totalling over 2500 vehicles by 1945. This example retains its British-made Boys anti-tank rifle, although the Bren Gun in the rear compartment has been replaced with a Soviet DP machine gun. Motor rifle battalions appreciated their low silhouette and used any that they could obtain as APCs, although US halftracks were generally preferred in this role due to their greater carrying capacity.

almost equal an average man's height, making it extremely awkward to handle in confined spaces, especially buildings and trenches. All rifles were zeroed in with the bayonet in place, so its removal seriously affected accuracy and effectively required the rifle to be re-zeroed.

The rifle's handling problems were partially solved by the introduction of a carbine version in 1938 (the M1938 carbine). It was much shorter than the rifle, measuring only 1020mm (40in) overall, but its greater handiness was marred by very heavy recoil due to its short barrel. No bayonet fitting was provided as it was originally intended for use by engineers and other specialists who were unlikely to be involved in bayonet fighting. However, as the weapon was increasingly issued to infantry, this capability became more important and its successor, the M1944 carbine, was produced with a permanently attached folding bayonet.

MACHINE GUNS

The DP light machine gun was the key weapon of each rifle squad. It was a bipod mounted weapon fed by a rather fragile 47-round pan magazine, from which it derived its nickname of '*proigryvatel*' (record player). Its theoretical rate of fire was 500-600rpm, but a more practical figure was around 80rpm. This allowed for magazine changes and firing short bursts to improve accuracy and minimise the risks of over-heating.

Most machine gun platoons were equipped with the Maxim M1910/30 which was essentially the same belt-fed machine gun which had entered service with the Imperial Russian Army in 1910. It was immensely strong and reliable, with a sustained rate of fire of 520–580rpm. Despite the type's bulk and weight – 63kg (139lb) – it only underwent relatively minor modifications during its production run which did not end until 1945.

SUBMACHINE GUN COMPANY

The submachine gun company was armed with the PPSh-41 (*Pistolet Pulemjot Shpagina* Model 1941 – Shpagin submachine gun Model 1941.) It was an effective, but rather crude weapon, which ideally matched Soviet wartime requirements. Its parts (excluding the barrel) could be produced by a relatively unskilled workforce with simple equipment readily available in small workshops, freeing more skilled workers for other tasks. The PPSh-41 comprised 87 components compared to 95 of the earlier PPD-40 submachine gun – the manufacture of each PPSh-41 required only 7.3 machining hours compared to 13.7 hours for each PPD-40. (From the spring of 1942 onwards, PPSh-41 production averaged 3000 weapons per day.)

The weapon had a crude compensator to lessen muzzle climb and a hinged receiver which facilitated field-stripping and cleaning the bore in battle conditions.

Tokarev SVT-40 semi-automatic rifle

Russian interest in self-loading rifles dated back to the Federov Avtomat of 1915. Research in the 1930s led to the development of Fedor Tokarev's SVT-38 which was withdrawn from service after it showed numerous faults in action during the Winter War against Finland in 1939/40. An improved version of the basic design, the SVT-40, entered production in July 1940 and it was intended that the type would largely replace the Mosin-Nagant 91/30 in front line infantry units. In the aftermath of the German invasion it was found that the type was just too complex for rapid mass production and that this complexity also made it difficult for hastily trained conscripts to use the weapon effectively. As a result, production was tapered off in favour of the old Mosin-Nagant rifles and PPSh submachine guns.

■ SPECIFICATIONS

Calibre: 7.62mm x 52R
Length: 1226mm (48.27in)
Weight: 3.90kg (8.6lb)
Feed/magazine capacity: 10-round detachable box magazine
Operation: Gas
Effective range: 500m (1640ft)

Though 35-round curved box magazines were available from 1942, the average infantryman would keep a higher-capacity, 71-round drum magazine as the initial load. This drum magazine was a near-copy of the Finnish M31 Suomi magazine which held 71 rounds, but in practice, misfeeds were likely to occur if it was loaded with more than 65 or so cartridges. A typical submachine gunner would probably carry one drum and a number of box magazines. Early magazines were made from 0.5mm sheet steel and were prone to distortion which caused jamming. This problem was largely solved by the use of 1mm sheet steel for later production batches.

The PPSh-41 was a highly-efficient close-range weapon – this was not fully appreciated at first and early guns featured elevation-adjustable rear sights, graduated up to 500 metres (1640ft); late production guns had flip-type 'L'-shaped rear sights set for ranges of 100 and 200 metres (328 and 656ft).

Thousands of PPSh-41s were captured and the weapon became a particular favourite of the German infantry who appreciated its low recoil, reliability and lethality at close range. Because of the similarities between the 7.62x25mm Tokarev and the cartridge used in the Mauser C96, captured examples were easily supplied with ammunition.

Mosin-Nagant M19/30 rifle

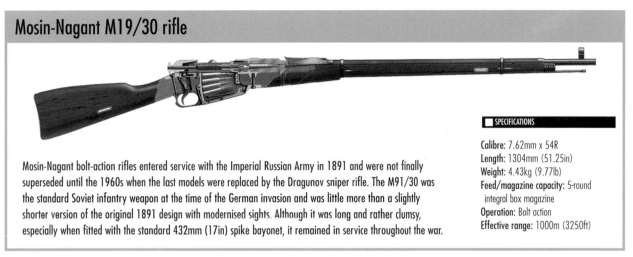

Mosin-Nagant bolt-action rifles entered service with the Imperial Russian Army in 1891 and were not finally superseded until the 1960s when the last models were replaced by the Dragunov sniper rifle. The M91/30 was the standard Soviet infantry weapon at the time of the German invasion and was little more than a slightly shorter version of the original 1891 design with modernised sights. Although it was long and rather clumsy, especially when fitted with the standard 432mm (17in) spike bayonet, it remained in service throughout the war.

SPECIFICATIONS

Calibre: 7.62mm x 54R
Length: 1304mm (51.25in)
Weight: 4.43kg (9.77lb)
Feed/magazine capacity: 5-round integral box magazine
Operation: Bolt action
Effective range: 1000m (3250ft)

PPSh-41 submachine gun

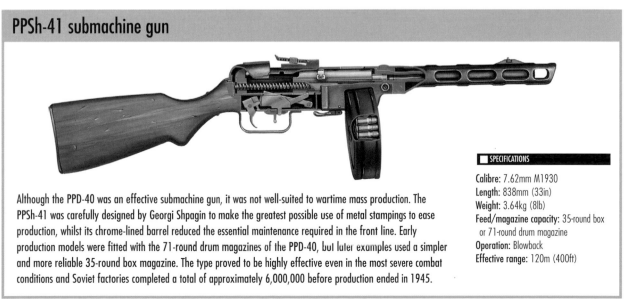

Although the PPD-40 was an effective submachine gun, it was not well-suited to wartime mass production. The PPSh-41 was carefully designed by Georgi Shpagin to make the greatest possible use of metal stampings to ease production, whilst its chrome-lined barrel reduced the essential maintenance required in the front line. Early production models were fitted with the 71-round drum magazines of the PPD-40, but later examples used a simpler and more reliable 35-round box magazine. The type proved to be highly effective even in the most severe combat conditions and Soviet factories completed a total of approximately 6,000,000 before production ended in 1945.

SPECIFICATIONS

Calibre: 7.62mm M1930
Length: 838mm (33in)
Weight: 3.64kg (8lb)
Feed/magazine capacity: 35-round box or 71-round drum magazine
Operation: Blowback
Effective range: 120m (400ft)

GAZ-AAA

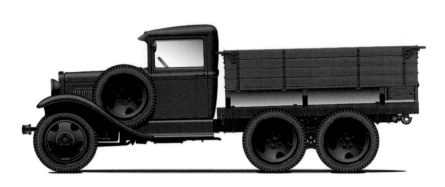

CREW

SPECIFICATIONS
Weight: 3.52 tonnes (3.46 tons)
Length: 5.34m (17ft 6in)
Width: 2.36m (7ft 9in)
Height: 2.1m (6ft 11in)
Engine: 37kW (50hp) GAZ-M 4-cylinder petrol
Speed: 35km/h (21.75mph)
Range: n/k

The GAZ-AAA was the first Soviet-designed 6x4 truck and was a familiar sight throughout the Red Army from the mid-1930s until 1945. Total production ran to roughly 37,000 vehicles.

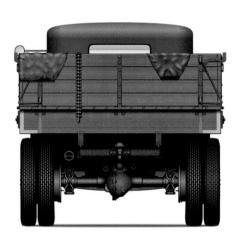

Mortar Company

Soviet mortars were especially valued weapons as they were simple to produce, relatively lightweight and thus easy to move (an important consideration given the Red Army's perennial shortage of gun tractors).

In offensive operations the mortar company's primary role was to lay down supporting fire for the battalion's leading rifle platoons. During the general artillery preparation preceding a Red Army infantry attack, the company concentrated on neutralising enemy infantry positions and clearing paths for the assault force by blowing gaps through minefields and wire entanglements. As the Soviet infantry deployed, the mortars joined with the artillery in providing general covering fire, whilst as the attack went in they fired concentrations against front-line enemy positions, known support weapons emplacements, and counter-attacking infantry.

When on the defensive, the mortar company provided normal supporting fire for the battalion and was also in readiness to:

■ Bombard enemy using concealed approaches at ranges of up to 2.5 kilometres (1.55 miles)

■ Fire barrages to separate attacking enemy infantry from their tanks and neutralise enemy support weapons.

If the assault force broke into the Soviet defences, the mortars were expected to aid its destruction by laying down fire to pin it down and support Red Army counter-attacks.

Defensive barrages against tank/infantry attacks were fired according to a pre-arranged plan. A series of phase lines between 274 and 366 metres (300–400 yards) apart were selected along the expected line of advance with the closest phase line being 274 metres (300 yards) from the forward positions. The range of each phase line was pre-determined and fire was brought down on the furthest phase line as soon as the lead tanks crossed it. Fire was then shifted to each succeeding phase line until the attack was either repulsed, or penetrated the final line.

When changing position, the company was preceded by a reconnaissance section which selected the firing positions and observation posts (OPs). Whenever possible, the company OP was set up alongside the motor rifle battalion OP to ease liaison between the company and battalion commanders. Each mortar platoon also established its own OP in front of its position, ensuring that it was close enough to allow verbal orders or signals to be passed between the OPs and their platoons. Field telephone lines were run from each of the platoon OPs to the rifle battalion OP and from there to the mortar company HQ back at the firing position. (The shortage of Red Army's chronic shortage of radios forced it to rely far more heavily on field telephones than its Western counterparts. Although this improved security, there was seldom time to bury the telephone lines which put them at considerable risk of being cut by artillery or mortar fire.)

Although the company lacked the tactical flexibility of its equivalent units in Western armies, its fire was particularly deadly as the casings of Soviet mortar bombs were cast iron which had better fragmentation characteristics than the forged steel used for Western mortar ammunition.

82mm (3.2in) Model 1937 mortar

Soviet design teams modified the French 82mm (3.2in) Model 1936 to produce the 82mm (3.2in) Model 1937. A number of changes were made, including the addition of recoil springs between the barrel and bipod to reduce the amount of re-laying required during prolonged firing. The most obvious alteration was the adoption of a new circular base plate which became one of the main recognition points of Russian mortars. In German hands the type was designated as the 8.2cm (3.2in) *Granatwerfer 274/2(r)*.

CREW

SPECIFICATIONS

Calibre: 82mm (3.228in)
Barrel length: 1320mm (51.97in)
Bore length: 1225mm (48.23in)
Weight in action: 57.34kg (126.3lb)
Elevation: 45° to 85°
Traverse: 6° to 11° depending on elevation
Maximum range: 3100m (3391 yards)
Bomb weight: 3.4kg (7.5lb)

Anti-tank Battery

The anti-tank battery was the motor rifle battalion's defence against enemy AFVs which managed to evade the tank brigade's own armour. By mid-1943, it was generally equipped with 76.2mm (3in) guns which were capable of dealing with most German AFVs and could also provide a useful volume of direct fire support when using HE.

The anti-tank batteries of motor rifle battalions had originally been equipped with 45mm (1.8in) Model 1937 anti-tank guns which were effective against most German tanks encountered in the early stages of Operation Barbarossa. However, they were outclassed by the newer up-armoured AFVs which began to appear from 1942 onwards.

The problem had been anticipated well before the German invasion, but unfortunately for the Red Army, Marshal Kulik had again muddied the waters of weapons development with his ill-informed meddling. His view was that the deployment of the prototype SMK, T-100 and KV-1 heavy tanks in the Winter War against Finland would have prompted the Germans to develop equivalent AFVs which would be immune to any Soviet 45mm (1.8in) or 76.2mm (3in) guns. It also seems likely that he was influenced by German propaganda which vastly inflated the numbers and capabilities of the experimental *Neubaufahrzeug* heavy tanks.

In early 1940, Vasiliy Grabin's artillery design team was ordered to begin work on a 57mm (2.2in) anti-tank gun capable of penetrating 90mm (3.5in) of armour at normal combat ranges. However, work was disrupted by Kulik's growing paranoia about German 'super tanks'. He soon believed that even the specified level of armour penetration would be inadequate and diverted Grabin's team to the development of a massive 107mm (4.2in) tank gun

Anti-tank Battery		
UNIT	VEHICLE	STRENGTH
Battery	Men	52
	76.2mm Towed Gun	4
	Trucks	4

which never entered service. Eventually, the excellent 57mm (2.2in) ZiS-2 Model 1941 entered production barely three weeks before the German invasion. This was easily capable of dealing with any German AFV of 1941/42, but it was not the easiest weapon to manufacture, especially in the chaotic conditions of the time, and only 371 guns had been completed when production was halted at the beginning of December 1941.

The appearance of the Tiger and Panther led to a modified version being adopted in mid-1943 as the ZiS-2 Model 1943, which had a formidable performance for its calibre, especially when firing tungsten-cored high velocity armour-piercing composite rigid (APCR) shot.

The problems with the ZiS-2 meant that a series of improvisations were adopted as it became clear that the 45mm (1.8in) anti-tank guns were becoming obsolescent. The various 76.2mm (3in) divisional guns were the most readily-available weapons and were used to equip anti-tank units from 1941 onwards. (Some 85mm (3.3in) AA guns

Anti-tank Battery

76.2mm towed guns: 4
Trucks: 4

COMMANDER

The anti-tank battery consisted of four 76.2mm (3in) anti-tank guns, towed by a light truck of some sort, in this case, the US-supplied Dodge WC51 weapons carrier.

were also deployed in the anti-tank role – whilst they had an impressive armour-piercing capability, they were large weapons which were difficult to move and conceal. These limitations and the pressing need for AA guns led to them being withdrawn from most anti-tank units by mid-1942.)

The 76.2mm (3in) divisional guns were high velocity weapons with a good anti-tank performance – almost 3000 examples of the Model 1936 (F-22) were completed between 1937 and 1939 when production switched to the modernised F-22USV, nearly 10,000 of which entered service between 1939 and 1941. The Germans captured several hundred guns of both types in 1941/42, and were so impressed with their armour-piercing performance that they converted many to dedicated anti-tank guns. The Red Army found these types equally effective in the anti-armour role, but it was also clear that they were too large and heavy to make ideal anti-tank guns. In addition, the sights and elevation controls were on opposite sides of the breech assembly, which hindered the rapid gun laying required to sight fast-moving enemy tanks.

THE ZIS-3

These problems were largely solved with the introduction of the ZiS-3, the best of the 76.2mm (3in) guns to see wartime service. It dated back to late 1940, when Grabin's team began unofficial design studies of a divisional gun combining the light carriage of the 57mm (2.2in) ZiS-2 anti-tank

gun and the 76.2mm (3in) barrel of the F-22USV divisional gun. A muzzle brake was fitted to decrease recoil and allow the barrel to be mounted on a relatively light carriage without the risk of over-stressing the mounting with prolonged firing. The ZiS-3 was far more suited to mass production than earlier divisional guns as many components were cast, stamped or welded in order to reduce the amount of machining required. A prototype performed extremely well and, following the German invasion, Grabin took the decision to order Artillery Factory 92 to begin production on his own authority. This was in contravention of Marshal Kulik's order for the production of F-22USVs and was an incredibly brave decision in the paranoid atmosphere of Stalin's Soviet Union.

Grabin experienced repeated frustration as supply authorities and military commanders refused to accept his offers of 'unauthorised' guns. Finally, he persuaded frightened supply officials to accept the ever-increasing stocks of ZiS-3s on his personal responsibility. Combat experience demonstrated the type's superiority over all other types of divisional guns, leading to its demonstration before Stalin and senior Red Army officers. Stalin was deeply impressed, remarking that: 'This gun is a masterpiece of artillery systems design.' His favourable impression was confirmed by the results of a five-day official state test run in February 1942 which resulted in the type's belated official entry into service.

76mm (3in) Zis-3 anti-tank gun

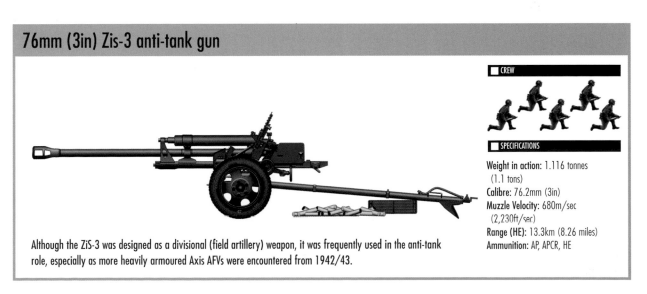

CREW

SPECIFICATIONS

Weight in action: 1.116 tonnes
(1.1 tons)
Calibre: 76.2mm (3in)
Muzzle Velocity: 680m/sec
(2,230ft/sec)
Range (HE): 13.3km (8.26 miles)
Ammunition: AP, APCR, HE

Although the ZiS-3 was designed as a divisional (field artillery) weapon, it was frequently used in the anti-tank role, especially as more heavily armoured Axis AFVs were encountered from 1942/43.

Medical Platoon

Soviet combat medicine was very basic in comparison with its Western counterparts, but some extraordinary successes were achieved by medical staff working with minimal equipment.

In theory, Soviet medical platoons were supposed to provide two doctors to man their battalion's aid post and two stretcher teams for each company. Combat injuries from large-scale actions could quickly swamp the limited front line medical facilities as transport to evacuate the more seriously wounded was always in short supply. In some respects, serious casualties from tank or motor rifle units were lucky as there was likely to be some form of motor transport to take them to one of the larger field hospitals. (Most other units were largely dependent on horse-drawn carts for casualty evacuation.)

However, tank crews were at greater risk of some types of injury than infantrymen or artillery crews. Despite the fact that many Soviet AFVs had diesel engines, making them less prone to fuel fires when hit, they were still at risk of burning or exploding

due to poorly protected ammunition. The results were often appalling – notably severe burns which were often fatal due to the lack of specialised medical facilities available close to the front line. (A few hardy individuals did survive extreme injuries – Lieutenant Nikolai Zheleznov recovered after being pulled from his blazing tank with a broken leg and 35 per cent burns. In typical Soviet field medical practice, he was given plenty of vodka as a rough and ready substitute for the rarely available morphine.)

Many of the Red Army's 800,000 women served in the Medical Corps. Female nursing staff were frequently in the front line, attempting to rescue those injured crewmen unable to 'bail out' from their stricken vehicles. Nina Vishnevskaya remembered how hard it was to deal with unconscious casualties: 'It was difficult to drag out a man, especially a turret gunner...' Dr Olga Borisenko was attached to the medical staff of Fifth Guards Tank Army and recalled the difficulties of treating wounded tank crewmen: 'Many of the men would come in covered in dirt. They'd tried to put out the flames by rolling on the ground. As a result their wounds got dirty and became infected.'

In general terms, the Red Army's medical services were well organised, but poorly equipped. Very few sulpha drugs or other antibiotics were available and infected wounds were commonplace. Some individual's experiences read like a journal from the Napoleonic Wars, rather than the mid-twentieth century. This was the case as late as 1944 when Colonel Sverdlov was wounded in the back by shell splinters. He was able to make his way to an aid post where he had to bend over holding his knees whilst being sewn up without any form of anaesthetic. The only beds were piles of straw in an open field, so he decided to return to his unit after laying down for a couple of hours.

Battlefield first aid: a Red Army nurse and medical orderly tend a wounded German corporal. This is likely to be a posed propaganda photograph as neither side was generally much concerned about treating wounded prisoners.

In many respects, illness was as serious a problem as wounds. Very few Red Army conscripts had received the inoculations which were increasingly common in Western armies – typhus, pneumonia, dysentery, meningitis, tuberculosis, diphtheria and malaria were all prevalent. In many cases, the only treatments available were a variety of peasant remedies of varying effectiveness.

Several illnesses (notably typhus) were largely due to the prevalence of lice – periodic checks were supposed to be made for lice with the results recorded on a 'Form 20'. In theory, the problem was to be kept under control by ensuring that all troops visited steam baths (*banyas*) at least every 10 days when their uniforms would be laundered

and steam-treated to kill any lice. However, this was frequently impossible under combat conditions and troops spent much of their time 'de-lousing' their uniforms. (One method used during the winter months was to bury the uniform with only the tip of the collar left above ground and burn the emerging lice with a cigarette as they crawled up the collar to escape from the frozen ground.)

A further hazard was posed by the often appalling quality of wartime rations which caused cases of scurvy. (Even the pre-war Red Army had to contend with food which was totally unfit for human consumption. In 1939 a consignment of rotten fish was served which led to 350 men from one unit being hospitalised with food poisoning.)

GAZ-55 ambulance

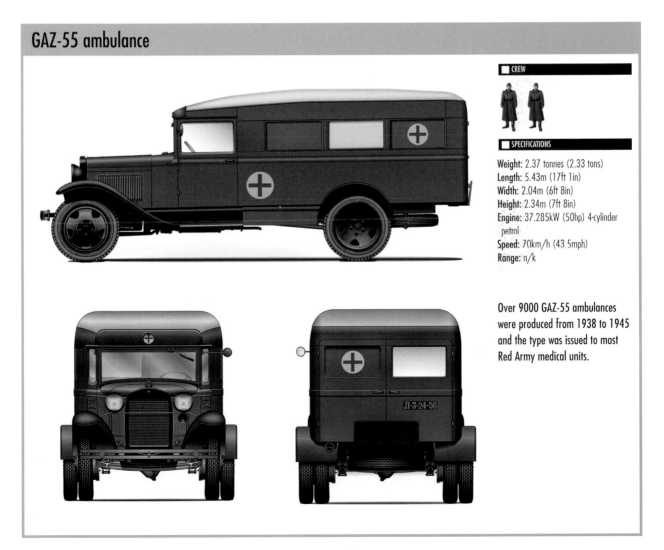

CREW

SPECIFICATIONS

Weight: 2.37 tonnes (2.33 tons)
Length: 5.43m (17ft 1in)
Width: 2.04m (6ft 8in)
Height: 2.34m (7ft 8in)
Engine: 37.285kW (50hp) 4-cylinder petrol
Speed: 70km/h (43.5mph)
Range: n/k

Over 9000 GAZ-55 ambulances were produced from 1938 to 1945 and the type was issued to most Red Army medical units.

Trains Company, 4th Guards Tank Brigade

'Logistics is the ball and chain of armoured warfare.' Heinz Guderian. Despite an understandable tendency to concentrate on the relative merits of AFVs, it's worth remembering that without fuel tankers and supply trucks they are little more than expensively-produced scrap metal.

The pre-war Soviet automotive industry was largely based on licence-built copies of US vehicles of the late 1920s. This was due to the contract signed with the Ford Motor Company in May 1929 by which the Soviet Union agreed to purchase vehicles and spares totalling $13,000,000. Ford also undertook to give technical assistance over a nine year period with the construction and running of a major vehicle production plant at Nizhny Novgorod. The factory began production in January 1932 – both it and the vehicles it produced were designated *Nizhegorodsky Avtomobilny Zavod* (NAZ). One of its first products was the light truck NAZ-AA, a licence-built copy of the Ford Model AA. The following year, the factory's name changed to *Gorkovsky Avtomobilny Zavod*, (GAZ) when the city was renamed in honour of Maxim Gorky – at the same time, all its products received the 'GAZ' prefix. The GAZ-AA proved to be so robust and reliable in both civilian and military service that an enlarged 6x4 version, the GAZ-AAA, was rapidly developed and put into production – over 37,000 vehicles were delivered between 1934 and 1943.

The other major pre-war Soviet truck was the ZiS-5, a close copy of the US Autocar Model CA. This was manufactured in a number of versions from 1933 until at least 1955, with total production figures of roughly 1,000,000 vehicles.

All these types were mechanically simple, extremely strong vehicles designed to operate with minimal maintenance on the Soviet Union's appalling roads in all weather conditions. They were under-powered, but their engines could run on the very low-octane petrol which was all that was available from Soviet refineries. Although the Red Army's total holdings in mid-1941 were impressive – possibly as high as 250,000 – many of these were destroyed or captured in the first chaotic months of the German invasion.

The horrendous losses of motor transport put huge pressure on the Soviet rail system at the very

Trains Company		
UNIT	VEHICLE	STRENGTH
(Manpower: 101 all ranks)	Cargo Trucks	36
	Workshop Vehicles	8
	Fuel Tankers	10
	Recovery Vehicles	4

time when it was working at full stretch to evacuate key factories from areas threatened by the German advance. However, the first Lend-Lease shipments arriving in late 1941 offered the hard-pressed Red Army a glimmer of hope for the future. The first batches of British, US and Canadian trucks to be unloaded were a world away from the obsolescent Soviet designs. In particular, the US 4x4 and 6x6 types were prized for their load-carrying ability and excellent cross-country performance.

However, the far more sophisticated Western trucks were tested to their limits as they required regular servicing and were designed to run on better fuel and lubricants than their Soviet counterparts. In practice, they were routinely over-loaded, rarely received proper maintenance and were casually refilled with whatever low-octane fuel was available. In the circumstances, it is hardly surprising that their performance was often well below the 'text-book figures' – indeed it is remarkable that so many kept running despite their rough handling.

Approximate annual figures for Soviet-produced transport vehicles are:
- 1940 – 145,000
- 1941 – 124,000
- 1942 – 32,000
- 1943 – 46,000
- 1944 – 57,000
- 1945 – 21,000 (until May)

Total Soviet production June 1941 – May 1945 amounted to 205,000 trucks, of which 150,400 were assigned to military use, with the remainder providing a bare minimum of essential road transport for the civil sector.

In comparison, the Lend-Lease totals for 1941–45 were:

- Light trucks – 151,000
- Heavy trucks – 200,000
- Jeeps – 51,000
- Tractors – 8070

In terms of usage, Lend-Lease trucks were generally issued direct to front-line combat units, whilst Soviet-built trucks were gradually relegated to use in rear areas. Significantly, the tables of organisation for anti-tank artillery units formed from 1943 onwards specified the use of Lend-Lease 'Willys' (¼ ton jeeps) 'Dodzhe' (¾ ton Dodge) and 'Studebekker' (2.5 ton 6x6 Studebaker) trucks. Since these were all-wheel drive vehicles, they had much

Trains Company

Workshop Vehicles: 8   Fuel Tankers: 10
Recovery Vehicles: 4   Cargo Trucks: 36

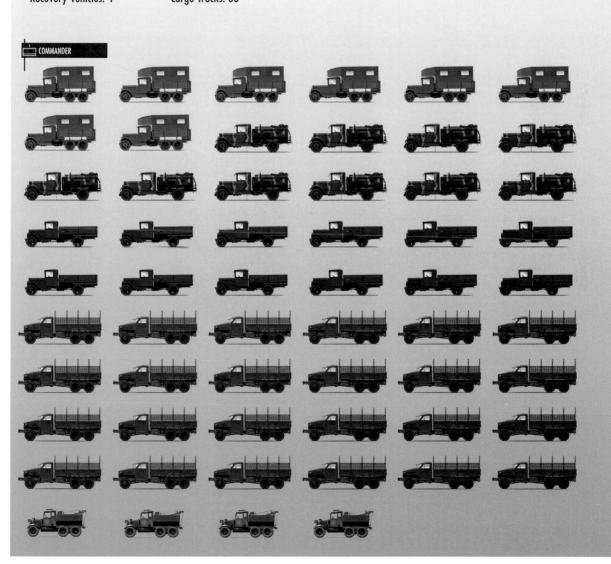

COMMANDER

better mobility than the majority of either Soviet or German trucks. (It was commonly asserted that the Studebaker could go through mud that would stop any other vehicle that wasn't tracked!) 76.2mm (3in) ZiS-3 and USV guns in anti-tank regiments equipped with Studebakers were able to keep pace with even the most advanced armoured spearheads and panzer officers became increasingly concerned at their exceptional mobility.

There were never enough Studebakers to meet the Red Army's needs and their issue was carefully controlled. Towed anti-tank artillery units had priority for these sought-after trucks, together with Guards Mortar units armed with BM-13 Katyusha rocket systems. In 1943 they were adopted as the standard mount for the BM-13 under the designation BM-13N (*Normalizovanniy*,

'standardised') and more than 1800 launchers of this type were produced by the end of the war.

US Lend-Lease support vehicles had considerable influence on post-war Soviet designs and were supplied in such vast numbers that they became a common sight throughout eastern Europe. (In the USSR, the popular belief grew up that the stencilled 'USA' prefixed serial numbers which were left on most vehicles stood for *Ubiyat Sukinsyna Adolfa* – Kill that Son-of-a-Bitch Adolf.)

The Red Army ended World War II with over 650,000 trucks in service of which 58 per cent were Soviet in origin, 33 per cent British or US and the remaining 9 per cent 'trophy vehicles' captured from the Germans. Throughout the war, Soviet motor transport carried over 101 million tonnes of freight in support of military operations.

Studebaker US6 U3 6x6 2.5 ton truck

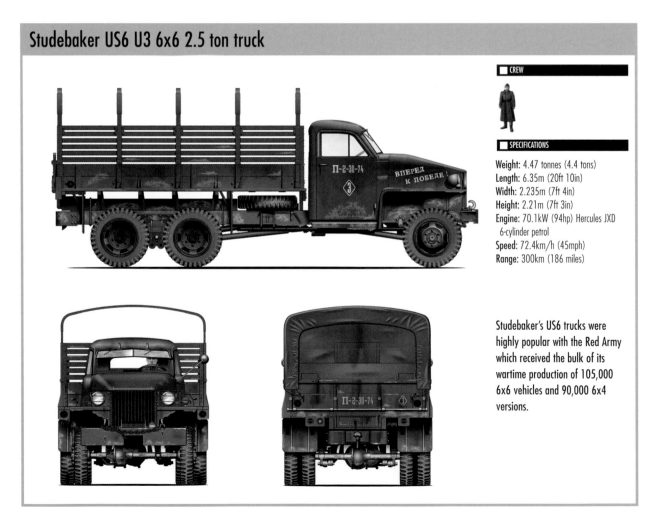

CREW

SPECIFICATIONS

Weight: 4.47 tonnes (4.4 tons)
Length: 6.35m (20ft 10in)
Width: 2.235m (7ft 4in)
Height: 2.21m (7ft 3in)
Engine: 70.1kW (94hp) Hercules JXD 6-cylinder petrol
Speed: 72.4km/h (45mph)
Range: 300km (186 miles)

Studebaker's US6 trucks were highly popular with the Red Army which received the bulk of its wartime production of 105,000 6x6 vehicles and 90,000 6x4 versions.

Scammell Pioneer SV2S 6x4 heavy recovery vehicle

CREW

SPECIFICATIONS

Weight: 9.74 tonnes (9.58 tons)
Length: 6.17m (20ft 3in)
Width: 2.64m (8ft 8in)
Height: 2.87m (9ft 5in)
Engine: 80kW (102hp) Gardner 6-cylinder diesel
Speed: n/k
Range: n/k

The Scammell Pioneer was supplied to the Red Army in small quantities early in the war. With its relatively powerful diesel engine and the ability to convert it to halftrack configuration by fitting tracks over the rear wheels, it was well suited to Soviet conditions.

ZiS-5-BZ fuel tanker

CREW

SPECIFICATIONS

Weight: 3.1 tonnes (3.05 tons)
Length: 6.06m (19ft 10.5in)
Width: 2.35m (7ft 9in)
Height: 2.16m (7ft 1in)
Engine: 54.43kW (73hp) ZiS-5M 6-cylinder petrol
Speed: 55km/h (34mph)
Range: n/k

Fuel tankers were always in high demand, but were exceptionally vulnerable to air attacks and artillery fire.

1500th Anti-Tank Artillery Regiment

Most Soviet wartime tactical publications are still not available in translation. Quoted below is a rare exception, which originally appeared in the US Military Intelligence Service's publication *Tactical and Technical Trends* (No. 31, 12 August 1943).

The following article from the *Red Star* shows the tactics employed by the Soviets in combating enemy tank attacks, as well as the organisation of a Soviet anti-tank regiment.

'There is no more powerful or deadly weapon in the struggle against tanks than the antitank gun, which can by its intensive and accurate fire frustrate the attack of great masses of tanks. This weapon is the basic means for the defense of troops, communications, and defensive objectives against tanks.

When the enemy, in organizing his attack concentrates his tanks on separate narrow sectors of the front, and uses them in masses as a battering ram, ruthless defense must be organized, and in the first place, antitank defense. Without powerful fighting units equipped for the purpose this would be difficult to achieve, and one such unit is the destroyer antitank artillery regiment. These regiments can operate independently, in the form of an army reserve, covering points of the front where there is a danger from tanks, or they can operate within the framework of an infantry division, supporting it at such points as may be necessary, and also operating with the supporting tank group.

In a sector where there is danger from enemy tank attack, the regiment can cover with its fire quite a large area, keeping a few batteries in a first echelon and a few in a second. Guns are usually sited so as to be mutually supporting. Each battery forms a separate antitank defense center mutually supporting, and within effective range of, the other batteries. This makes it possible to increase the field of fire.

Anti-tank Artillery Regiment: Weapons

UNIT	LIGHT MGS	AT RIFLES	76MM AT GUNS
Regiment HQ	0	0	0
HQ Platoon	0	0	0
Anti-tank Battery x5			
Battery HQ	0	0	0
HQ Platoon	0	1	0
Firing Battery			
Firing Battery Group	0	0	0
Platoon x2	1	1	2
Ammunition Platoon	0	0	0
Logistics Section	0	0	0
Other Trains elements	0	0	0
TOTAL	10	10	20

ORBAT: 1500th Anti-Tank Artillery Regiment

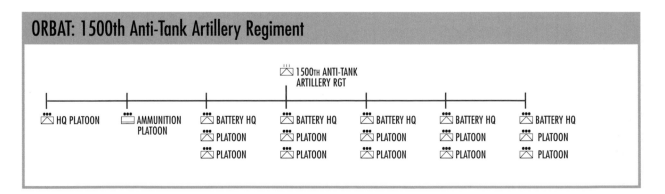

a. The Antitank Regiment in Action

The mission of the antitank regiment is to stop at nothing in its battle against tanks, even if it involves the sacrifice of a considerable part of its strength. The regiment will be carrying out its task even if it loses its guns, provided that it destroys and puts out of action a large number of enemy tanks, and provided that against the loss of the guns can be offset the time gained, the holding of territory, or the restoring of a position.

In any circumstances, guns will only open fire on tanks from a distance of 500 to 600 yards, and will do nothing before that to disclose their position. In order to attack the gun position, a tank, allowing for a speed of 12 miles per hour, will require two minutes. During this time, allowing for average conditions of fire, 12 to 14 shots can be fired. Let us suppose that the percentage of effective hits will be 20 to 25. This means that each gun will put out of action two to three tanks, before it is annihilated, assuming that the enemy continues to advance with complete disregard for losses. The whole regiment under such conditions can put out of action several dozen tanks in one attack, and moreover, only the batteries in the first echelon will suffer substantial losses.

Anti-tank Artillery Regiment: Personnel (April 1943)

UNIT	OFFICERS	POLITICAL OFFICERS	WARRANT OFFICERS	NCOS	OTHER RANKS
Regiment HQ	7	3	7	2	4
HQ Platoon	1	0	0	6	28
Anti-tank Battery x5					
Battery HQ	2	1	0	2	0
HQ Platoon	1	0	0	5	14
Firing Battery					
Firing Battery Group	0	0	0	2	1
Platoon x2	1	0	0	6	11
Ammunition Platoon	1	0	0	2	18
Logistics Section	0	0	2	5	13
Other Trains elements	0	0	4	9	15
TOTAL	34	8	13	129	263

Anti-tank Artillery Regiment: Vehicles (April 1943)

UNIT	FIELD CARS	GAZ-AA	ZIL-5	SPECIALS	TRACTORS
Regiment HQ	1	1	0	0	0
HQ Platoon	0	2	0	0	0
Anti-tank Battery x5					
Battery HQ	0	0	0	0	0
HQ Platoon	0	1	0	0	0
Firing Battery					
Firing Battery Group	0	0	0	0	1
Platoon x2	0	0	1	0	2
Ammunition Platoon	0	0	12	0	0
Logistics Section	0	4	2	2	0
Other Trains elements	0	2	3	3	0
TOTAL	1	14	27	5	25

Lunch break: the crew of a ZiS-3 76.2mm (3in) gun have lunch – probably black bread and *shchi* (cabbage soup) – whilst a sentry stands guard in the background.

Such is the destructive potentialities of the tank-destroying regiment, and they have not in any way been exaggerated. The correctness of these calculations has been borne out by actual combat. In addition there have been not a few cases where one gun has put out of action not two, but six, or eight or even more tanks. A few batteries have thus shattered a German attack.

b. How the Regiment is Organized in Defense

Let us examine the organization for defense within the regiment. The most usually adopted battle formation for the regiment is a diamond shape center of resistance, consisting of nests of resistance each of battery strength, with all-around defense within each battery. In the case of such a formation it is useful to keep one

battery in reserve, because the possibility exists that the enemy tanks will go around the flanks of one of the batteries within the first echelon. The speed with which the reserve of fire power can be developed and brought into action is an important factor in success.

Each battery has its main and its alternate positions, for which all data are prepared; dummy positions are prepared if there is time. When a battery has to leave its main position for its alternate position, the former becomes the dummy position. Changing position must only take place during a lull in the fighting, and in all circumstances under cover of darkness. Before the battle positions are taken up, daylight reconnaissance is necessary. During this reconnaissance, the directions from which tank attacks are threatened are noted, battery control points and the tasks of each are fixed, and fire is coordinated. When the batteries take up their positions, the rearward elements of the regiment are moved back sufficiently far for

Anti-tank Artillery Regiment

Field Cars: 1
ZiS-5 (3 ton) truck: 27
Tractors: 25

GAZ-AA (1.5 ton) truck: 14
Special Trucks: 5
76.2mm Zis-3 Field Gun: 20

A typical anti-tank regiment employed 46 trucks and 25 tractors to serve just 20 field guns. This made perfect sense, when considering the regiment had to transport 263 personnel.

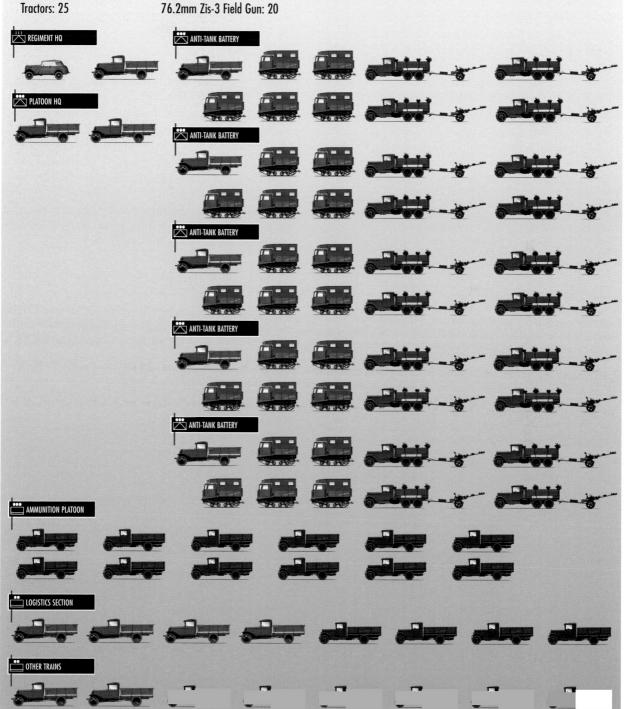

them to be out of range of fire of enemy tanks and artillery in an attack.

To ensure more effective and flexible control over the regiment, the commander has, in addition to his command post, an observation post in the area of the batteries of the second echelon (in the center of this defensive area, or on its flank). It is very important that it should be possible to observe from the OP the approach of tanks at every point within the regimental area. If this is not possible, the OP is chosen to cover the most vital parts of the defended area.

The regimental commander coordinates the fire of the batteries, ordering them to switch or concentrate their fire as the situation requires. He also determines the time and place for the reserve battery to come into action. If communications with the batteries break down, staff officers are immediately sent out to the batteries to ensure coordination.

c. The Reserve Battery

It is desirable to discuss in greater detail the employment of the reserve battery, since the question is one of importance. This battery can be employed in the following tasks: it can be brought into action at a point where the enemy has made a mass tank attack, in order to stiffen resistance; or on a flank which is open and where enemy tanks would get through to the rear; finally, to prevent further penetration at a point where the enemy tanks have driven a wedge into our lines. In all these cases, the time at which the reserve battery is deployed for action is of decisive importance; this is what determines both its position and the route by which it moves over to the required point.

The reserve battery can either be in the center of the defensive zone (the second echelon) as a whole, or can be split into its platoons and used nearer the flanks. The latter is possibly the better method. For example, if one of the flanks should become exposed, one platoon immediately goes into action, while the second can come up under cover of its fire. In case of a forward move, both platoons can converge simultaneously on the prearranged position.

If a battery (or platoon) is being moved any distance up to about 500 yards, it is best to move the guns by hand, since to bring up the prime movers will take nearly as long. Often, in order to conceal movement of guns, it is better to move them forward several times a short distance by hand, rather than to use the prime movers to move them a considerable distance in a single bound. Moving the reserve battery by prime movers is practicable when the time is available, when the distance to be moved exceeds 600 yards and when the movement is lateral. (A diversion rearwards is desirable in the interests of concealment.)'

76.2mm (3in) ZiS-3 field gun

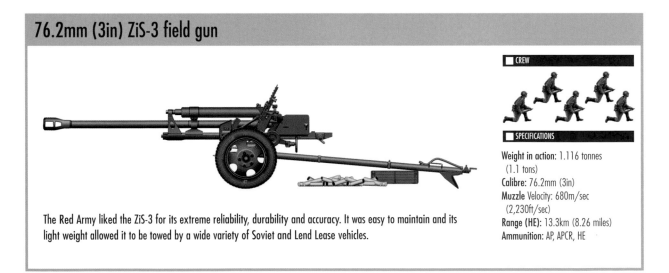

The Red Army liked the ZiS-3 for its extreme reliability, durability and accuracy. It was easy to maintain and its light weight allowed it to be towed by a wide variety of Soviet and Lend Lease vehicles.

CREW

SPECIFICATIONS

Weight in action: 1.116 tonnes (1.1 tons)
Calibre: 76.2mm (3in)
Muzzle Velocity: 680m/sec (2,230ft/sec)
Range (HE): 13.3km (8.26 miles)
Ammunition: AP, APCR, HE

755th Independent Anti-Tank Battalion

The following is another rare translation of wartime Soviet notes on the tactical handling of anti-tank rifles which was originally published in the US Military Intelligence Service's publication *Intelligence Bulletin* Vol. I, No. 5: January 1943.

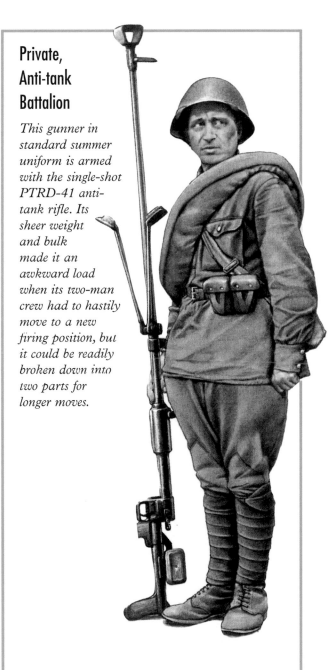

Private, Anti-tank Battalion

This gunner in standard summer uniform is armed with the single-shot PTRD-41 anti-tank rifle. Its sheer weight and bulk made it an awkward load when its two-man crew had to hastily move to a new firing position, but it could be readily broken down into two parts for longer moves.

The following information about the use of the Soviet anti-tank rifle was originally published in the *Red Star*, official Soviet Army publication:

'A Soviet artillery battery was on the march when the column was suddenly attacked by six enemy tanks. A Red Army private armed with an antitank rifle jumped off a caisson, took position behind a mound, and opened fire. He inflicted sufficient damage on the leading tank to cause the remainder of the enemy tanks to delay their attack for a few minutes. The battery was given a chance to deploy and open fire, and the surprise attack was beaten off. Four of the six German tanks were put out of action.

In many similar instances antitank rifles have proved effective against enemy tanks. The light weight, portability, and rapid fire power of this weapon permit its crew to go into action in so short a time that it can cover units on the march, at rest, or in battle.

...The greatest success has been attained by squads consisting of two or three antitank rifles placed 15 to 20 yards apart. Such units can bring effective fire to bear on a target, and have a greater chance of putting it out of commission than fire by a single rifle would have.

In selecting positions for antitank titles, detailed reconnaissance of the target area should be made, in addition to the usual local

ORBAT: 755th Independent Anti-Tank Btn

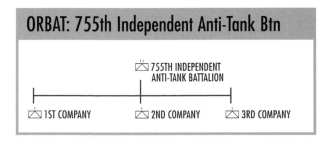

755TH INDEPENDENT ANTI-TANK BATTALION

1ST COMPANY   2ND COMPANY   3RD COMPANY

Awaiting the panzers: a PTRS-41 anti-tank rifle team photographed in a dangerously exposed firing position. (Anti-tank rifles needed good cover in order to survive long enough to open fire at their effective range.)

reconnaissance. Eliminating dead spots and protecting against the most likely routes of enemy tank approach are most important considerations. The positions should be echeloned so as to be mutually supporting with fire from the flanks. Antitank rifles in artillery batteries are generally grouped on the most exposed flank of the gun positions. In all cases, the squad leader should select his own position so as to have maximum observation and, at the same time, personally control the actions of the antitank rifles.

In fortifying these positions, it has proved impracticable to construct emplacements with roofs because of increased visibility to the enemy air force and lack of 360° traverse. The best types of emplacements are open and circular in shape, with a diameter large enough to permit free movement of the crew for all-around traverse and to protect the gun and crew from being crushed by enemy tanks. Narrow communication trenches connect the gun positions with each other as well as with the rear. Both emplacements and trenches are constructed without parapets; the extra dirt is utilized in building false installations to draw enemy fire. It is practically impossible for tanks to spot such fortifications, and the rifles are able to fire on them for the longest possible time. Also, protection against aerial bombardment is increased.

In the preparation of antitank fire, the rifleman should select five or six key reference points at different ranges, measure the distance to them, and study the intervening terrain. When actually firing, he should fire at stationary tanks whenever possible and not take leads at ranges over 400 yards. Aim should always be taken at the vulnerable parts, taking advantage of any hesitation or exposure of the sides of the enemy tanks.

Antitank defense must be drawn up so as to protect the antitank rifle units fully, by means of all available obstacles, mines, and fire power.'

273rd Mortar Regiment

The 120mm (4.7in) mortar blurred the distinction between infantry weapons and light artillery pieces. The German Army first encountered this monster the hard way as the Red Army had pioneered the concept with the 120mm Model 1938. The Germans had a taste of its effectiveness in the early stages of Operation Barbarossa and were sufficiently impressed to simply copy the type instead of producing the usual equivalent 'Germanic' design.

Soviet 120mm (4.7in) mortars were essentially cheap but effective regimental artillery. In common with virtually all other mortars, they sacrificed range for simplicity, but their firepower was devastating – a 120mm (4.7in) mortar bomb has about the same explosive capacity as a 155mm (6.1in) artillery shell. (This is due to the fact that mortar bombs have thinner casings than conventional artillery shells as they are fired at much lower velocities and do not have to withstand such high pressures. The thinner casing leaves more space for explosives, enhancing the bomb's blast effect.)

Although their rate of fire could not match that of the 82mm (3.2in) mortar ('only' 6rpm compared to

12rpm), they provided much-needed short-range firepower for the Red Army. This was especially true in 1941/42 when production of conventional artillery was badly disrupted by the evacuation of war industries – the mortars proved to be so useful and cost-effective that they remained in production after the crisis eased and over 46,000 were completed by the end of the war.

Whilst the 82mm (3.2in) mortar bomb was largely ineffective against all but the lightest AFVs (or those with open-topped fighting compartments) the 120mm (4.7in) had sufficient blast effect to damage or destroy most German tanks with a direct hit or very near miss. As with all mortars, they were most effective when combined with direct fire anti-tank weapons. Mortar fire forced AFV crews to 'button up', reducing their visibility and preventing them from firing any externally mounted machine guns. This fire also played a major role in separating AFVs from their supporting infantry, allowing Soviet infantry tank-hunting teams to close in and use their hand-held anti-armour weapons.

A further advantage of the 120mm (4.7in) mortar bomb was that it was far less affected by terrain or cover than those from lighter weapons. (Soft ground limits the effectiveness of HE rounds

273rd Mortar Regiment: Strength	
UNIT	STRENGTH
Men	848
Motor vehicles	135
120mm (4.7in) Mortars	36

from light, medium and heavy mortars, with the small bombs of light mortars being the most badly affected. Thirty centimetres (1ft) of soft ground, mud, or sand, or 1 metre (3ft) of snow can reduce the effectiveness of ground-burst HE rounds by up to 80 per cent. Light mortar rounds can land within a few yards of a target on this type of ground and still have no effect.)

Light and medium mortar fire was also relatively ineffective against field fortifications with overhead cover, whereas 120mm (4.7in) bombs had sufficient blast effect to damage or destroy all but the deepest and most strongly constructed bunkers.

The regiment's 36 mortars could lay down a formidable concentration of fire (approximately 216rpm for short periods). When operating in conjunction with conventional artillery and *Katyusha* rockets, they were even more terrifying.

120mm (4.7in) Model 1938 mortar

The 120mm (4.7in) Model 1938 was one of the best mortar designs of the war, firing a heavy bomb to a good range. It was also highly mobile and could be brought into action very quickly. The Germans not only took it into service as the 12cm (4.7in) *Granatwerfer* 378(r) but also copied the design and produced it as the 12cm (4.7in) *Granatwerfer* 42. The modernised Model 1938/1943 was essentially similar to the Model 1938 but used a single shock absorber on the barrel-bipod mounting.

CREW

SPECIFICATIONS

Calibre: 120mm (4.72in)
Barrel length: 186 mm (73.3 in) (L/15.5)
Bore length: 1536mm (60.47in)
Weight in action: 280.1kg (617lb)
Weight travelling: 477.6kg (1.052lb)
Elevation: 45° to 80°
Traverse: 6°
Muzzle velocity: 272m/sec (892ft/sec)
Maximum range: 6000m (6564 yards)
Bomb weight (HE): 16kg (35.3lb)
Ammunition: HE, Smoke

273rd Mortar Regiment

120mm Mortar Model 1938: 36
GMC CCKW-352 trucks: 135

A huge trains group was reuqired to carry the ammunition, supplies and 800-plus men of a typical mortar regiment in 1943.

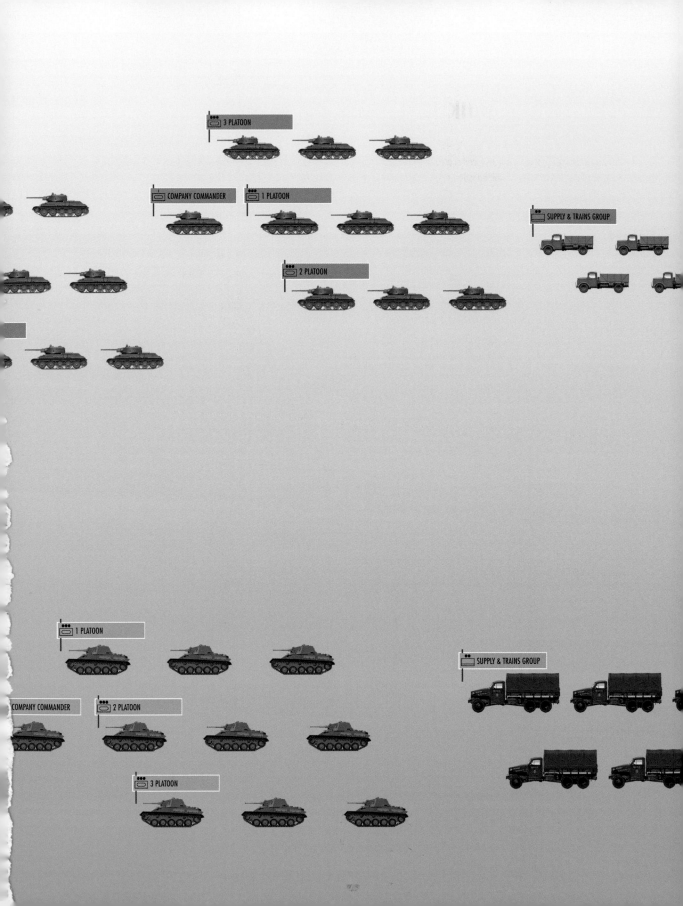

3 PLATOON

COMPANY COMMANDER

1 PLATOON

SUPPLY & TRAINS GROUP

2 PLATOON

1 PLATOON

SUPPLY & TRAINS GROUP

COMPANY COMMANDER

2 PLATOON

3 PLATOON

4th Guards Tank Brigade

At full strength, a typical Soviet tank brigade in 1943 numbered over 50 tanks. However, II Guards Tank Corps was involved in heavy fighting on 8th July, and sources suggest that the corps's total strength on 12th July was approximately 80 AFVs shared amongst three tank brigades, suggesting each tank brigade was severely under strength.

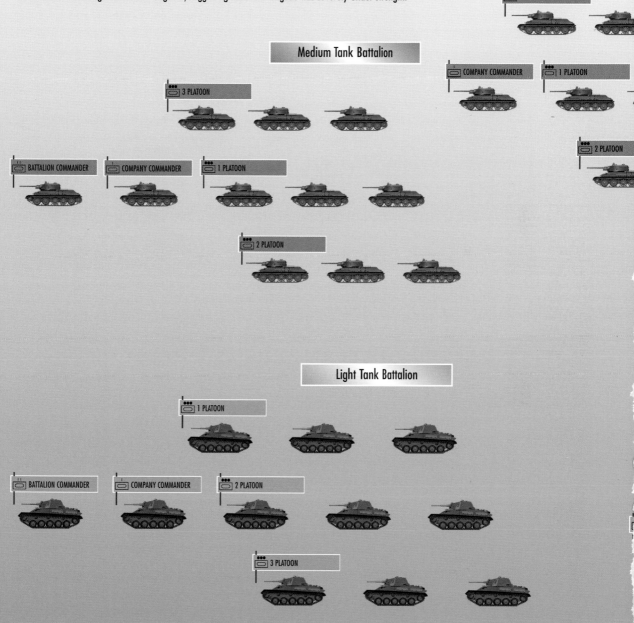

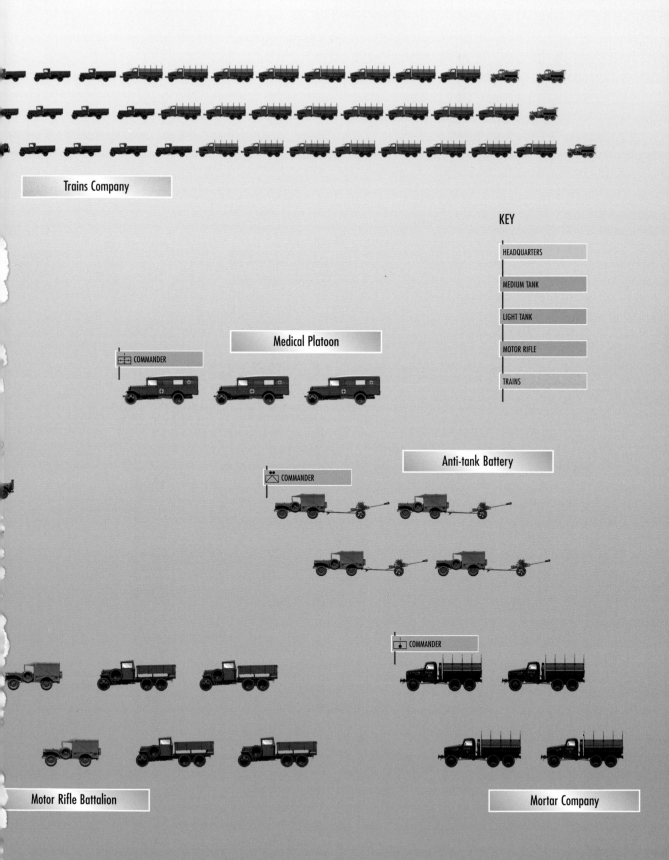

Trains Company

KEY

HEADQUARTERS

MEDIUM TANK

LIGHT TANK

MOTOR RIFLE

TRAINS

Medical Platoon

COMMANDER

Anti-tank Battery

COMMANDER

COMMANDER

Motor Rifle Battalion

Mortar Company

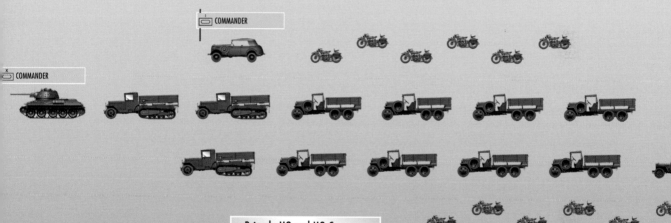

COMMANDER

COMMANDER

x
COMMANDER

Brigade HQ and HQ Company

COMMANDER

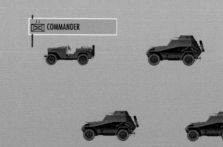

1695th Anti-aircraft Regiment

In mid-1943 the *Luftwaffe* still posed a major threat to the Red Army. The poorly-equipped Soviet air defence system meant that formations relied heavily on their integral AA units to provide protection from air attacks.

By 1943, German ground forces in the Soviet Union had come to rely on tactical air power both as a supplement to their over-stretched heavy artillery and as a key part of their anti-tank defences. *General der Flieger* Paul Diechmann recalled that: 'Even during quiet spells, the army command insisted on the constant commitment of air power against enemy targets within the battle areas in order to conceal their own weaknesses in …numbers and weapons.'

As the *Luftwaffe* was heavily dependent on fighter-bombers and dive bombers, the emphasis in equipping Soviet air defence units was to provide as much light and medium AA firepower as possible. It was unfortunate for the Red Army that it never received any equivalent of the multiple 20mm (0.79in) cannon used so effectively by German light AA batteries. It had to get by with quadruple rifle calibre Maxim machine guns and 12.7mm (0.5in) DShK heavy machine guns – whilst both were good, reliable weapons, they lacked the punch and the effective explosive shells of 20mm (0.79in) cannon.

TOKAREV 4M MODEL 1931

This was the earliest light AA weapon to be produced for the Red Army. It comprised four of the venerable 7.62mm (0.3in) Maxim Model 1910/30 machine guns on a heavy pedestal mount. These were manually operated, but were quite successful, although rather limited by the low effective ceiling of their rifle calibre rounds. The AA role demanded a good sustained fire capability and most effort went into improving this aspect of the gun's performance. The mounting incorporated special ammunition boxes with a capacity of 500 rounds each instead of the standard 250-round belt boxes. It is likely that the guns used in this role were issued with non-disintegrating metal-link ammunition belts which could be relatively easily joined together. The earlier cloth belts seem to have only been produced in 250-round lengths and it would have required considerable work to link

these strongly enough to resist the strain of firing. There would also have been a real risk of an 'untidy' join jamming the feed mechanism. The guns retained their original water cooling systems and the prolonged firing likely to be required in the AA role posed problems of potential over-heating. (The water would begin to boil after 500-600 rounds of rapid fire and the resulting steam escaped through a valve in the cooling jacket.)

To minimise this problem, detachable rubber hoses were fitted running from the four water jackets to carry the steam to condensers so that much of the water could be recycled. The massive weight of the Tokarev mount – 80kg (176lb) for the four guns alone, without water – meant that it was restricted to use on trucks or in permanent AA emplacements to defend point targets.

The guns were aimed using simple ring AA sights – not a particularly accurate method of sighting, but simple and efficient enough given the dispersion of rounds from four barrels and their combined rate of fire (approximately 2100rpm). The real problem with the system lay in the fact that it gradually became less and less effective as the *Luftwaffe* deployed better protected aircraft. Even relatively light armour offered a considerable degree of protection from the Maxim's rifle calibre bullets and the heavily armoured ground attack

1695th Anti-Aircraft Regiment: Weapons

UNIT	GUN	STRENGTH
1st Battery	Quadruple Maxim 7.92mm	4
2nd Battery	Quadruple Maxim 7.92mm	4
3rd Battery	Quadruple Maxim 7.92mm	4
4th Battery	DShK 12.7mm Heavy	4
5th Battery	DShK 12.7mm Heavy	4
6th Battery	37mm AA	4
7th Battery	37mm AA	4
8th Battery	37mm AA	4

1695th Anti-Aircraft Regiment

Quadruple Maxim 7.92mm machine guns: 12
DShK 12.7mm heavy machine guns: 8
37mm AA guns: 12

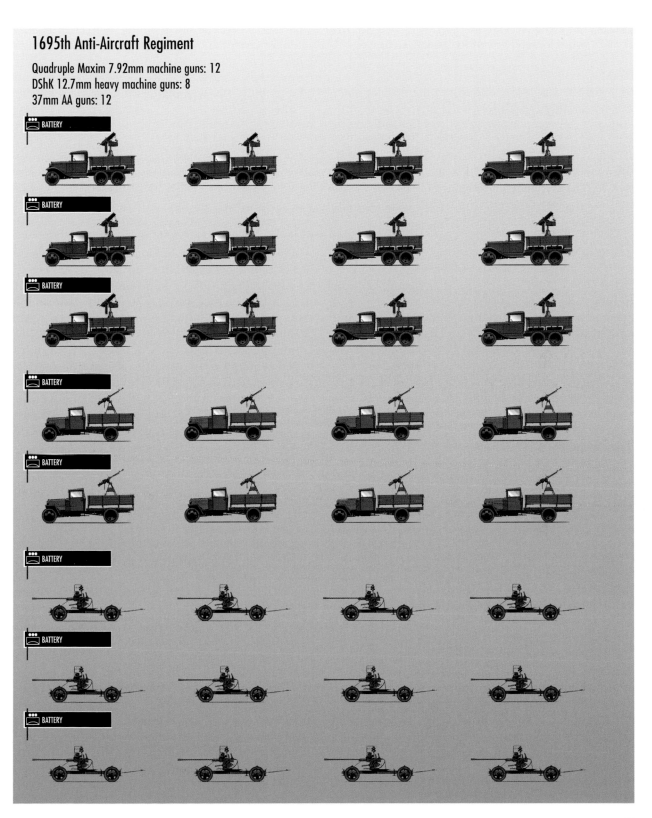

aircraft entering service in 1942/43 such as the Hs 129 were virtually immune to these rounds.

DSHK

In 1925 the Red Army requested the development of a large calibre machine gun, primarily as an anti-tank and AA weapon. As a first step, an indigenous 12.7mm (0.5in) round was developed. Unlike the standard Soviet 7.62mm (0.3in) rifle ammunition, the new 12.7x108 round had a rimless case and was remarkably similar to the ammunition of the US .50in Browning machine gun, although the Soviet round had a somewhat longer case.

By 1930 Degtyarov had developed what was basically an enlarged DP machine gun, known as the DK (*Degtyarov Krupnokalibernyj* – Degtyarov large calibre). This was a large, gas operated, air cooled weapon fed from top-mounted 30-round detachable drum magazines. The type went into limited production in 1933, and armed some light AFVs, small naval craft and river patrol boats. In service the heavy 30-round drum magazine proved to be unsatisfactory as it was emptied in a few seconds' firing. Its weight made the frequent magazine changes an awkward and exhausting business for the gun crew. It was clear that a belt-feed was needed to transform the design into a practical service weapon and by 1938 the gun designer Shpagin had developed an 'add-on' belt feed unit for the DK.

This modified DK was adopted as DShK-38 (*Degtyarov – Shpagin Krupnokalibernyj* – Degtyarov & Shpagin large calibre, model 1938). Whilst it was a satisfactory weapon with reasonable power (at least to deal with low-flying aircraft and light AFVs), it had some peculiar properties, of which the most notable was the very heavy universal wheeled mount which, despite its weight (157kg (346lb) including the gun), failed to provide the necessary stability and vibration-dampening for accurate long-range fire. Although this was a potential drawback when firing against ground targets, the dispersion of fire actually helped when the DShK was employed as an AA weapon on a lighter tripod mounting.

37MM (1.45IN) 61-K M1939

By the early 1930s, the rapid improvements in aviation technology made it clear that machine

guns were in danger of becoming ineffective against the next generation of attack aircraft. Soviet design teams came up with several weapons, the earliest being the 45mm (1.8in) K-21 of 1934, an adaptation of the Red Army's anti-tank gun.

The 21-K was a very simple design which involved little more than fitting the barrel of the 53-K anti-tank gun to a high-angle pedestal mount. On firing, its semi-automatic breech automatically ejected the cartridge case and locked open, ready for the next round. This hand-loaded, single shot mechanism was less than ideal for an anti-aircraft weapon of this calibre as it limited the practical rate of fire to no more than 25–30rpm.

There were problems with the breech mechanism in early production guns, a number of which lacked the semi-automatic breech mechanism, further slowing the already inadequate rate of fire. As a final blow to the gun's AA performance, it was never issued with time-fused ammunition and had to rely on impact-fused shells which required a direct hit on the target aircraft. Unsurprisingly, the gun was rejected by the Red Army, but it was adopted by the Soviet Navy and remained in production until 1947.

Something better than the 21-K was clearly needed and a small batch of Bofors 25mm (0.98in) Model 1933 AA guns were bought for trials in 1935. These were far more sophisticated weapons and it was decided to use the design as the basis for the development of a 45mm (1.8in) version designated 49-K. The result was apparently quite successful, but the Red Army felt that a 45mm (1.8in) gun was rather too large for optimum mobility in the field.

The development of a 'home-grown' 37mm (1.45in) automatic AA gun had in fact already begun. This was a 1935 design produced by a team headed by Boris Shpitalny, the Chief Designer at Kaliningrad's Artillery Factory No. 8. Production of his gun began in 1936 and ended two years later after only a small number had been completed as it was quite heavy for its calibre and had a low rate of fire. The failure of this gun led to the development of a 37mm (1.45in) version of the 49-K which was also influenced by the 40mm (1.57in) Bofors guns.

Work on a new gun, which was designated 61-K, began in January 1938 and the prototype underwent successful firing trials in October of that

37mm (1.45in) 61-K M1939 AA gun

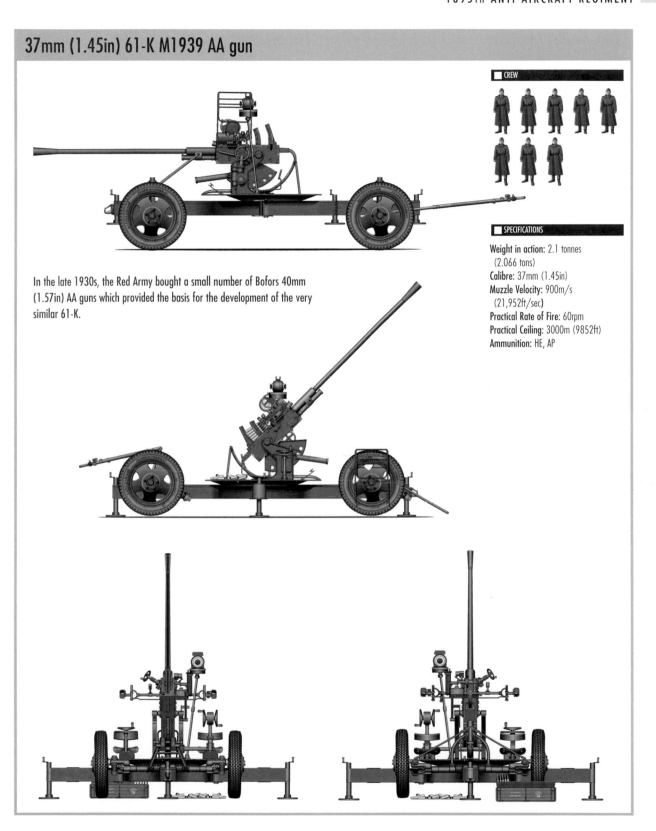

CREW

SPECIFICATIONS

Weight in action: 2.1 tonnes
(2.066 tons)
Calibre: 37mm (1.45in)
Muzzle Velocity: 900m/s
(21,952ft/sec)
Practical Rate of Fire: 60rpm
Practical Ceiling: 3000m (9852ft)
Ammunition: HE, AP

In the late 1930s, the Red Army bought a small number of Bofors 40mm (1.57in) AA guns which provided the basis for the development of the very similar 61-K.

Watch duty: the crew of a camouflaged 12.7mm (0.5in) DShK machine gun scan the skies for the *Luftwaffe*. The gun is fitted with a detachable AA ring sight.

year. The gun was mounted on a four-wheeled ZU-7 carriage and closely resembled the 40mm (1.57in) Bofors guns in general appearance. The ammunition seems to have been derived from that used by the contemporary US 37mm (1.45in) Browning AA gun and was loaded in five-round clips. The initial order for 900 guns was quickly increased and by the time that Soviet production ended in 1945, a total of almost 20,000 guns had been completed.

The Red Army carried out pre-war comparative trials with the Bofors 40mm (1.57in) gun and concluded that its performance was virtually identical to that of the 61-K. (The type was an effective AA gun, although not the wonder weapon of Soviet propaganda which claimed that the 61-K batteries shot down a total of 14,657 enemy aircraft, averaging 905 rounds per aircraft destroyed. As the

best estimate of the total *Luftwaffe* combat losses in the Soviet Union between March 1942 and December is less than 8400 aircraft, this would seem to be highly optimistic!)

Although it was designed as an AA gun, the 61-K's potential in the anti-tank role was also appreciated and priority was given to developing armour-piercing (AP) ammunition – penetration at 500 metres (1640ft) range was recorded as 37mm (1.45in) of armour sloped at 60 degrees. (The 61-K's high rate of fire in comparison to conventional anti-tank guns would make it a more potent 'tank-killer' than these figures suggest. Especially at short ranges, it had a good chance of achieving multiple hits by firing short bursts at attacking AFVs.)

This was an important secondary role for almost all AA weapons at Kursk – as the Soviet General Staff Study of the battle noted: 'Anti-aircraft artillery firing positions were selected taking into account direct firing against tanks with an all-round

ZiS-5V with 12.7mm (0.5in) DShK HMG

In common with many other Soviet trucks, the ZiS-5 was modified soon after the German invasion to simplify production, the most obvious change being the adoption of a wooden cab. This vehicle serving with an AA battery has been fitted with a 12.7mm (0.5in) DShK heavy machine gun.

CREW

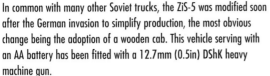

SPECIFICATIONS

Weight: 3.1 tonnes (3.05 tons)
Length: 6.1m (20ft)
Width: 2.25m (7ft 4.5in)
Height: 2.16m (7ft 1in)
Engine: 54/57kW (73/76hp) ZiS-5/ZiS-5M
Speed: 60km/h (37.3mph)
Armament: 1 x 12.7mm (0.5in) DShK heavy machine gun

GAZ-AAA 1937 with Maxim M4M

CREW

SPECIFICATIONS

Weight: 3.52 tonnes (3.46 tons)
Length: 5.34m (17ft 9in)
Width: 2.36m (7ft 9in)
Height: 2.1m (6ft 11in)
Engine: 37kW (50hp) GAZ-M 4-cylinder
Speed: 35km/h (21.75mph)
Armament: Quadruple 7.62mm (0.3in) machine guns on 4M pedestal AA mounting

The 6x4 GAZ-AAA was produced in vast numbers – over 37,000 vehicles were delivered between 1934 and 1943. One of its many roles was that of air defence armed with the 4M system, quadruple 7.62mm (0.3in) machine guns on a pedestal AA mounting.

field of fire to a distance of 800–1000 metres. Each battery was assigned a field of fire sector in accordance with the general anti-tank defence plan. All AA guns were supplied with an adequate number of armour-piercing shells…Tank destroyer teams armed with anti-tank grenades, clusters of hand grenades and Molotov cocktails were formed in all batteries from administrative personnel.'

36th Guards Heavy Tank Regiment

The regiment was formed in March 1943 in Moscow Military District with Lend-Lease Churchill IV tanks and was assigned to XVIII Tank Corps in June 1943.

The Churchill tanks which entered service with the Red Army in 1942/43 had a curious history. Their design had its origins in the Phoney War of 1939/40 when it was confidently expected that future combat would be almost identical to the trench warfare of World War I. In September 1939 outline specifications were issued for a tank designated A20 which was intended to be a modern equivalent of the heavy tanks of 1918. The specifications stressed the need for immunity to the standard 37mm (1.45in) German anti-tank gun together with the ability to cross shell-torn, water-logged ground. Initially it was intended to fit the new tank with the turret of the Matilda II infantry tank, although a number of other weapons fits were proposed as development progressed. As it was primarily intended to operate in the infantry support role, a maximum speed of no more than 16km/h (10mph) was required. Two prototypes were completed in early 1940 before the project was terminated in the aftermath of the Dunkirk evacuation.

In July 1940, development began of the A22, essentially an updated version of the A20, which was to become the Infantry Tank Mark IV, Churchill. The threat of a German invasion was very real at the time and the desperate need for tanks led to the initial batch of 500 A22s being ordered 'straight off the drawing board' with no preliminary trials of any prototypes. (One veteran engineer did remark that this meant that there would in fact be 500 prototypes!) Although the

36th Guards Heavy Tank Regiment

TANKS	OPERATIONAL	REPLACEMENT AWAITED	UNDER REPAIR
Churchill Mk IV	31	0	0

decision was understandable, it was the primary cause of the Churchill's troubled early history.

EARLY CHURCHILLS

Although it had been intended to arm the tank with the 57mm (6-pounder) gun, which was ready for production in mid-1940, its manufacture was postponed in order to concentrate on production of the 40mm (2-pounder) during the post-Dunkirk invasion scare. This meant that the first production model, the Churchill Mark I, was armed with a 40mm (2-pounder) gun and co-axial Besa machine gun in a small cast turret supplemented by a 76.2mm (3in) howitzer in a limited traverse mounting alongside the driver.

This was a somewhat archaic armament fit which harked back to the original A20 concept and was soon revised by fitting a second Besa in place of the howitzer in what became the Mark II. All these early vehicles which entered service in the summer of 1941 suffered from their rushed development – there were severe problems with the engine, transmission, tracks and steering. (These were so bad that Vauxhall Motors who built the tanks issued a detailed booklet with each vehicle which listed

ORBAT: 36th Guards Tank Regiment

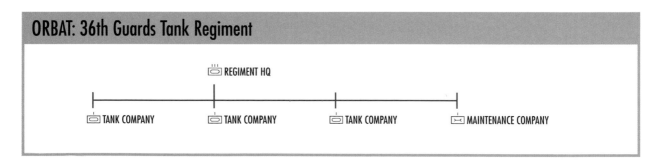

REGIMENT HQ

TANK COMPANY   TANK COMPANY   TANK COMPANY   MAINTENANCE COMPANY

36th Guards Heavy Tank Regiment

Combat vehicles: Churchill Mk IV: 31
                     BA-64: 1

Unlike most heavy tank regiments, the 36th Heavy Guards Tank Regiment was organized with a total of 31 Churchills instead of the standard heavy tank regiment's establishment of 21 tanks.

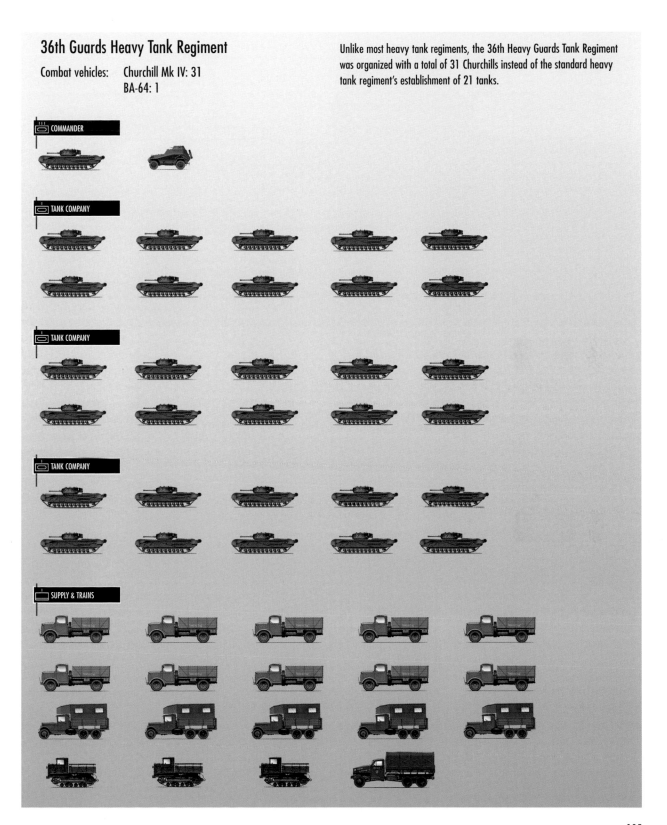

A British-built Churchill Mk IV from the Fifth Guards Tank Army passes a destroyed SdKfz 232, Kursk area, July 1943. There is a degree of uncertainty regarding the extent of the regiment's role at Prokhorovka — some sources indicate that it saw little action as it was held in reserve for much of the battle, but there is photographic evidence of captured or destroyed Churchills on *Das Reich's* sector of the front.

potential faults, essential precautions to minimise breakdowns and future changes in design which were intended to improve matters.) One of the few good points was the armour protection of up to 102mm (4in) which was far better than that of any other contemporary British tank.

Despite these problems, a total of 45 Mark IIs (26 of which arrived safely) were shipped to the Soviet Union in late 1941 on the Arctic convoys. Understandably, the Red Army was not impressed with these slow, unreliable tanks, but they had to be used operationally given enormous losses of Soviet AFVs in the opening stages of Operation Barbarossa.

CHURCHILL MARK III

Whilst British and Soviet tank crews struggled to cope with the mechanical problems of the early Churchills, considerable effort was being put into designing a new turret to mount the 57mm (6-pounder) gun which was finally coming off the production lines. In August 1941, Babcock and Wilcox began construction of an enlarged welded turret for the new gun, but the first example failed in firing trials as its flat plates flaked badly when hit.

After improving quality control standards, the problem was solved, allowing production of the up-gunned Churchill Mark III to begin in the spring of 1942. Although it was still not entirely mechanically reliable, the new gun had a good armour-piercing performance (87mm at 472 metres – 3.42in at 500 yards) making the Mark III a far more potent tank than its predecessors.

CHURCHILL MARK IV

Despite the effort which had gone into perfecting the welded turret, there were doubts about the future supply of suitable quality weldable plate and a cast turret was hastily designed to ensure that production could continue in the event of a complete supply failure. This cast turret version was designated Churchill IV and was otherwise virtually identical to the Mark III.

'TANKS FOR RUSSIA'

The Marks III and IV formed the vast majority of the Red Army's Lend-Lease Churchills. Both types were shipped on the Arctic convoys of 1942 and 1943, the probable totals being:
- Mark III – 151 sent, 24 lost, 127 received.
- Mark IV – 105 despatched, all of which arrived.

Although these represented a significant improvement in comparison with the initial shipment of Mark IIs, the Red Army was still highly critical of the Churchill, comparing it unfavourably to the KV-1 in terms of speed and firepower. (The 57mm's (6-pounder) armour piercing performance was at least as good as that of most Soviet 76.2mm (3in) tank guns, but the latter had a much better HE capability.)

There was also criticism of the Churchill's mobility in snow or icy conditions and some attempts were made to improve its performance by modifying the tracks, but these were at best no more than partially successful. (Plans for future shipments of Churchills were cancelled in favour of increased deliveries of the Valentine infantry tank

which was much preferred by the Red Army. A total of almost 4000 Valentines were supplied under Lend-Lease by 1945.)

RED ARMY CHURCHILLS

The allocation of the handful of Churchill Mark IIs to reach the Red Army is unknown, but the Marks III and IV were issued to the following regiments:

■ **15th Guards Heavy Tank Regiment** – Formed on 26 October in Moscow Military District from 137th Tank Brigade. It was initially assigned to I Guards Mechanized Corps, but was removed from the corps in July 1943 and thereafter served as an independent infantry support regiment. It was disbanded in February 1944 to provide cadres for new heavy assault gun regiments.

Infantry Tank Mk IV, Churchill Mark IV

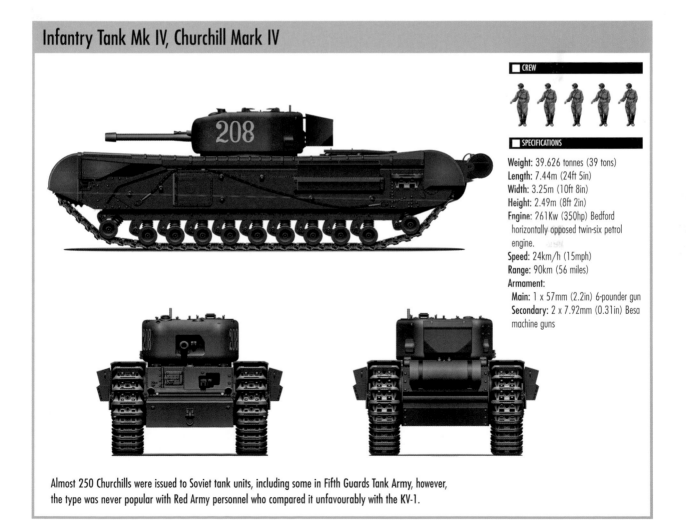

CREW

SPECIFICATIONS

Weight: 39.626 tonnes (39 tons)
Length: 7.44m (24ft 5in)
Width: 3.25m (10ft 8in)
Height: 2.49m (8ft 2in)
Engine: 261Kw (350hp) Bedford horizontally opposed twin-six petrol engine.
Speed: 24km/h (15mph)
Range: 90km (56 miles)
Armament:
  Main: 1 x 57mm (2.2in) 6-pounder gun
  Secondary: 2 x 7.92mm (0.31in) Besa machine guns

Almost 250 Churchills were issued to Soviet tank units, including some in Fifth Guards Tank Army, however, the type was never popular with Red Army personnel who compared it unfavourably with the KV-1.

■ **36th Guards Heavy Tank Regiment** – Formed in March 1943 in Moscow Military District. Unusually, it was organized as an ordinary tank regiment with a total of 31 Churchills instead of the standard heavy tank regiment's establishment of 21 tanks. It was assigned to XVIII Tank Corps in June 1943 and took part in the fighting around Prokhorovka. In the subsequent reorganisation of Fifth Guards Tank Army it was removed from XVIII Tank Corps and was deployed in the infantry support role until mid-1944.

In June/July 1944 it re-equipped with JS-2 heavy tanks before joining IX Tank Corps in October 1944 where it served for the rest of the war.

■ **48th Guards Heavy Tank Regiment** – Formed in November 1942 in Moscow Military District. It first saw action in the infantry support role with Twenty-First Army at Stalingrad in January 1943. It was transferred to V Guards Tank Corps in June 1943, before going into Stavka reserve in Moscow Military District. During the first half of 1944 it re-equipped with JS-2 heavy tanks before being assigned to VIII Guards Mechanized Corps where it served for the rest of the war.

■ **59th Guards Heavy Tank Regiment** – Formed in July 1943 in Volga Military District and was assigned to IX Mechanized Corps. There is a degree of uncertainty about its equipment, but it is likely to have formed with Churchills and re-equipped with JS-2 heavy tanks during 1944.

1st Guards Motorcycle Regiment

In common with many other European armies, the Red Army made extensive use of motorcycles as cheap reconnaissance machines during the inter-war years. Although motorcycle troops were highly vulnerable to any well-directed enemy fire, the addition of armoured support elements made them a useful and highly mobile force.

In the pre-war Red Army, motorcycle battalions had been an integral part of the tank corps and tank brigades. The upheavals of Stalin's purges had affected them as badly as other units and, although the mechanized corps of 1941 each had a motorcycle regiment, plus motorcycle companies and platoons at divisional and brigade level, very few were at anything like their official strength. This was unsurprising as each of the planned 29 mechanized corps should have had a total of 1700 motorcycles – it is likely that few units had more than 20 per cent of the machines which they should have held at the time of the German invasion.

The massive losses sustained in the first months of Operation Barbarossa meant that by the end of 1941 there were only seven operational motorcycle regiments. Each of these comprised:

■ Three motorcycle rifle companies, each with a total of 180 men in three rifle platoons and a submachine gun platoon. (Each company fielded nine light and four medium machine guns.)

■ A mortar company with 18 x 50mm (1.97in) light mortars.

1st Guards Motorcycle Rgt: Equipment

EQUIPMENT	OPERATIONAL	REPLACEMENT AWAITED	UNDER REPAIR
T-34	6	2	2
M3A1 Scout Car	12	0	1
M2 Half Track	5	0	0

■ An anti-tank battery with four 45mm (1.8in) anti-tank guns

■ An armoured company with four armoured cars and four light tanks.

(In the chaotic conditions of late 1941/early 1942, the armoured companies were likely to be equipped with a strange mixture of different types of pre-war armoured cars and light tanks. Whilst every effort would be made to try to ensure that no more than one type of each was held by any given unit, this was probably not always possible.).

In March 1943 new motorcycle regiments were raised, similar to the 1941 regiment but with the anti-tank battery expanded to a battalion with three

1st Guards Motorcycle Regiment

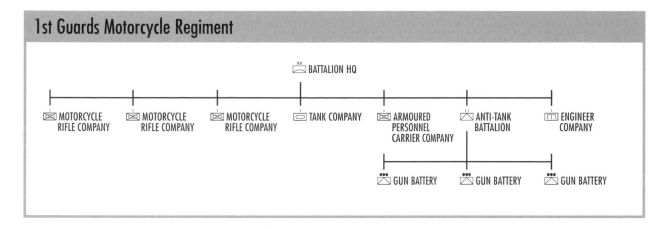

4-gun batteries (two with 45mm (1.8in) and one with 76.2mm (3in)). The armoured company became a tank company, initially with 16 x T-70, which were later replaced by 10 x T-34.

Unusually for the wartime Red Army, these new regiments included an armoured personnel carrier (APC) company, which was generally equipped with Lend-Lease M3A1 scout cars.

An engineer company was also added to each regiment, which became a near equivalent of the German *kampfgruppe* (battle group) capable of undertaking a variety of duties such as deep penetration raids in addition to its primary reconnaissance role.

MOTORCYCLES

Soviet military motorcycles of the late 1930s were obsolescent machines based on Western designs of almost 10 years earlier. Unsurprisingly, these types performed badly during the Winter War against Finland and as part of the review of Red Army equipment, it was decided to standardise on a single new motorcycle type. This was the period of the Molotov-Ribbentrop Pact and its associated trade agreements, so it was natural that German motorcycles should be considered and the BMW R 71 was chosen as the basis for the new Soviet design.

Although accounts differ, it seems likely that, rather than arranging for production under licence

M2 halftrack

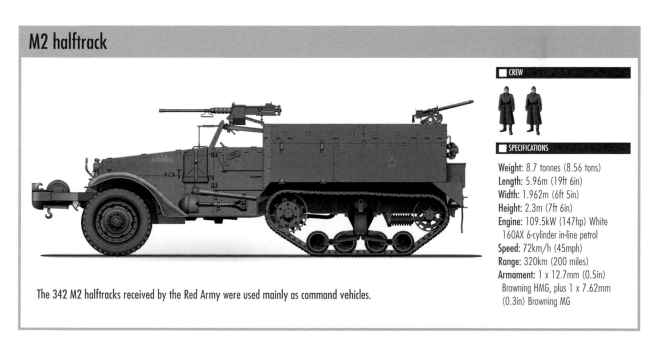

The 342 M2 halftracks received by the Red Army were used mainly as command vehicles.

CREW

SPECIFICATIONS

Weight: 8.7 tonnes (8.56 tons)
Length: 5.96m (19ft 6in)
Width: 1.962m (6ft 5in)
Height: 2.3m (7ft 6in)
Engine: 109.5kW (147hp) White
160AX 6-cylinder in-line petrol
Speed: 72km/h (45mph)
Range: 320km (200 miles)
Armament: 1 x 12.7mm (0.5in)
Browning HMG, plus 1 x 7.62mm
(0.3in) Browning MG

in the USSR, five R 71s were covertly purchased through Swedish intermediaries and shipped to Moscow where they were dismantled and reverse engineered to produce the M-72 motorcycle. The prototypes were demonstrated to Stalin in early 1941 and approved for service.

However, mass production had barely begun before the German invasion forced the evacuation of the Moscow factory, which was re-established at Irbit in the Urals. A total of almost 10,000 M-72s were produced during the war years – although this was nowhere near sufficient for the Red Army's needs, the balance was met by a total of 34,000 British and US Lend-Lease machines.

M3A1 SCOUT CAR

The White Motor Company of Cleveland, Ohio began design studies of what would become the M3 Scout Car in 1937. For its time, it was a sophisticated vehicle with permanent four-wheel drive, a four-speed manual constant-mesh (non-synchromesh) transmission (with one reverse gear) and two-speed transfer case, leaf spring suspension and (unusually for the period) vacuum-assisted (power) brakes.

The initial order was for 64 vehicles, all of which were assigned to the 7th Cavalry Brigade, which

was later expanded to become the 1st Armored Division. Whilst the type performed quite well in the major exercises of the period, such as the Louisiana manoeuvres, it was decided to adopt a new version, designated M3A1, which entered production in 1940. This had a longer and wider hull, with a spring-mounted roller fitted to the front bumper to improve its obstacle-crossing performance. The M3A1 could carry up to seven infantry and provide fire support with three Browning machine guns – one 12.7mm (0.5in) and two 7.62 mm (0.3in) – mounted on a skate rail which ran right around the hull.

Over 3300 Lend-Lease M3A1s were supplied to the Red Army – their four-wheel drive and carrying capacity made them invaluable in a variety of roles. Many of these were the M3A1E1, a diesel-powered derivative which was designed to improve the vehicle's range – this was far better suited to Russian conditions than the petrol engine of the original M3A1 which suffered badly from the very low octane petrol used by the Red Army.

The design influenced the later US halftrack designs such as the M2 and M3 halftracks and the post-war Soviet BTR-40 wheeled APC. The M2 halftrack copied the armour layout as well as the skate rail machine gun mounts.

Harley-Davidson 42WLA with sidecar and mortar

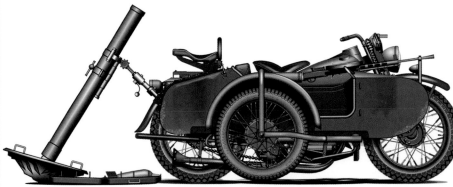

■ CREW

■ SPECIFICATIONS

Weight: 245kg (540lb)
Length: 2.24m (7ft 4in)
Width: 1.04m (3ft 5in)
Height: n/k
Engine: 17kW (23hp) V-2 air-cooled petrol
Speed: 105km/h (65.2mph)
Range: 161km (100 miles)

Most of the Red Army's WLAs were fitted with the M72 sidecar and a proportion of these combinations were modified to mount the standard 82mm (3.2in) mortar.

1446th Assault Gun Regiment

The versatility of the German StuG III assault guns deployed in the early stages of Operation Barbarossa impressed the Red Army and when the up-gunned StuG III Ausf. F demonstrated its effectiveness in the anti-tank role, a requirement was issued for a Soviet equivalent.

In the spring of 1942, design studies were begun for a light assault gun based on the hull of the T-60 light tank dubbed the OSU-76 (*Opytnaya Samokhodnaya Ustanovka*: Experimental Mechanized Mounting). The prototype was armed with a standard ZiS-3 76.2mm (3in) divisional gun on a limited traverse mounting in an open-topped fighting compartment. The project was abandoned when trials showed that the gun was too powerful for the small hull of the T-60 and attention turned to investigating the potential of the new T-70 light tank in this role.

Even the larger T-70 proved to be too small – the hull had to be lengthened and fitted with an extra pair of road wheels to provide a stable mount for the gun. The design was approved for service as the SU-76, but the initial production batches used the peculiar automotive design of the early T-70 light tanks. Two GAZ-202 truck engines were fitted, one on each side of the hull with each engine powering one track via separate, unsynchronised transmissions. This was hopelessly unreliable and an urgent redesign was undertaken to fit the far better engine and transmission layout of the T-70M.

The modified vehicle was officially designated SU-76M, but, as so few of the original design were completed, it was generally known simply as the SU-76.

Crews hated the type for its discomfort and poor protection, dubbing it *Suka* (bitch), or *Suchka* (little

1446th Assault Gun Regiment: Equipment			
EQUIPMENT	OPERATIONAL	REPLACEMENT AWAITED	UNDER REPAIR
SU-76	10	0	0
SU-122	11	0	0

bitch). This was understandable as the open-topped fighting compartment was cramped and bitterly cold in the depths of winter. The driver had the opposite problem as he sat alongside the engine compartment which was not fitted with any bulkheads, so that temperatures in his position often soared to almost unbearable levels in summer. The vehicle's thin armour could be penetrated by almost any anti-tank weapon, whilst the open-topped fighting compartment was vulnerable to grenades and even small arms fire.

The SU-76M virtually replaced infantry tanks in the close support role as it was far cheaper and better suited to mass production. Soviet infantry appreciated its firepower and the open-topped design made it easy to communicate with the crew. In addition to the infantry support role, it was also used for anti-tank work as the ZiS-3 could penetrate most German AFVs, with the exception of the Panther's frontal armour, the Tiger and the Ferdinand. Tungsten-cored armour-piercing composite rigid (APCR) shot and hollow charge

ORBAT: 1446th Assault Gun Regiment

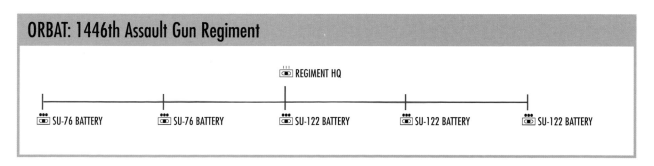

REGIMENT HQ

SU-76 BATTERY   SU-76 BATTERY   SU-122 BATTERY   SU-122 BATTERY   SU-122 BATTERY

shells were developed to give the SU-76M a better chance against such heavily-armoured opponents, but this ammunition was not generally available until late 1943/early 1944.

Despite the limitations of the design, the SU-76M remained in production until late 1945, by which time almost 14,000 vehicles had been completed.

SU-122

In April 1942 a requirement was issued for an assault gun armed with the 122mm (4.8in) M-30 howitzer to operate primarily in the infantry support role. In order to make use of the growing numbers of captured German AFVs, it was proposed to adapt hulls of StuGs and Panzer IIIs. A

prototype and ten pre-production vehicles designated SG-122 were completed, but there were concerns about the inability to guarantee a steady supply of spares and hulls for conversion and the project was cancelled in early 1943.

During the summer of 1942 the U-35, a T-34 based design, was developed which utilised the gun mounting already developed for the SG-122. The howitzer was mounted in a fully-enclosed fighting compartment protected by a well-sloped frontal plate of 45mm (1.8in) armour, a layout which may have influenced the design of the later German *jagdpanzers*. The M-30S howitzer had had an elevation range of -3° to +26° and a total traverse of 10°. The five-man crew comprised a driver, gunner, commander and two loaders.

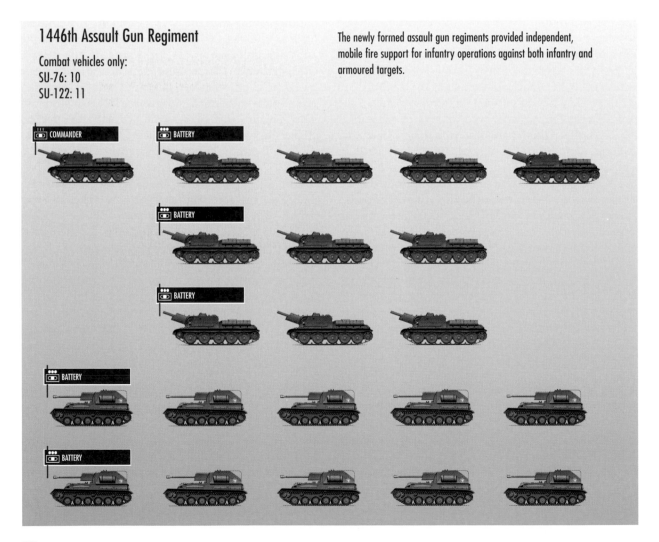

1446th Assault Gun Regiment

Combat vehicles only:
SU-76: 10
SU-122: 11

The newly formed assault gun regiments provided independent, mobile fire support for infantry operations against both infantry and armoured targets.

SU-76M assault gun

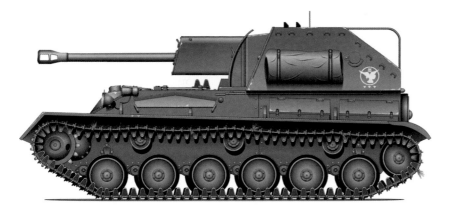

■ **CREW**

■ **SPECIFICATIONS**

Weight: 10.2 tonnes (10.04 tons)
Length: 5m (16ft 5in)
Width: 2.7m (8ft 10in)
Height: 2.1m (6ft 11in)
Engine: 2 x GAZ 203 totalling 126.8kW (170hp)
Speed: 45km/h (28mph)
Range: (Road): 320km (199 miles) (Cross-Country): 190km (118 miles)
Radio: 9RM (When fitted — even by 1945, not all Soviet AFVs had radios.)
Armament: 1 x ZiS-3 76.2mm (3in) gun

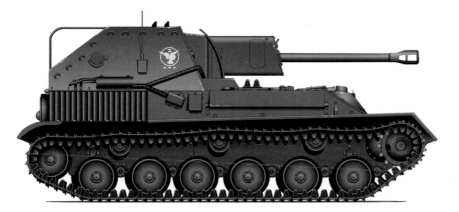

The SU-76M was developed from the T-70M light tank. Although its ZiS-3 76.2mm (3in) gun had a maximum range of over 13,000m (14,217 yards), the type was most often used in the infantry support and anti-tank roles.

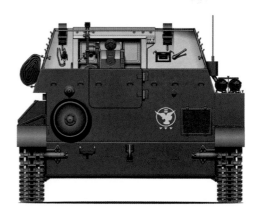

The first U-35 prototype was completed in late 1942 and was subjected to a series of trials between 30 November and 19 December which revealed various shortcomings including insufficient gun elevation, poor fighting compartment ventilation and an awkward division of crew duties. Despite these problems, the U-35 was accepted for service with the Red Army as the SU-35 (later renamed SU-122). However, it was recognized that some modifications were essential and production SU-122s were based on a later, improved prototype incorporating several modifications including slightly less sharply sloped frontal armour to simplify production and a modified fighting compartment with a periscope for the commander, plus rearranged ammunition stowage and crew

SU-122 self-propelled gun

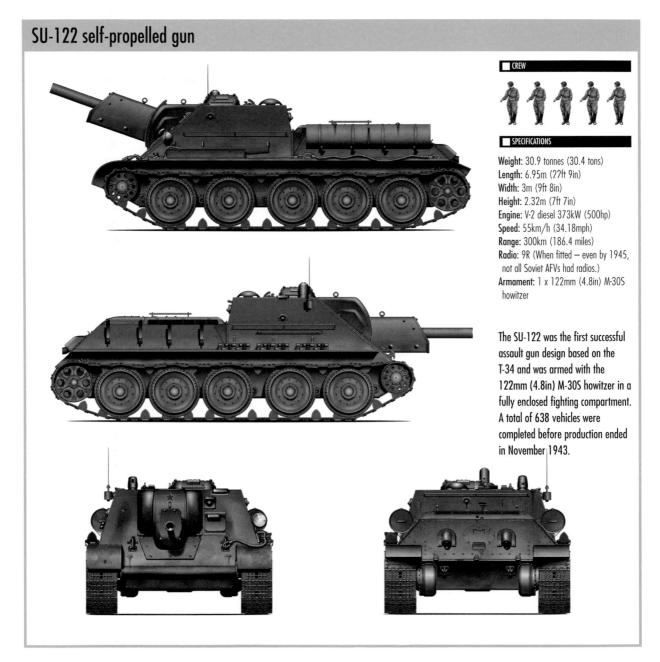

■ CREW

■ SPECIFICATIONS

Weight: 30.9 tonnes (30.4 tons)
Length: 6.95m (22ft 9in)
Width: 3m (9ft 8in)
Height: 2.32m (7ft 7in)
Engine: V-2 diesel 373kW (500hp)
Speed: 55km/h (34.18mph)
Range: 300km (186.4 miles)
Radio: 9R (When fitted — even by 1945, not all Soviet AFVs had radios.)
Armament: 1 x 122mm (4.8in) M-30S howitzer

The SU-122 was the first successful assault gun design based on the T-34 and was armed with the 122mm (4.8in) M-30S howitzer in a fully enclosed fighting compartment. A total of 638 vehicles were completed before production ended in November 1943.

positions. Production began in December 1942 and continued until mid-1944, by which time 1150 vehicles had been completed.

COMBAT

The first SU-122s went into action in January 1943 and proved to be effective fire support vehicles although combat experience quickly led to them being assigned to the second wave in the attack where their very limited traverse was not a major limitation. (They would generally advance 400–600 metres (1300–1970ft) behind the tanks, but sometimes this distance was shortened to 200–300 metres (650–1000ft).)

The SU-122 proved effective in its intended role of direct fire on strongholds. The massive concussion of the 122mm (4.8in) HE round was reportedly enough to blow the turret off even a Tiger I if a direct hit was scored at close range, although longer range penetration against heavier German AFVs remained poor, a trait it shared with the 152mm (6in) howitzer. The theoretical armour-piercing performance of the howitzer improved with the introduction of the new BP-460A HEAT shell

in May 1943, but this was poorly designed and only marginally more effective than the brute concussive effects of the HE shell at close range.

1446TH ASSAULT GUN REGIMENT

In common with the other early assault gun regiments, the 1446th comprised batteries of both SU-76Ms and SU-122s. This mix imposed a considerable strain on the small unit workshop crews which had to hold two entirely different sets of spares and on the supply system which had to manage demands for 76.2mm (3in) and 122mm (4.8in) ammunition.

The tactical handling of these mixed units was equally difficult as the well-protected SU-122s with their low-velocity howitzers needed to engage targets at close range, whilst the thinly armoured SU-76Ms stood a far better chance of survival by using their high-velocity 76.2mm (3in) armament at longer ranges. Unsurprisingly, the process of reorganising assault guns into separate light and medium regiments began as early as April 1943, although the process was not complete until the autumn and many mixed regiments fought at Kursk.

1529th Assault Gun Regiment

Whilst the KV-2 heavy artillery tank had proved to be too unwieldy to survive in the sort of armoured warfare which developed in 1941/42, there remained a need for a heavy AFV with similar firepower for dealing with increasingly sophisticated German field defences.

This gap in the Red Army's capability was emphasised by the bitter street fighting in Stalingrad, where both sides discovered just how difficult it was to demolish factories and other large buildings. Conventional tanks and assault guns lacked the necessary firepower, whilst towed medium and heavy artillery had the required 'punch', but really needed to be brought up to close range and use direct fire. Even with the heaviest covering fire, gun crews were horribly vulnerable in these circumstances and there was no certainty that they would survive long enough to destroy their target. In November 1942 the State Defence Committee ordered the development of a heavy

self-propelled gun armed with the 152mm (6in) ML-20 howitzer. The KV-2 heavy artillery tank armed with the 152mm M-10 howitzer had proved the value of this type of AFV, although it had a very short service life due to numerous design flaws. These included an enormous slab-sided turret which brought the vehicle's total height to 3.65 metres (12ft), a sluggish manual turret traverse which was virtually impossible to operate on anything other than level ground, a slow rate of fire and a high centre of gravity which made the vehicle horribly unstable when moving across country. Production of KV-2s was halted in July 1941 and a few survived until late 1942. The new vehicle was

KV-1S heavy tank

■ CREW

■ SPECIFICATIONS

Weight: 42.5 tonnes (41.8 tons)
Length: 6.8m (22ft 3.7in)
Width: 3.25m (10ft 8in)
Height: 2.64m (8ft 8in)
Engine: V-2 diesel 447.42kW (600hp)
Speed: 45km/h (28mph)
Range: 250km (155 miles)
Radio: 9R (When fitted — even by 1945, not all Soviet AFVs had radios.)
Armament:
 Main: 1 x 76.2mm (3in) ZiS-5 gun
 Secondary: 3 x 7.62mm (0.30in) DT machine guns

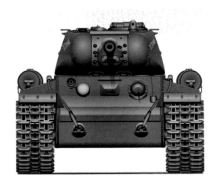

The KV-1S (*Skorostniy*: Speedy) was a final attempt to update the KV-1 which was rapidly becoming out-classed by improved German AFVs and anti-tank guns. The turret layout was re-arranged and the transmission up-rated to improve road speed and cross-country performance. This example was deployed as a command vehicle for the SU-152s of 1529th Assault Gun Regiment.

intended for a similar role, but with improved mobility, heavier armour and the more powerful and accurate ML-20 152mm (6in) gun. The problems of the KV-2 led to the rapid conclusion that a turret mount for the ML-20 was impractical and that the new vehicle should have a fixed fighting compartment with limited traverse main armament.

The situation was complicated by the service debut of the Tiger I in September 1942. A single example was captured very shortly afterwards and it was realized that the new heavy assault gun would have to be capable of dealing with this formidable opponent. The most promising projects were two designs based on the hull of the KV-1S heavy tank. The first was designated KV-12 and broke new ground by mounting the massive 203mm (8in) B-4 Model 1931 howitzer, whilst the more modest KV-14 was armed with the ML-20. The KV-12 was considered to be too risky and the project was cancelled to concentrate resources on the KV-14. Construction of the prototype began on 31 December 1942 and work was completed within 25 days. Factory testing began on 25 January 1943, followed by more stringent state tests. On 14 February 1943 the State Defence Committee formally accepted the type for Red Army service ordered it into production as the SU-152.

Only minor modifications were incorporated at this stage, primarily slight alterations to the controls of the ML-20, which became the ML-20S. (The muzzle velocity and ballistics were identical to the original towed ML-20 gun-howitzer.)

ARMOUR PIERCING PERFORMANCE

Although the SU-152's armament had never been designed as an anti-tank gun, it proved to have surprisingly good armour-piercing performance due to its heavy HE projectiles. Purpose-built AT guns of the period relied on relatively small calibre high velocity projectiles, optimised for punching through armour. However, tests performed on captured Tiger tanks in early 1943 showed that the SU-152 was able to destroy them at any range with a fair degree of reliability (the only vehicle then in Soviet service capable of doing so) by simply blowing the turret off the vehicle through sheer blast effect.

The problem lay in surviving long enough to score such hits – the ML-20 was a relatively low velocity gun-howitzer which was inaccurate at anything other than short range – its effective direct fire range has been quoted as 700 metres (2300ft), but it seems likely that 500 metres (1640ft) would be more realistic. The SU-152's armour was only adequate; the 75mm (3in) sloped frontal armour still left it vulnerable to the Tiger, Panther and Ferdinand at long range and to the Panzer IV and StuG III/IV at medium and short ranges.

Later production batches of the SU-152 included modest improvements – as originally designed, the type lacked a machine gun, which was recognized as a dangerous omission, especially in urban warfare and other close combat situations. To solve this problem a DShK 12.7mm (0.5in) AA installation was developed in the summer of 1943 and fitted to a number of SU-152s. Other drawbacks of the design could not be rectified so readily – little could

1529th Assault Gun Regiment: Equipment

EQUIPMENT	OPERATIONAL	REPLACEMENT AWAITED	UNDER REPAIR
KV-1	1	0	0
SU-152	11	0	1

ORBAT: 1529th Assault Gun Regiment

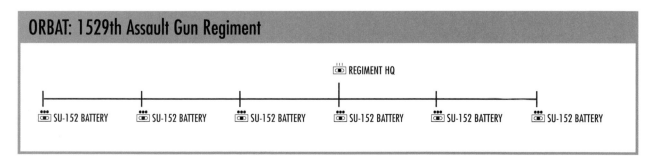

be done to improve the ML-20's slow rate of fire of two rounds per minute, which was due to the difficulties in handling the heavy, two-part ammunition in the confines of a cramped fighting compartment. The SU-152 only carried 20 rounds of the massive, two-piece ammunition. The HE shells weighed 43.6kg (96lb), whilst the AP rounds were 49kg (108lb) each and the propellant charge was a further 6kg (13lb). The weight and bulk of the ammunition also meant that no more than 20 rounds could be stowed which was liable to cause acute problems in prolonged actions. Despite these problems, the SU-152 was highly successful and a total of roughly 700 were completed before production switched to the improved JSU-152 in late 1943.

1529TH ASSAULT GUN REGIMENT AT KURSK

The 1529th was one of the first units to be equipped with the SU-152 and was sent to join Fifth Guards Tank Army as it formed up in the spring of 1943. According to some sources, the unit was the only SU-152 regiment at Kursk – whilst this is unproven, it is safe to say that very few SU-152s saw action during the offensive. They were certainly effective against the newer German AFVs and

Soviet propaganda played up their successes, dubbing the type *Zveroboy* ('beast killer') in recognition of its ability to knock out Panthers, Tigers and Ferdinands.

Soviet claims included the destruction of at least seven Ferdinands by SU-152s. One SU-152 commander, Major Sankovskiy, was awarded the title of Hero of the Soviet Union for the destruction of 10 German tanks in a single day. Such claims are at best dubious – no Ferdinands were deployed in the southern sector of the Kursk salient, so they could not have fallen victim to the 1529th. However, if SU-152s were indeed in action against Model's forces in the north of the salient, it is likely that they did make at least some of the claimed kills. A possible explanation for some of the apparent discrepancies lies in the then novel German practice of fitting *Schurzen* (armoured skirts) to many of their AFVs. These dramatically altered the appearance of familiar types such as the StuG III and the Panzer IV, making it all too easy for Soviet crews to misidentify them as Ferdinands and Tigers in the stress of combat.

Battle experience confirmed the results of the early tests against captured Tigers – although inaccurate at anything other than short range, the

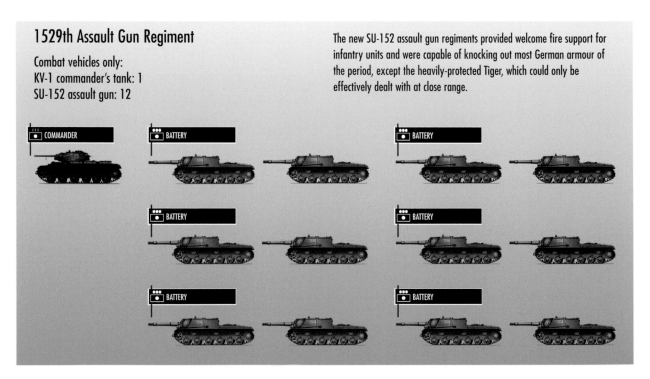

1529th Assault Gun Regiment

Combat vehicles only:
KV-1 commander's tank: 1
SU-152 assault gun: 12

The new SU-152 assault gun regiments provided welcome fire support for infantry units and were capable of knocking out most German armour of the period, except the heavily-protected Tiger, which could only be effectively dealt with at close range.

COMMANDER

BATTERY   BATTERY

BATTERY   BATTERY

BATTERY   BATTERY

SU-152 heavy self-propelled gun

■ **CREW**

■ **SPECIFICATIONS**

Weight: 45.5 tonnes (44.78 tons)
Length: 8.95m (29ft 4in)
Width: 3.25m (10ft 8in)
Height: 2.45m (8ft)
Engine: V-2 diesel 447.42kW (600hp)
Speed: 43km/h (27mph)
Range: 330km (205 miles)
Radio: 9R (When fitted – even by 1945, not all Soviet AFVs had radios.)
Armament: 1 x 152mm (6in) ML-20 howitzer

The SU-152 was developed under a crash programme to produce a heavy tank destroyer on the KV-1S chassis. In the type's first actions at Kursk, the 152mm (6in) ML-20's armour-piercing rounds proved to be capable of destroying even the latest German AFVs at normal battle ranges.

ML-20's HE shell was quite capable of blowing the turret completely off a Tiger.

No AFV crew could expect to survive a direct hit from a 152mm (6in) shell, which even if it failed to penetrate, would cause major internal damage and casualties from spalling (splintering) of the inner face of the armour. There was also a strong possibility that such non-penetrating hits would detonate stowed ammunition and the certainty of considerable external damage as the blast smashed vision blocks and sights, ripped off aerials and broke tracks.

In the aftermath of Kursk, SU-152 units began to receive armour-piercing ammunition – this seems to have been of two types, Model 1915/1928 semi-armour piercing (SAP) shells and 53-BR-540 armour-piercing HE (APHE) rounds. Both these had a similar performance, penetrating approximately 125mm (4.9in) of armour at 500 metres (1640ft), but were in short supply and little more effective against AFVs than the standard HE shell. In view of the limited ammunition stowage of the SU-152, it is likely that many crews opted to carry HE only, even when AP rounds were available.

678th Heavy Artillery Regiment

The Red Army followed the tradition of the Imperial Russian Army in giving high priority to the development of a powerful artillery arm, which Soviet propaganda dubbed 'the God of War'.

The equipment of the 678th Heavy Artillery Regiment was the ML-20 152mm (6in) gun-howitzer, the final derivative of the 152mm (6in) Model 1910 howitzer with which the Tsar's army had gone to war in 1914. The Model 1910 had been subjected to two earlier updates to produce the Model 1910/30 and the Model 1910/34, but these were still regarded as insufficiently mobile to meet the demands of future warfare and the ML-20 was accordingly developed in 1936/37.

The ML-20 was a typical Soviet design, capable of functioning in the worst extremes of the Russian climate and of withstanding considerable rough handling from poorly trained conscripts. In common with all the Red Army's artillery, it was frequently used as a direct fire weapon and even as an anti-tank gun. (In the desperate fighting to contain II SS Panzer Corps advance, ML-20s frequently had to become ad hoc anti-tank guns – their slow traverse and low rate of fire were far from ideal for the task, but a hit from one of their APHE shells could penetrate up to 125mm of armour and even the standard 43.5kg HE shell was quite capable of knocking out all but the heaviest German AFVs.)

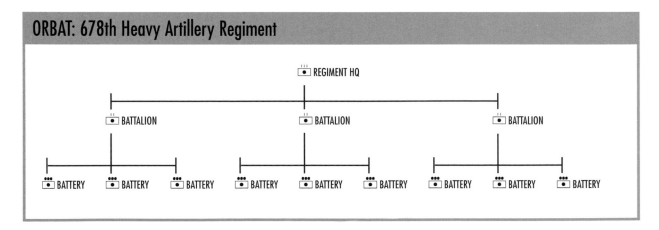

ORBAT: 678th Heavy Artillery Regiment

REGIMENT HQ

BATTALION   BATTALION   BATTALION

BATTERY BATTERY BATTERY   BATTERY BATTERY BATTERY   BATTERY BATTERY BATTERY

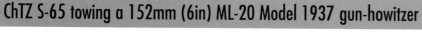

ChTZ S-65 towing a 152mm (6in) ML-20 Model 1937 gun-howitzer

The S-65 was a diesel-engined derivative of the Caterpillar 60 design. Although initially intended as a civilian vehicle, many of the 37,626 S-65s built from 1937–41 were brought into service as artillery tractors.

■ SPECIFICATIONS

Weight: 11.2 tonnes (11.02 tons)
Length: 4.086m (13ft 5in)
Width: 2.416m (7ft 11in)
Height: 2.151m (7ft 1in)

Engine: 55.87kW (75hp) diesel
Speed: 7km/h (4.35mph)
Range: 90km (55.82 miles)

■ CREW

The Soviets, like the artillerymen of Western armies, have always placed great emphasis on the achievement of heavy concentrations of fire as well as of weapons. However, during much of World War II they were unable or unwilling to create the sort of fire control system which enabled US, British and German artillery to concentrate the fire of widely dispersed batteries on a single target, but achieved the same effect by massing huge numbers of guns on small sectors of the front. Western armies emphasised flexibility of fire coupled with comparatively rigid command structures. The Soviets, on the other hand, combined relative inflexibility of fire with highly flexible command structures.

FIRE-PLAN
The Red Army formed artillery groups for specific combat operations, but the composition of these groups was very fluid. Different groups were sometimes formed for each successive phase of a single attack and in general, the detachment of battalions and batteries from these groups began as early as the end of the bombardment preceding the assault. This process of decentralisation continued as the attack progressed, with the result that the artillery groups underwent a steady shrinkage. The

678th Heavy Artillery Regiment: Equipment

UNIT	STRENGTH
Men	1120
Tractor	35
152mm ML-20 gun-howitzer	18

Soviets found it preferable to shift artillery pieces rather than to shift fire in many situations. Whilst this practice did make batteries more vulnerable to air attack, the risk steadily declined as the VVS gained an increasing degree of air superiority from 1943 onwards.

Detailed planning at army level was another important characteristic of the Red Army's artillery. Eventually, a detailed artillery fire-plan was drawn up on the basis of the information available about the enemy and the overall Soviet attack plan. Targets were assigned to individual batteries, battalions or groups. Barrages were carefully planned and 'on call' signals arranged for firing them. Especially important targets in the forward areas were singled out for destruction by direct-fire guns where possible, or by heavy concentrations of indirect fire where direct fire was not feasible. Subordinate artillery commanders were assigned portions of the fire-plan to fulfil. They were also assigned blocks of 'empty' concentration numbers, which they could assign to targets they wished to destroy or neutralise. However, although they could add targets to those already given, they were not permitted to neglect assigned targets in favour of ones which they had selected.

Finally, every artillery commander and his subordinates were required to make a reconnaissance of the sector of the front on which his units were to fire, personally observing all possible targets. By planning the initial phases of the artillery action at army level, the Soviets were able to reduce the chances that errors made by inexperienced subordinates would ruin the development of an offensive at the very outset.

DIRECT AND INDIRECT FIRE

Another prime characteristic of Soviet artillery was its combination of direct and indirect fire. Indirect fire of conventional artillery, mortars and rocket-launchers was employed primarily against area targets, although in some instances destruction of

A 152mm (6in) M1937 howitzer prepares to fire shortly before the Kursk offensive, somewhere near Kharkov.

point targets was ensured by sheer weight of metal. Where possible, however, the Red Army preferred to utilise direct fire of individual field artillery pieces, anti-tank or anti-aircraft guns, or even assault guns to eliminate key point targets.

The system worked out very well in practice; it not only reduced the effect of Soviet fire-control weaknesses, but also helped to conserve ammunition. One or two rounds of direct fire could do the work of 20 rounds of indirect fire. It is significant that whilst the Soviets were extremely lavish in their ammunition expenditure whenever and wherever a main effort was being made, they were extremely parsimonious in doling out ammunition to the batteries at other times.

Even as late as the autumn of 1944, the German batteries, although greatly outnumbered, often fired more rounds in a given week on the Eastern Front than the Red Army – and neither expended the vast quantities of ammunition commonly fired by US artillery batteries.

SHORT, SHARP SHOCK

As the war went on, Soviet artillery bombardments became steadily shorter, but more intense, sometimes lasting for as little as 40 minutes. No set

678th Heavy Artillery Regiment

152mm ML-20 gun-howitzers: 18
Tractors: 35

Roughly two tractors were required to serve each gun-howitzer. Precise figures are not available for the many dozens of trucks used to carry the regiment's supplies and personnel.

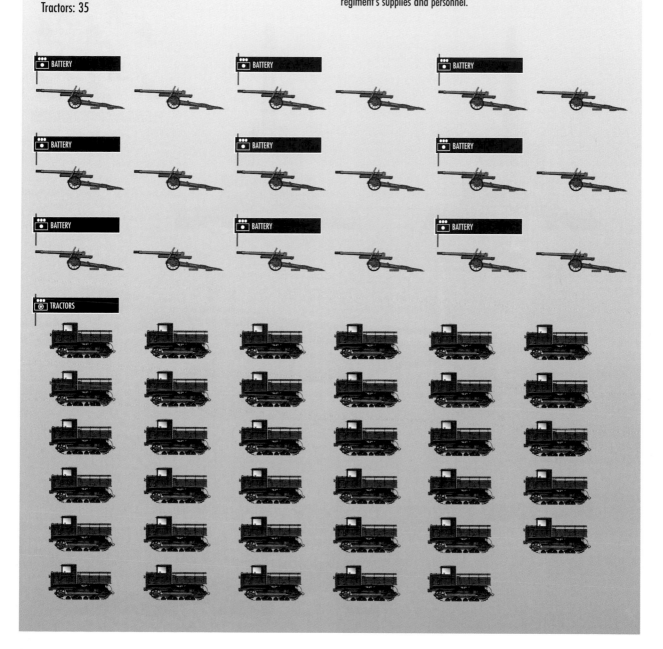

timetable was followed, and all sorts of ruses were employed. In many cases the barrage would be temporarily halted in the hope of luring local German reserves forward, so that they could be brought under fire for the remainder of the bombardment. Another favourite trick was the creation of 'channels' of safety in their bombardments by halting the fire of one or more batteries or battalions. Infantry units then advanced swiftly through these lanes to the very edge of the

152mm (6in) ML-20 Model 1937 gun-howitzer

CREW

SPECIFICATIONS

Weight in action: 7.27 tonnes (7.155 tons)
Calibre: 152mm (6in)
Muzzle Velocity: 680m/sec (2,231ft/sec)
Range: 17.23km (10.7 miles)
Ammunition: HE, HEAT, Shrapnel, Illuminating, Smoke

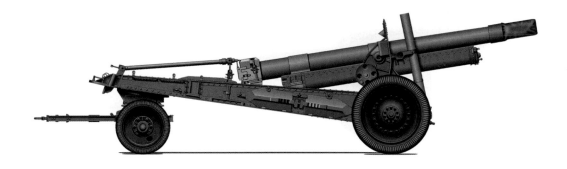

The ML-20 had a range of over 17 kilometres (11 miles) with a standard 43.5kg (96lb) HE shell. It later became one of the principal weapons of the Breakthrough Artillery Divisions, each of which fielded 32 ML-20s. Later examples had disc wheels and pneumatic tyres to allow high-speed towing as the original spoked wheels and solid tyres severely restricted towing speeds.

enemy's position, and often caught the enemy troops still in their bunkers, deceived into believing that their area was still under fire.

The support of the attack phase began when the infantry assault was launched. The artillery then passed over from preparatory fire to direct support fire, which normally took the form of an accompanying rolling barrage combined with area concentrations. At this point the mortar units of infantry formations reverted to local control and some field artillery units were assigned close direct-support missions, which called for them to follow the infantry and deliver support fire from the nearest defilade behind them. Other light artillery pieces were manhandled forward with the infantry and together with the anti-tank guns, helped to knock out point targets.

The accompanying rolling barrage consisted of a series of linear barrages spaced 50 to 100 metres (165 to 330ft) apart. The barrage moved deeper into enemy position as the infantry advanced. The rolling wall of fire conformed to the enemy's defensive system as it moved, and was subject to control by the infantry who were expected to advance closely behind it and catch the enemy still shaken and under cover.

FINAL PHASE

The Red Army believed that it was preferable to suffer some casualties from their own artillery fire than to allow the Germans to recover from the initial shock and disorganisation of the artillery bombardment. Once the breakthrough of the main German defence line had been accomplished, and Soviet armour was committed, the final phase of the artillery attack began. This amounted to support of the attack in the depth of the enemy position. In this phase the control of artillery was highly decentralised, with each combined-arms formation commander having full control of organic and attached artillery and assault gun units.

Mobile reserves were formed at each echelon from regiment up. These reserves, which were normally composed of anti-tank artillery, engineers, infantry tank-killer teams, and heavy field-pieces or assault guns, were used to break up German counter-attacks. Employed successfully in depth, such reserves proved their worth on many occasions.

76th Guards Mortar Regiment

Soviet artillery rockets, generally known as *Katyushas*, were developed under the tightest security in the late 1930s. They were deployed by what were officially referred to as 'guards mortar breakthrough' units, more usually termed 'guards mortar units'.

In June 1938, the Red Army's Main Artillery Directorate (GAU) ordered the Soviet Jet Propulsion Research Institute (RNII) to develop a multiple rocket launcher for the new 82mm (3.2in) RS-82 and 132mm (5.2in) RS-132 air-launched rockets (RS - *Reaktivnyy Snaryad*, 'rocket-powered shell'). Initial efforts were concentrated on the RS-132 which was fitted with a larger warhead and designated M-13. A total of 233 prototype rockets were test-fired in late 1938 from ZiS-5 trucks and it was found that a salvo could straddle an area target at a range of 5500 metres (18,000ft). These test-firings were made from 24-rail launchers firing over the sides of ZiS-5 trucks, but this firing arrangement was unstable and the problem was only solved when longitudinally-mounted launch rails were adopted.

The modified vehicles were completed in August 1939 as the BM-13 (BM – *Boyevaya Mashina*, 'combat vehicle' for M-13 rockets). Further trials took place throughout 1940 and the BM-13-16 with launch rails for 16 rockets was ordered into production, but only 40 vehicles were completed by the time of the German invasion.

M-13 ROCKET

The system consisted of an elevating frame which carried a bank of eight parallel rails on which the rockets were mounted (eight on top of the rails and a further eight hung beneath them). The 132mm (5.2in) diameter M-13 rocket of the BM-13 system had an overall length of 180cm (5ft 11in) and weighed 42kg (92lb). It was stabilised by pressed-steel cruciform fins and powered by a solid nitrocellulose-based propellant, venting through a single central nozzle at the base. Maximum range was just under 8500 metres (28,000ft), but the M-13-DD rocket, introduced in 1944, used two standard motors which gave a maximum range of 11,800 metres (39,000ft). This was the best range achieved by any solid-fuel artillery rocket of the war, but the type could only be launched from the upper rails of the launcher.

FURTHER DEVELOPMENTS

As the war progressed more types of M-13 warhead were introduced, including armour-piercing to break up tank formations, flare for night illumination, incendiary and signal. Most warheads were simple 22kg (48.5lb) impact-fused HE-fragmentation types, although there is a possibility that HEAT warheads may have been developed for use against tank concentrations. (Some reports indicate that illuminating and incendiary warheads were also used in small numbers.)

Whilst the weapon was slow to reload and was far less accurate than conventional artillery, it had immense firepower. In 7–10 seconds, a battery of four BM-13 launchers could fire a salvo which delivered 4.35 tonnes of HE over a four-hectare impact zone. Well-trained crews could then redeploy in a matter of a few minutes to avoid counter-battery fire.

The multiple rocket launchers were considered top secret at the beginning of the war and were operated under close NKVD supervision. They were assigned various code names such as 'Kostikov Guns', before being officially designated Guards Mortars. However, to the troops they were *Katyushas*, the name coming from a popular song of the time and this was the title by which they would become world-famous.

THE M8 AND M30

On 7 July 1941, an experimental battery of seven launchers was first used in combat at Orsha – the bombardment was spectacular, destroying the important railway junction together with German troop and supply trains. Following this success, the Red Army began priority production of the system and developed additional types of *Katyusha*. In August 1941, the 82mm (3.2in) M-8 rocket entered service. Much smaller and lighter than the M-13, it could be fired from vehicles as small as a jeep, which could carry eight M-8s. Medium trucks mounted a bank of rails for no less than 48 rockets. The M-8's overall length was 66cm (26in), weight 8kg (17lb) (including a 5.4kg (12lb) HE-fragmentation warhead) and its maximum range was just over 5000 metres (16,500ft). In 1944, an improved version of the rocket came into service with a maximum range of 5500 metres (18,000ft).

These light and medium rockets were highly effective, but there was a need for a heavier version,

76th Guards Mortar Regiment: Equipment

UNIT	MANPOWER	EQUIPMENT
Headquarters	58	
1 Battalion	191	3 batteries of 4 x salvo rocket launchers
2 Battalion	191	3 batteries of 4 x salvo rocket launchers
3 Battalion	191	3 batteries of 4 x salvo rocket launchers
AA Battery	–	4 x 37mm guns

ORBAT: 76th Guards Mortar Regiment

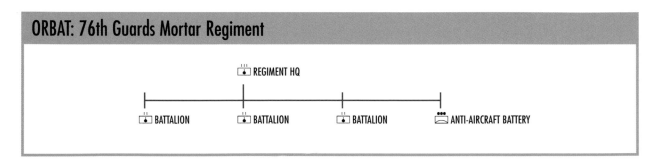

REGIMENT HQ

BATTALION   BATTALION   BATTALION   ANTI-AIRCRAFT BATTERY

which was initially met by the M-30. This used a modified version of the M-13's rocket motor which was fitted with a bulbous 300mm (12in) HE warhead containing 28.9kg (64lb) of explosive. Maximum range was only 2800 metres (9200ft), but this was considered acceptable in view of the warhead's devastating blast effect. The M-30 was fired directly from its packing case, four of which could be mounted on a firing frame, referred to as a *Rama*. In late 1942, the improved M-31 was adopted. This was very similar to its predecessor, but a new rocket motor gave it a maximum range of

4300 metres (14,100ft). (The later M-13-UK was modified to give a degree of spin-stabilisation, which greatly improved accuracy.) Initially the firing method was the same as that of the M-30, but in March 1944 a mobile version entered service consisting of launchers for 12 M-31s on a ZiS-6 6x6 truck. Later production batches were mounted on Lend-Lease Studebaker US-6 6x6 trucks. These had such a good cross-country performance that in 1943 they were adopted as the standard mount for the BM-13 under the designation BM-13N (*Normalizovanniy*, 'standardized').

Studebaker US6 U3, 2½-ton, 6x6, with BM-13-16 *Katyusha* salvo rocket launcher

■ CREW

■ SPECIFICATIONS

Weight: 4.47 tonnes (4.4 tons)
Length: 6.19m (20ft 4in)
Width: 2.23m (7ft 4in)
Height: 2.79m (9ft 2in)
Engine: 70kW (94hp) Hercules JXD 6 cylinder petrol
Speed: 72.4km/h (45mph)
Range: n/k
Armament: 16 x 132mm (5.2in) M-8 fin-stabilised rockets

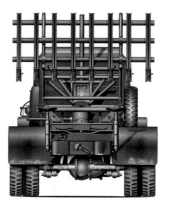

In early 1943, the Red Army adopted the Studebaker 6x6 as the standard vehicle to mount the BM-8 and BM-13 salvo rocket launchers. A total of almost 105,000 Studebaker vehicles were delivered to the Soviet Union by the end of the war, many of which were adapted to give the *Katyusha* a high degree of cross-country mobility.

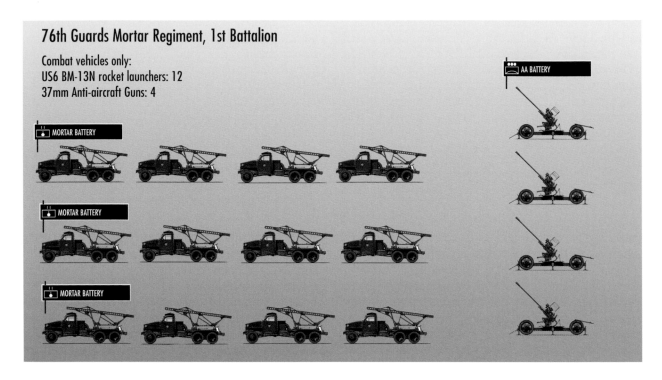

76th Guards Mortar Regiment, 1st Battalion

Combat vehicles only:
US6 BM-13N rocket launchers: 12
37mm Anti-aircraft Guns: 4

AA BATTERY

MORTAR BATTERY

MORTAR BATTERY

MORTAR BATTERY

Red Army artillery crew load 132mm (5.2in) rockets onto the 1- rail launcher of an M-13 *Katyusha*, mounted on a Lend-Lease supplied 6x4 Studebaker 2½ ton truck.

All *Katyushas* were simple, cheap weapons and could be manufactured in workshops and small factories which lacked the specialist machinery for producing conventional artillery or ammunition. This simplicity allowed fast construction times – over 3000 launchers of all types were produced during 1942. By the end of the year, 57 regiments were operational; together with the independent battalions, they equated to 216 batteries: 21 per cent BM-8 light launchers, 56 per cent BM-13, and 23 per cent M-30 heavy launchers.

Whilst the majority of *Katyushas* were truck-mounted, a bewildering variety of other vehicles were also used in small numbers, including STZ-5 artillery tractors, plus the hulls of T-60 and KV-1 tanks. A few launchers were even fitted to armoured trains and river gunboats.

The Red Army's initial enthusiasm for the new weapon led to the creation of a large number of small units. The very first batteries had seven launchers each, but this was soon reduced to four per battery. On 8 August 1941, Stavka ordered the formation of eight rocket regiments, each of three battalions, with three four-vehicle batteries per battalion. (A total of 36 launchers per regiment). By the end of 1941, a total of 554 launchers were operational, equipping eight regiments, 35 independent battalions and two independent batteries. The increasing numbers of BM-13s allowed a battalion of eight launchers to be added to each tank corps from July 1942.

In June 1942 20 independent battalions were formed to operate the new M-30 rockets, with each having 96 launchers in three batteries. These units were gradually concentrated into larger formations, finally leading to the establishment of seven full divisions in 1943, each of which had 864 launchers firing a total of 3456 rockets. (In 1944 these divisions were supplemented by motorized heavy battalions, each equipped with 48 BM-31 launchers.)

KATYUSHAS AT KURSK

Although *Katyushas* were most frequently employed in their usual indirect fire role, the threat posed by the German armoured assaults was such that many batteries had to be used for direct fire. As the cab of the launch vehicle prevented the rockets being fired at 'zero elevation', ramps were prepared to cover the probable lines of advance of panzer units. Launch vehicles were backed up onto the ramps, bringing their rocket launch rails down to the horizontal so that they could use direct fire against targets within a couple of thousand metres.

Although the chances of a single rocket hitting a 'tank-size' target were remote, the impact of even a single 12-vehicle battalion's fire was impressive – the target area would be saturated with 192 HE-fragmentation warheads.

Whilst these 5.4kg (12lb) warheads would be unlikely to destroy anything other than light AFVs, they were quite capable of disabling tanks and assault guns by breaking tracks, shattering vision blocks and blowing away radio aerials. Naturally, the *Katyushas* would never be deployed in isolation and such disabled vehicles would then become prime targets for Soviet tanks, anti-tank guns and infantry anti-tank teams.

The Soviet General Staff Study of the battle concluded: 'The experience in the July battles of using M-13s to fight enemy tanks was extraordinarily valuable. The successful use of guards mortars for direct fire and the good results obtained by salvo fire against tanks expanded the possibilities of using guards mortars for fighting not only enemy personnel but also tanks.'

A brief rest halt for a BM-13-16 *Katyusha* battery. The rocket launchers are mounted on US Studebaker truck chassis, whilst a jeep overtakes the column – a vivid illustration of the Red Army's reliance on Lend-Lease support vehicles.

Chapter 3
Soviet Air Support at Kursk

The pre-war Red Air Force (VVS) was administered as a branch of
the Red Army and was subjected to considerable interference from Stalin. His interest
had the malign effect of ensuring that all reports on it were wildly optimistic. This
'spin' became outright faking where statistics were concerned, with false figures being
routinely submitted for everything from aircraft production to aircrew training.
Unsurprisingly, the VVS had a horrifying accident rate, which remained at
a very high level throughout the war.

The endemic faking of data throughout the Stalin era means that
statistics relating to the VVS are even more uncertain than those for the Red Army,
but it had at least 10,000 front-line aircraft at the time of the German invasion, of
which roughly half were serviceable. *Luftwaffe* attacks on the first day of Operation
Barbarossa destroyed roughly 800 of these on the ground, whilst German fighters shot
down a further 400 in the same period.

OPPOSITE: Yakovlev Yak-9s fly a mission sometime in 1943. The Yak-9 was one of the most successful Soviet fighters of
World War II and the most mass-produced Soviet fighter of all time. It remained in production from 1942 to 1948, with
14,579 being built during the war.

Soviet Air Power

Although the VVS had favoured strategic bombing during the 1930s and included 800 TB-3 four-engine bombers, the demands of war compelled it to develop into a force dedicated to providing close air support to the Red Army.

Pre-war Soviet military doctrine emphasised the need for combined arms operations involving full coordination of air and ground forces. The 1939 Field Service Regulations stressed that aviation should '...act in close operational-tactical contact with ground forces' besides carrying out attacks on deep objectives and air superiority missions. The Field Regulations of 1940 re-emphasised this requirement, but as the war began, there was a vast gap between theory and reality.

THE STRUGGLE FOR SURVIVAL: 1941–42

In practice, the VVS was as unprepared as the rest of the Red Army for the German attack in June 1941. Over 43 per cent of its pilots and 90 per cent of its formation commanders had completed less than six months service. Although some aircrew had gained combat experience during the Spanish Civil War and the Winter War against Finland, the majority of pilots were inexperienced and poorly trained. Its equipment varied wildly, ranging from the modern to the antique – early examples of the ultra-modern Pe-2 bomber were in service alongside more than 1000 I-15bis fighter biplanes dating from the mid-1930s.

In the immediate aftermath of the German invasion, the VVS and the Red Army struggled to rebuild basic close air support and air defence systems. Initially, ground armies controlled aircraft assets, but operational close air support procedures were primitive. Ground forces were untrained in aircraft identification and no system of forward command posts existed to control aircraft. In order to minimise the risk of 'friendly fire' incidents, pilots seldom attacked targets closer than 10 kilometres (6 miles) to the Soviet front line.

A dire shortage of radios forced the adoption of a variety of improvized recognition and target designation methods. Ground troops would mark the front line by signal panels, smoke grenades, coloured signal rockets, bursts of tracer bullets, and vehicle headlights. When rockets, smoke grenades and signal panels were unavailable, troops resorted to even more rough and ready expedients to mark their positions.

Soviet air defence was equally primitive at this stage of the war. So many fighters had been lost in the first weeks of Operation *Barbarossa* that a motley collection of obsolete and obsolescent types

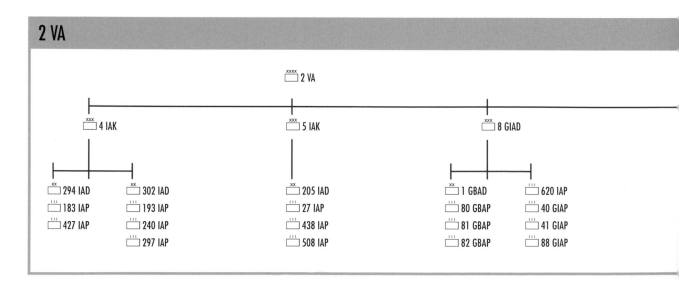

2 VA

Soviet Ground Attack Aircraft, 1941–45

YEAR	STRENGTH
1941	1543
1942	8219
1943	11,177
1944	11,110
1945	c. 5500
TOTAL	37,549

such as the I-16 had to be kept in service to provide some semblance of air cover for the front line. Soviet air defence radar development had been badly disrupted by Stalin's purges and there was nothing comparable to the sophisticated British and German radar systems. Although a number of Lend-Lease British and US radars were received from 1942 onwards to supplement a handful of Soviet sets, these were totally insufficient to provide coverage for anything more than a few high value targets well behind the front line.

As a result, Soviet fighters had to fly standing patrols little different from those of World War I – a highly inefficient form of air cover. This ineffectiveness was compounded by very low standards of pilot training – the *Luftwaffe* came to regard the Eastern Front as an operational training area for its fighter aircrew and several German aces (such as Erich Hartmann with 352 victories) ran up phenomenal scores of VVS aircraft.

RECOVERY: 1942–43

In April 1942, Stavka appointed General Novikov as commander of the VVS and Deputy Commissar for Aviation. He immediately set about rejuvenating the Red Air Force by combining Front and Army air units into combined air armies. These large formations maximised the effective use of frontal aviation, to allow concentrations of air power in support of ground operations. Each air army was allocated to support a Front.

Close cooperation was ensured by placing the air army's deputy commander and his staff with the Front HQ. The Front and air army commanders jointly worked out operational plans, with the Front commander determining the priority of missions.

The first air armies were formed in May 1942 with others following in June, July, August and November, by which time 13 separate air armies had been formed. Each air army consisted of two

2VA Aircraft Strength

TYPE	SERVICEABLE	NOT SERVICEABLE	TOTAL
Fighters	389	85	474
Shturmoviks	276	23	299
Day bombers	172	18	190
Night bombers	34	15	49
Reconnaissance	10	8	18
Totals	881	149	1030

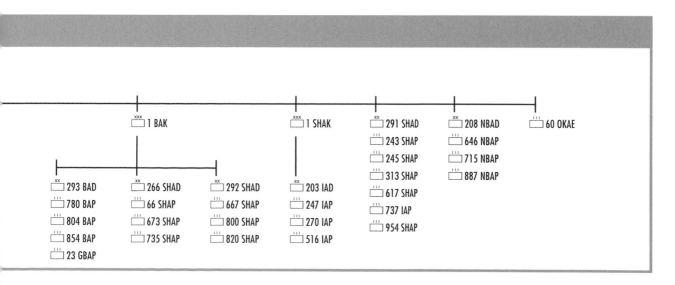

fighter divisions, each with four regiments, and two mixed air divisions, each formed from two fighter and two ground attack regiments. Additional units were soon added, generally a bomber regiment, an air reconnaissance regiment, a night bomber regiment and a training regiment. A gradual process of standardization ensured that each regiment was equipped with a single type of aircraft, to eliminate the logistic problems inherent in trying to maintain a variety of aircraft types during combat operations.

The strength of each air regiment was increased from two squadrons to three, giving a total of 32 aircraft per regiment. The centralisation of air

2 VA

UNIT	COMMANDER	AIRFIELD	AIRCRAFT
4 IAK	Gen-Maj I. Podgomyy	Pestunovo	Yak-1
294 IAD	Polkovnik (Colonel) V. Sukhoryabov		Yak-1
183 IAP	Maj A. Oboznenko		Yak-1
427 IAP	Maj A. Yakimenko		Yak-1
302 IAD	Polkovnik (Colonel) B. Litinov	Shirokiy Gul	La-5
193 IAP	G.M. Pyatakov		La-5
240 IAP	Maj S. Podorozhnyy		La-5
297 IAP	–		La-5
5 IAK	Gen-Maj D. Galunov	Sukho-Solotno. Kochetovka	Yak-1
205 IAD	Polkovnik (Colonel) Y. Nemstevich		Yak-1
27 IAP	Maj V. Bobrov		Yak-1
438 IAP	Podpolkovnik (Lt-Col) Y. Utkin		Yak-1
508 IAP	Podpolkovnik (Lt-Col) S. Zaychenko		Yak-7B
8 GIAD	Gen-Maj D. Galunov	Trubezh, Oboyan, Ivniya	La-5
620 IAP	–		La-5
40 GIAP	Maj M. Tokarev		La-5
41 GIAP	Maj P. Chupikov		La-5
88 GIAP	Maj S. Rymsha		La-5
1 GBAD	Polkovnik (Colonel) F. Dobysh	Liyinka	La-5
80 GBAP	–		Pe-2
81 GBAP	Podpolkovnik (Lt-Col) V. Gavrilov		Pe-2
82 GBAP	–		Pe-2
1 BAK	Polkovnik (Colonel) I. Polbin	Trostanka, Ostrogozhsk	Pe-2
293 BAD	Polkovnik (Colonel) G. Gribakin		Pe-2
780 BAP	–		Pe-2
804 BAP	Maj A.M. Semyonov		Pe-2
854 BAP	Maj A.A. Novikov		Pe-2
23 GBAP	–		Pe-2
266 ShAD	Polkovnik (Colonel) F. Rodyakin	Dubkiy, Valuyki, Urazovo	Pe-2
66 ShAP	Maj V. Lavrinenko		Il-2
673 ShAP	Podpolkovnik (Lt-Col) A. Matikov		Il-2
735 ShAP	Maj S. Bolodin		Il-2
292 ShAD	Maj F. Agaltstov	Kulma, Novyy Oskol	Il-2
667 ShAP	Maj G. Shuteyev		Il-2
800 ShAP	Maj A. Mitrofanov		Il-2
820 ShAP	Maj I.N. Afanasyev		Il-2

regiments also simplified operational planning, logistics, training, maintenance and command.

VVS corps HQs were co-located with those of army commanders, with a VVS detachment assigned to each army corps HQ. (Smaller detachments were stationed at divisional HQs.) Whilst this was a vast improvement on earlier practice, there was no equivalent to the sophisticated German system in which *Luftwaffe* officers – *Fliegerverbindungsoffizier* (air liaison officers, or Flivos) commanded small teams attached to panzer units. These teams travelled in armoured halftracks carrying high-powered radios tuned to *Luftwaffe* frequencies, speaking directly to pilots in the air to direct them against point targets sometimes less than 100 metres (330ft) from the German front line.

THE AIR BATTLE OVER THE SOUTHERN SECTOR

Even by mid-1943, Soviet aircrew training was minimal. The 13,383 Soviet pilots who were trained in 1942 averaged 13–15 flying hours before being posted to combat units. *Shturmovik* and bomber pilots received an average of just 18 and 15 hours flight training respectively and their survival prospects were worsened by their inexperience – only 7 per cent of them had seen action prior to

Kursk. Most Soviet pilots were trained on the aircraft they would fly in combat and unsurprisingly the VVS lost an estimated 10,600 aircraft in training accidents between 1941 and the summer of 1943.

Despite these shortcomings, the Red Air Force opened the air campaign on 6 May when waves of 300–400 aircraft from several air armies attacked *Luftwaffe* airfields around the Kursk salient over a three day period. (At the time, Stavka anticipated that Operation Citadel would be launched no later than 12 May and ordered the raids in the hope of crippling the *Luftwaffe* before the offensive.) Although the initial attacks achieved a measure of surprise and damaged or destroyed 22 *Luftwaffe* aircraft on the ground, the later raids were mauled by thoroughly alerted German defences which shot down a total of 101 Soviet aircraft.

Soviet raids on German communications, supply lines and assembly points around the salient were more effective – the Second and Sixteenth Air Armies flew 9896 sorties against these targets with some spectacular successes such as the detonation of 1200 tonnes of ammunition in the marshalling yards at Bryansk.

The repeated delays to the start date of Operation Citadel allowed the *Luftwaffe* to

2VA continued

UNIT	COMMANDER	AIRFIELD	AIRCRAFT
1 ShAK	Gen V. Ryazanov	Ostapovka	Il-2
203 IAD	Gen-Maj K. Baranchuk		Il-2
247 IAP	*Podpolkovnik* (Lt-Col) Y. Kutikhin		Yak-1
270 IAP	Maj V. Merkushev		Yak-1
516 IAP	–		Yak-1
291 ShAD	*Polkovnik* (Colonel) A. Vitruk	Shumakovo	Il-2
243 ShAP	Maj A. Nakonechnikov		Il-2
245 ShAP	–		Il-2
313 ShAP	Maj I.D. Borodin		Il-2
617 ShAP	Maj D. Lomovtsev		Il-2
737 IAP	*Polkovnik* (Colonel) N. Varchuk		Il-2
954 ShAP	–		Il-2
208 NBAD	*Polkovnik* (Colonel) L. Yuzeyev	Kalinovka	Il-2
646 NBAP	*Podpolkovnik* (Lt-Col) A. Letuchiy		Il-2
715 NBAP	*Podpolkovnik* (Lt-Col) I.I. Zamyatin		Il-2
887 NBAP			Il-2
60 OKAE			Il-2

17VA Aircraft Strength

TYPE	SERVICEABLE	NOT SERVICEABLE	TOTAL
Fighters	163	43	206
Shturmoviks	239	27	266
Day bombers	76	2	78
Night bombers	60	1	61
Reconnaissance	–	–	–
Totals	538	73	611

undertake a limited strategic bombing campaign with a series of night attacks against Soviet war industries throughout much of June 1943. These raids were primarily directed against the GAZ tank factories in Gorkiy, the rubber industry at Yaroslavl and the oil refineries at Saratov. These provoked a series of Soviet retaliatory raids on *Luftwaffe* bomber airfield which inflicted only limited damage.

These preliminaries at least provided some combat experience for the novice Soviet aircrews, but the much-delayed opening of the German offensive on 5 July proved that they still had much to learn. Soviet intelligence sources provided so much detail about German preparations for their offensive that the air armies had planned a series of pre-emptive strikes against *Luftwaffe* airfields as early as May. These plans had been regularly updated and it was confidently expected that the attacks would cripple German air power in the sector during the first crucial days of Operation 'Citadel'.

Unfortunately for the VVS units involved, by the time that they were on their way to their targets, most of the *Luftwaffe* aircraft based at those airfields were already airborne in readiness to make their own attacks in support of the German offensive. A further factor was the effective *Luftwaffe* radar coverage of this sector of the front – Freya radars at Belgorod and Kharkov detected the Soviet aircraft and directed fighters against them which were able to break up many of the formations before they reached their targets.

For much of the remainder of 5 July, the VVS continued to launch repeated attacks, primarily by Il-2s and Pe-2s with fighter escorts, all of which took heavy losses from the far more experienced *Luftwaffe* fighters. At air army level, there was particular concern at their lack of success in preventing the *Luftwaffe* from making devastating

17 VA

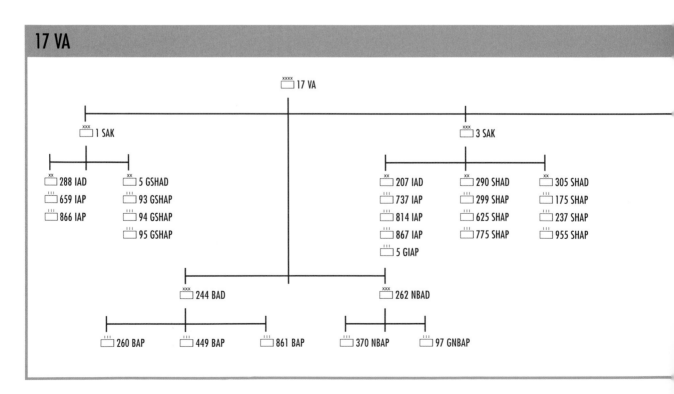

attacks against key sectors of the front – one Soviet account referred to the sector attacked by II SS Panzer Corps '...an area measuring 6 x 4 kilometres in the sector of 52nd Guards Rifle Division... was subjected to 15 hours of uninterrupted air attacks ... during this time as many as 20 bombers were continuously in the air. Such intense enemy air operations...made it considerably easier for the Germans to penetrate our defence and advance 6-8 kilometres into the depth of our positions.' (The division sustained 8500 casualties on 5 July, the majority due to these near-continuous air attacks.)

For the remainder of the offensive, the VVS began to operate more efficiently as reinforcements began to flow in. Repeated attacks by formations of up to 40 Il-2s and Pe-2s with fighter escort proved to be far more effective than earlier strikes flown by no more than eight aircraft. (The balance of air power was also affected by the first signs of a fuel shortage which increasingly restricted *Luftwaffe* operations.) The *Luftwaffe* never lost its qualitative and technological advantage, and ran up an impressive tally of victories, but it was a wasting asset, unable to win the battle of attrition to which

it had been committed. In contrast, the Red Air Force could absorb its tremendous losses, thanks to high rates of production of proven aircraft types, backed up by large scale Lend-Lease deliveries.

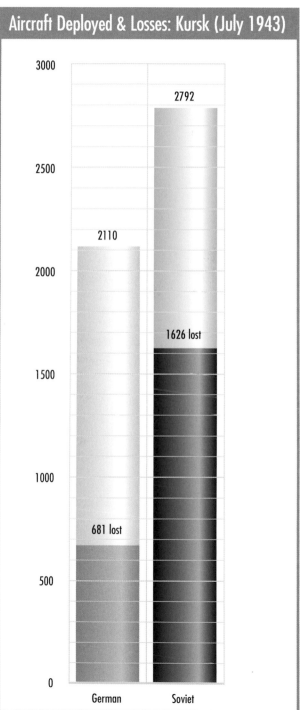

Aircraft Deployed & Losses: Kursk (July 1943)

German: 2110 (681 lost)
Soviet: 2792 (1626 lost)

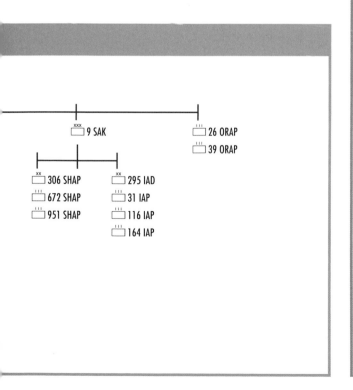

9 SAK

26 ORAP
39 ORAP

306 SHAP   295 IAD
672 SHAP   31 IAP
951 SHAP   116 IAP
                164 IAP

OPPOSITE: RED AIR FORCE AND *LUFTWAFFE* DEPLOYMENT, SOUTHERN SECTOR

The Red Air Force (VVS) assembled an enormous concentration of air power in defence of the Kursk salient. The force may well have totalled 6000 aircraft of all types, roughly the equivalent of the strength of the entire *Luftwaffe* in 1943. Although the VVS never matched the operational skills of the *Luftwaffe* and suffered far higher losses throughout Operation Citadel, these losses were swiftly replaced by a combination of Soviet-produced and Lend-Lease aircraft.

17VA

UNIT	COMMANDER	AIRFIELD	AIRCRAFT
1 SAK	Gen-Maj V. Shevchenko		Yak-7B
288 IAD	*Polkovnik* (Colonel) B. Smimov		Yak-7B
659 IAP	—		Yak-7B
866 IAP	Maj P. Ivanov		Yak-7B
5 GShAD	*Podpolkovnik* (Lt-Col) L. Kolometytsev	Novo-Pskov	Il-2
93 GShAP	—		Il-2
94 GShAP	—		Il-2
95 GShAP	—		Il-2
3 SAK	Gen-Maj V. Aladinski	Novsosinovka, Aleksandrovka	Yak-7B
207 IAD	*Polkovnik* (Colonel) A. Osadchiy		Yak-7B
737 IAP	Maj N. Varchuk		Yak-7B
814 IAP	Maj M. Kuznetsov		Yak-1
867 IAP	Maj S. Indyk		Yak-1
5 GIAP	Maj V. Zaytsev		La-5
290 ShAD	*Polkovnik* (Colonel) P. Mironenko		Il-2
299 ShAP	Maj S. Ananin		Il-2
625 ShAP	—		Il-2
775 ShAP	Maj N. Zubanev		Il-2
305 ShAD	*Polkovnik* (Colonel) N. Mikhyevichev	Pokrovskoye, Lantratovka, Nizhni Budyonnovka, Olshana, Duvanka	Il-2
175 ShAP	—		Il-2
237 ShAP	—		Il-2
955 ShAP	—		Il-2
9 SAK	Gen-Maj O. Tolstikov	Budyonnovka	Il-2
306 ShAD	*Polkovnik* (Colonel) A. Miklashevskiy		Il-2
672 ShAP	—		Il-2
951 ShAP	—		Il-2
295 IAD	*Polkovnik* (Colonel) N. Balanov	Olshana	La-5
31 IAP	—		La-5
116 IAP	—		La-5
164 IAP	Maj A. Melentyov		La-5
244 BAD	Gen-Maj V. Kievtsov	Beloltsk	DB-7B, Boston Mk III
260 BAP	—		BDB-7B, Boston Mk III
449 BAP	Maj M.I. Malov		DB-7B, Boston Mk III
861 BAP	*Podpolkovnik* (Lt-Col) N.A. Nikiforou		DB-7B, Boston Mk III
262 NBAD	*Polkovnik* (Colonel) G. Belitskiy	Zapadnoye, Vasilyevka	U-2
370 NBAP	*Podpolkovnik* (Lt-Col) A. Vasilyevskiy		U-2
97 GNBAP	Maj A.B. Styazhkov		U-2
26 ORAP	—		U-2
39 ORAP	*Podpolkovnik* (Lt-Col) A. Fyodorov		U-2

Red Air Force and *Luftwaffe* Deployment: Kursk, southern sector

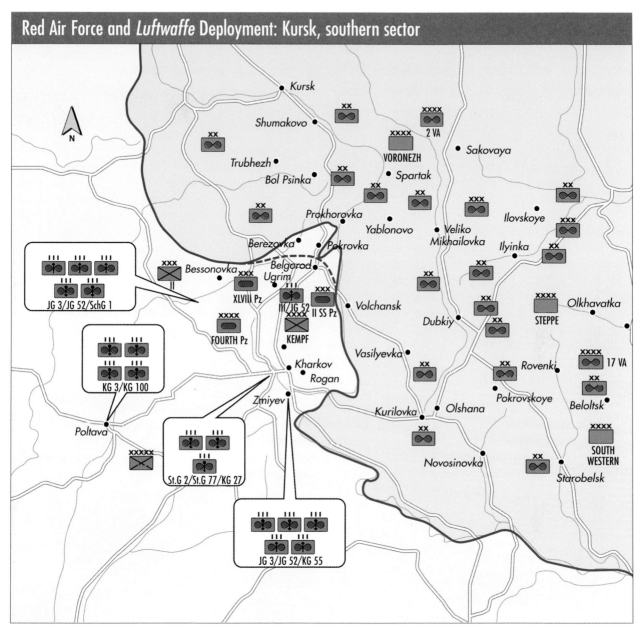

KEY

German army		Soviet army	
German panzer corps		Soviet air army	
Luftwaffe bomber units (regiment)		Soviet air division	
Luftwaffe fighter units (regiment)		Front line, 12th July 1943	
		Original front line, 5th July 1943	

UNIT DEFINITIONS:

Luftwaffe

JG – *Jagdgeschwader* (Fighter)

KG – *Kampfgeschwader* (Bomber)

St.G – *Stukageschwader* (Dive bomber)

SchG – *Schlachtgeschwader* (Ground attack)

Soviet:

VA – Soviet aviation army

Aircraft, Weapons and Tactics

Soviet aircraft were crude in comparison to their Western equivalents, but this lack of sophistication was offset by a robustness which allowed them to operate with minimal maintenance from ill-equipped forward airfields in the worst extremes of the Russian climate.

The main types employed at Kursk included the highly effective Iluyshin IL-2M3 *Shturmovik*, the Petlyakov Pe-2, the Yak-1B and the La-5FN.

ILUYSHIN IL-2M3 *SHTURMOVIK*

The type was entering service at the time of the German invasion when just under 250 aircraft had been delivered. The initial single-seat version proved to be highly vulnerable to German fighters although its good armour protection allowed it to absorb multiple hits from small calibre AA fire. Despite its limitations, it was quickly recognized that the type

was particularly well-suited to the sort of war being fought in the Soviet Union and its production was given the highest priority.

In common with the rest of the Soviet aircraft industry, the factories producing the Il-2 had to be hastily evacuated and re-established east of the Urals as the German armies overran much of European Russia in the summer and autumn of 1941. When Stalin saw an unusually honest report on the slow rate of Il-2 production at the new sites he sent a furious telegram to the factory managers:

'You have let down our country and our Red Army. You have the nerve not to manufacture Il-2s

Ilyushin Il-2M3 *Shturmovik*

The initial single-seat version of the Il-2 entered service in May 1941 and a total of 249 were operational at the time of the German invasion. The aircraft's armour gave good protection from light AA fire, but it proved to be vulnerable to attack by *Luftwaffe* fighters. This vulnerability was significantly reduced by the introduction of the two-seat Il-2M in September 1942 which remained in service throughout the war. Total production of all variants exceeded 36,000.

■ CREW

■ SPECIFICATIONS

Type: Ground attack aircraft
Length: 11.6m (38ft 1in)
Wingspan: 14.6m (47ft 11in)
Height: 4.2m (13ft 9in)
Wing area: 38.5m^2 (414ft^2)
Empty weight: 4360kg (9,612lb)
Loaded weight: 6160kg (13,580lb)
Powerplant: 1x Mikulin AM-38F liquid-

cooled V-12, 1285kW (1,720hp)
Maximum speed: 414km/h (257 mph)
Range: 720km (450 miles)
Service ceiling: 5500m (18,045ft)
Rate of climb: 10.4m/s (2050ft/min)
Wing loading: 160kg/m^2 (31.3lb/ft^2)
Power/Weight Ratio: 0.21kW/kg (0.13hp/lb)

Armament: 2 x fixed forward-firing 23mm VYa-23 cannons, 150 rpg 2 x fixed forward-firing 7.62mm (0.3in) ShKAS machine guns, 750rpg 1 x manually aimed 12.7mm (0.5in) Berezin UBT machine gun in the rear cockpit, 150 rounds; up to 600kg (1,320lb) of bombs and/or 8 x RS-82 rockets or 4 x RS-132 rockets

until now. Our Red Army now needs Il-2 aircraft like the air it breathes, like the bread it eats. Shenkman produces one Il-2 a day and Tretyakov builds one or two MiG-3s daily. It is a mockery of our country and the Red Army. I ask you not to try the government's patience, and demand that you manufacture more Ils. This is my final warning.

Stalin'

Initially, the type was not particularly effective, but tactics changed as Soviet aircrew became used to the Il-2's strengths. Instead of a low-level direct attacking run at a height of 50 metres (165ft) or so, a formation of up to 12 aircraft would usually approach the target from one side before turning to attack from a shallow 30° dive.

However, such tactics could do nothing to improve the type's survivability when intercepted by *Luftwaffe* fighters, which had a far higher performance than the lumbering *Shturmoviks*. The only answer seemed to be some sort of rearwards firing armament and a number of front-line units took matters into their own hands, modifying their aircraft by cutting a hole in the fuselage behind the cockpit. This provided a very exposed position for a gunner sitting on a canvas sling manning a 12.7mm (0.5in) UBT machine gun on an improvised mounting. Although these field modifications made the aircraft difficult to handle and lacked any protection for the rear gunner, they did significantly reduce losses to *Luftwaffe* fighters. (Later versions of the Il-2 incorporated a properly-designed rear gunner's position with amour protection.)

Although the Il-2s RS-82 and RS-132 rockets could destroy AFVs with a single hit, they were so inaccurate that experienced Il-2 pilots mainly relied on their cannon. It was soon recognized that the type's 20mm (0.79in) or 23mm (0.9in) cannon

Shturmovik Tactics: Attacking a column

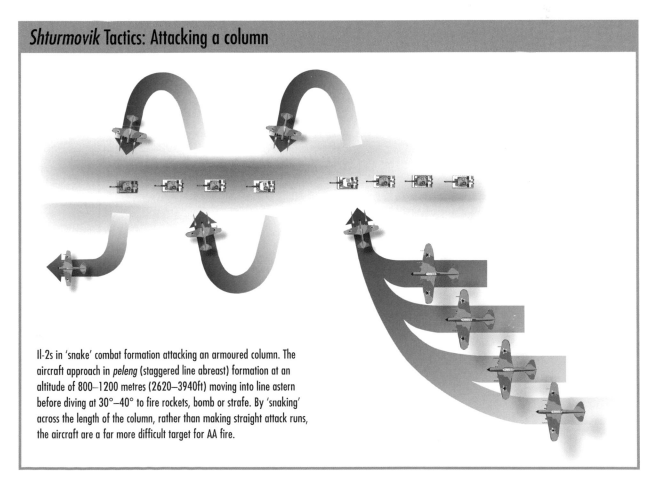

Il-2s in 'snake' combat formation attacking an armoured column. The aircraft approach in *peleng* (staggered line abreast) formation at an altitude of 800–1200 metres (2620–3940ft) moving into line astern before diving at 30°–40° to fire rockets, bomb or strafe. By 'snaking' across the length of the column, rather than making straight attack runs, the aircraft are a far more difficult target for AA fire.

were ineffective against any but the lightest AFVs and by the time of the Kursk offensive, a number of Il-2s were re-armed with a pair of 37mm (1.45in) Nudelman-Suranov NS-37 cannon in under-wing fairings as dedicated anti-tank aircraft. However, although these had a good armour-piercing performance, they were highly inaccurate. This was due to difficulties in synchronising their fire, which coupled with their heavy recoil, made it extremely difficult for the pilot to keep his sights on the target.

One of the type's most potent anti-tank weapons was the 2.5kg (5.5lb) PTAB bomblet (*Protivotankovaya aviabomba*, Anti-Tank Aviation Bomb) which was first used at Kursk. Up to 192 were carried in four external dispensers or up to 220 in the internal weapon bays and released from altitudes of around 100 metres (328ft), creating a beaten zone roughly 70 metres (229ft) long and 15 metres (49ft) wide. Its 65mm (2.5in) diameter HEAT charge could penetrate 55–65mm

(2.1in–2.5in) of armour – more than enough to deal with the upper armour of German AFVs.

PETLYAKOV PE-2

The Pe-2 *Petlyakov* (nick-named the *Peshka*) dive bomber was designed by a team headed by Vladimir Petlyakov in a *sharashka* (one of the secret research and development centres of the Soviet Gulag labour camp system). The type was originally intended as a two-seat long-range fighter capable of escorting bombers on deep penetration raids, but was hastily redesigned as a three-seat dive-bomber which entered service in December 1940. Although the type required careful handling, its high speed gave it a considerable degree of protection from the German fighters of 1941. As the *Luftwaffe* introduced more potent interceptors, the Pe-2 was updated with more powerful engines and heavier defensive armament to improve its survivability.

In the first months of the war, the type's dive-bombing capability was not fully exploited as crews

Shturmovik Tactics: Circle of Death

The 'Circle of Death' could be highly effective against panzer units caught in the open. The circle allowed each pilot to pick a target, before attacking in turn from a shallow dive with rockets, bombs or cannon fire. It also provided a fair degree of protection against marauding *Luftwaffe* fighters as each aircraft covered the one in front. Repeated attacks would be made until the *Shturmoviks* had fired off all their ammunition.

had never been trained in the technique. However, tactics were gradually devised at unit level, principally by Colonel Ivan Polbin, the commander of the 150th Bomber Regiment.

By early 1942, he had perfected the *Vertushka* (Dipping wheel) attack in which the Pe-2s approached the target in a 'Vee of Vees' formation before moving into line astern with about 610 metres (2000ft) between each aircraft. They would circle the target before making individual attacks from 70° dives, which would be maintained until all bombs had been dropped.

YAK-1

The Yak-1 was ordered into production on 19 February 1940. Simultaneous manufacturing and testing of a design that required as many improvements as I-26 wreaked havoc on the production lines. Almost 8000 changes were made to the aircraft's blueprints by 1941 with an additional 7000 implemented the following year and 5000 more changes coming in 1942. Production was further slowed by shortages of engines, propellers, radiators, wheels and cannon. Shortages of quality materials resulted in the plywood skins being torn off the wings of several

aircraft. Due to loose tolerances, each aircraft was essentially unique with workers performing the final assembly having the unenviable task of mating what often proved to be dissimilar components. (At unit level, the problems could be even worse as parts were frequently not interchangeable between aircraft.) Production of the Yak-1 ended in July 1944 with somewhere around 8700 built.

At the outbreak of war, 425 Yak-1s had been completed, although only 92 machines were fully operational in the Western Military Districts and most were lost in a matter of days. The type was primarily designed as an escort for Il-2 *Shturmoviks* and was designed for maximum performance at altitudes below 4000 metres (13,123 ft).

The Yak-1 was better than the Bf 109E encountered in 1941, but inferior to the later Bf 109F and Bf 109G in rate of climb at all altitudes. It took an experienced pilot to get good results from its light armament, but a number of aircraft were modified by removing the 7.62mm (0.3in) ShKAS machine guns, leaving only the single ShVAK cannon. These lighter aircraft were popular with expert pilots, for whom the reduction in armament was acceptable and combat experience in November 1942 showed a much improved kill-to-loss ratio.

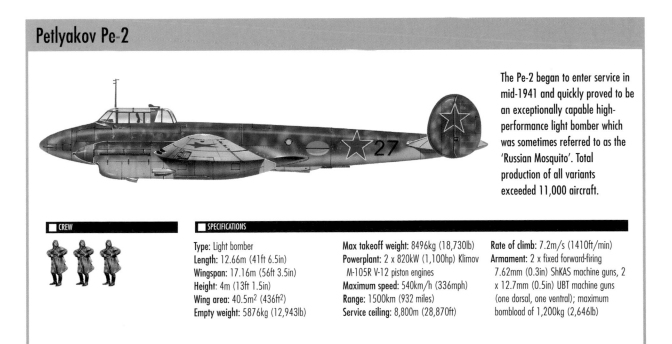

Petlyakov Pe-2

The Pe-2 began to enter service in mid-1941 and quickly proved to be an exceptionally capable high-performance light bomber which was sometimes referred to as the 'Russian Mosquito'. Total production of all variants exceeded 11,000 aircraft.

CREW

SPECIFICATIONS

Type: Light bomber
Length: 12.66m (41ft 6.5in)
Wingspan: 17.16m (56ft 3.5in)
Height: 4m (13ft 1.5in)
Wing area: 40.5m² (436ft²)
Empty weight: 5876kg (12,943lb)

Max takeoff weight: 8496kg (18,730lb)
Powerplant: 2 x 820kW (1,100hp) Klimov M-105R V-12 piston engines
Maximum speed: 540km/h (336mph)
Range: 1500km (932 miles)
Service ceiling: 8,800m (28,870ft)

Rate of climb: 7.2m/s (1410ft/min)
Armament: 2 x fixed forward-firing 7.62mm (0.3in) ShKAS machine guns, 2 x 12.7mm (0.5in) UBT machine guns (one dorsal, one ventral); maximum bombload of 1,200kg (2,646lb)

LA-5FN

The La-5FN was derived from the unsuccessful LaGG-1 and LaGG-3 fighters which had experienced constant problems with their underpowered in-line engines. During the winter of 1941/42 Lavochkin unofficially redesigned the LaGG-3 to accept the more powerful ASh-82 radial engine which transformed the type's performance. The new aircraft deeply impressed test pilots and it was rapidly ordered into production as the La-5.

Whilst the La-5 was still inferior to the newest German fighters at high altitudes, its low-level performance was outstanding. Pilots also appreciated its armament of two 20mm (0.79in) cannon which provided a welcome increase in firepower compared to earlier Soviet fighters.

POLIKARPOV U-2/PO-2

The Soviet inability to seriously contest the *Luftwaffe*'s air superiority until mid-1943 forced a search for radical solutions to provide some degree of air support for the hard-pressed Red Army. One such measure was the formation of night ground attack units, equipped with a variety of aircraft drawn from communications and training units, such as the Polikarpov U-2 or Po-2, a reliable,

uncomplicated and forgiving aircraft, powered by a 74kW (99hp) Shvetsov air-cooled radial engine which had first flown in January 1928. German troops referred to it as the *Nähmaschine* (sewing machine) after its rattling sound. Its low cost and easy maintenance led to a production run of over 40,000, and manufacture continued into the 1950s.

The U-2 equipped the 588th Night Bomber Regiment, a unit with all-women pilots and ground crew, which became famous for its daring low-altitude night raids on German rear-areas. Its veteran pilots often flew several such short-range missions in a single night and won numerous Hero of the Soviet Union and dozens of Order of the Red Banner medals – most survivors had flown nearly 1000 combat missions at the end of the war. Their usual tactics involved flying only a few metres above the ground, climbing for the final approach before cutting the engine and making a gliding bombing run, leaving the targeted troops with only the eerie whistling of the wind in the wings' bracing-wires as an indication of the impending attack. The type's maximum load of 6 x 50kg (110lb) bombs was unlikely to inflict major damage on any given target, but the disruption caused by constant harassment

Yak-1B

The Yak-1 was the first Soviet fighter comparable to Western designs to be produced in significant numbers. Although its firepower was unspectacular, it was a rugged design which was well-suited to the primitive conditions of Soviet airfields.

■ CREW

■ SPECIFICATIONS

Type: Single-seat fighter
Length: 8.5m (27ft 11in)
Wingspan: 10m (32ft 10in)
Height: 2.75m (9ft)
Wing area: 17.2m² (185.1ft²)
Empty weight: 2394kg (5,267lb)
Loaded weight: 2883kg (6,343lb)

Max takeoff weight: N/k
Powerplant: 1x 880kW (1180hp) Klimov M-105PF V-12 engine
Maximum speed: 563km/h (350mph)
Range: 700km (435 miles)
Service ceiling: 10,050m (32,972ft)
Rate of climb: 15.4m/s (3038ft/min)

Wing loading: 168kg/m² (34lb/ft²)
Armament: 1 x 20mm (0.79in) ShVAK cannon, plus 1 x 12.7mm (0.5in) Berezin UBS machine gun; bombload of up to 200kg (440lb)

raids night after night steadily sapped the combat capability of even the best units.

In order to counter these Soviet attacks, the *Luftwaffe* commissioned urgent studies to find an aircraft suitable for conversion as a night fighter. (Conventional types of aircraft already deployed in this role such as the Bf 110 and Ju 88 could not be used as their stalling speeds were higher than the Soviet biplanes' maximum speed!) Eventually, about 30 Fw 189 tactical reconnaissance aircraft were fitted with cannon and radar and proved to be effective in combating the U-2 raids.

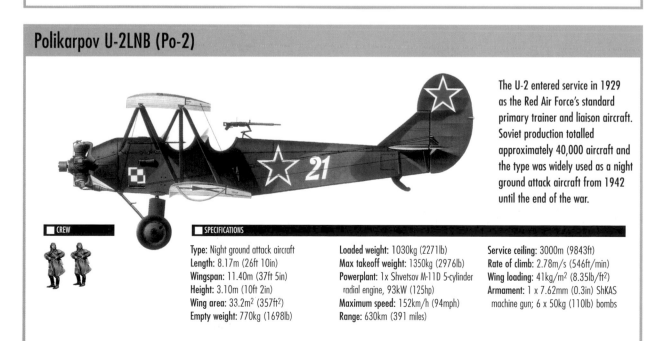

La-5FN

The La-5 entered service in 1942 and quickly proved to be a highly effective low-altitude fighter, capable of taking on both the Bf-109 and Fw-190. The type equipped 15 fighter regiments tasked with the air defence of the Kursk salient.

■ CREW

■ SPECIFICATIONS

Type: Single-seat fighter
Length: 8.67m (28ft 5in)
Wingspan: 9.8m (32ft 1.75in)
Height: 2.54m (8ft 4in)
Wing area: 17.5m² (188ft²)
Empty weight: 2605kg (5743lb)

Loaded weight: 3265kg (7,198lb)
Max takeoff weight: 3402kg (7,500lb)
Powerplant: 1 x 1385kW (1,850hp)
Shvetsov ASh-82FN radial engine
Maximum speed: 648km/h (403mph)
Range: 765km (475 miles)

Service ceiling: 11,000m (36,089ft)
Rate of climb: 16.7m/s (3,280ft/min)
Wing loading: 186kg/m² (38lb/ft²)
Armament: 2 x 20mm (0.79in) ShVAK
cannon, 200rpg; plus up to 2 x 100kg
(220lb) bombs

Polikarpov U-2LNB (Po-2)

The U-2 entered service in 1929 as the Red Air Force's standard primary trainer and liaison aircraft. Soviet production totalled approximately 40,000 aircraft and the type was widely used as a night ground attack aircraft from 1942 until the end of the war.

■ CREW

■ SPECIFICATIONS

Type: Night ground attack aircraft
Length: 8.17m (26ft 10in)
Wingspan: 11.40m (37ft 5in)
Height: 3.10m (10ft 2in)
Wing area: 33.2m² (357ft²)
Empty weight: 770kg (1698lb)

Loaded weight: 1030kg (2271lb)
Max takeoff weight: 1350kg (2976lb)
Powerplant: 1x Shvetsov M-11D 5-cylinder
radial engine, 93kW (125hp)
Maximum speed: 152km/h (94mph)
Range: 630km (391 miles)

Service ceiling: 3000m (9843ft)
Rate of climb: 2.78m/s (546ft/min)
Wing loading: 41kg/m² (8.35lb/ft²)
Armament: 1 x 7.62mm (0.3in) ShKAS
machine gun; 6 x 50kg (110lb) bombs

Chapter 4
The Test of Battle: Prokhorovka

During much of the winter of 1942/43, it seemed that the Red Army was on the verge of achieving a decisive victory. Hitler had characteristically refused to allow Sixth Army to break out from Stalingrad and insisted that Kleist's Army Group A should hold its positions in the Caucasus, despite its grossly over-stretched supply lines.

Even *Generalfeldmarschall* von Manstein's genius could not compensate for this folly – ordered by Hitler to relieve Stalingrad, he launched the 'Winter Storm' offensive that pushed to within 50 kilometres (30 miles) of the city, before being beaten back. The last remnants of the garrison surrendered on 2 February, releasing substantial Soviet forces for further advances, which threatened to cut off Army Group A. Kleist was forced to order a hasty retreat to the Taman Peninsula, which was subjected to a series of ferocious but unsuccessful Soviet attacks.

Within a week of the final surrender at Stalingrad the Voronezh and Southwestern Fronts had retaken Kursk and Belgorod. Kharkov fell on 14 February and Soviet armour was threatening the Dnieper crossings at Zaporozhe.

OPPOSITE: Surrendered with honour. The surviving crew members of a disabled T-34 surrender to a Waffen-SS trooper during the German drive on Prokhorovka. This photograph was taken for the German armed forces magazine *Signal*, and was used for propoganda purposes.

Reverse at Kharkov

The seemingly irresistible Red Army offensive was pushed too far, out-running its supply lines and providing an opportunity for a devastating German counter-attack.

By mid-February, there was very little time left before the mud of the spring thaw made major operations impossible, but von Manstein showed just what could be achieved in the most threatening situation. By getting a shaken Hitler to authorise a mobile defence and release the necessary resources (the SS Panzer Corps, five *Wehrmacht* panzer divisions and the elite *Grossdeutschland* Division) he was able to shorten his front and concentrate the panzers to take advantage of Soviet overconfidence. This overconfidence was understandable – Soviet armour had advanced as much as 300 kilometres (185 miles) in a month and seemed poised to re-conquer the entire Ukraine. Such spectacular successes brought their own problems as the tanks outran their supply lines and had to struggle forward with totally inadequate reserves of fuel and ammunition. By this time, Lieutenant General Popov's 'mobile group' of four tank corps spearheading the advance had been reduced to 53 serviceable tanks.

Like their German counterparts, Soviet divisions were seriously under-strength – Fortieth Army's divisions had an average strength of 3500–4000 men each, whilst some of those in Sixty-Ninth Army were down to as few as 1000–1500 combat troops. This shortage in manpower and equipment led Vatutin's South-Western Front to request over 19,000 troops and 300 tanks, while it was noted that the Voronezh Front had only received 1600 replacements since the beginning of operations in January 1943. By the time von Manstein launched his counter-offensive, Voronezh Front had lost so much manpower and had over-extended itself to the point where it could no longer offer assistance to the neighbouring Southwestern Front.

On 20 February, von Manstein unleashed four panzer corps supported by a 'maximum effort' from the *Luftwaffe* which rapidly established air superiority over the battlefield, flying up to 1000 sorties per day. The concentrated panzer thrusts achieved massive local superiority of up to 7:1 over the scattered and depleted Red Army armoured forces, rapidly defeating each in detail. The SS Panzer Corps recaptured Kharkov on 15 March, going on to take Belgorod three days later, wiping out much of the Soviet gains of the previous month.

SWIFT RESPONSE

The swift German recapture of Kharkov came as a tremendous shock to Stalin who ordered Zhukov to fly to the Voronezh Front and stabilise the rapidly deteriorating situation. Zhukov's initial report stressed the seriousness of the crisis and the very real threat that von Manstein's counter-offensive could go on to recapture Kursk. Stalin reacted swiftly, reinforcing the Kursk sector with Twenty-First and Sixty-Fourth Armies from Stavka reserve, together with General Katukov's First Tank Army which was hastily withdrawn from operations around Demyansk. These formations, coupled with the spring thaw and German exhaustion, were just enough to prevent Kursk going the same way as Kharkov and Belgorod.

After coming tantalisingly close to winning a major victory, the Red Army had been badly mauled – the South-Western Front had lost 23,000 men, 615 AFVs and 354 guns, whilst the Voronezh Front's casualties were even worse, totalling 40,000 men, 600 tanks and 500 guns. German forces once again held much of the territory lost during the winter except for a large salient centred on the small provincial city of Kursk.

THE MILITARY BALANCE

By the spring of 1943, there was no doubt about Soviet numerical superiority on the Eastern Front

OPPOSITE: The German winter counter-offensive achieved both strategic and tactical surprise. On the strategic level, this was due to the fact that all the operational planning was carried out at Manstein's HQ, which gave immunity from the Soviet 'Lucy' spy ring which had infiltrated OKH. At the tactical level, on the other hand, the Red Army had become overconfident, believing that the *Wehrmacht*'s losses at Stalingrad had left it incapable of making any significant counter-attacks.

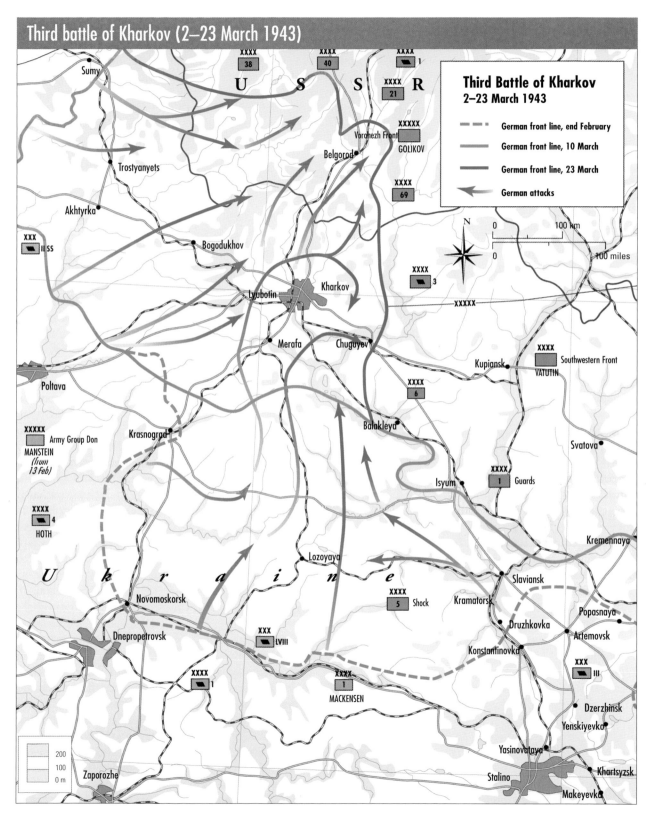

Third battle of Kharkov (2–23 March 1943)

Sumy

U   S   S   R

XXXX
38

XXXX
40

XXXX
1

XXXX
21

Voronezh Front
XXXXX
GOLIKOV

Third Battle of Kharkov
2–23 March 1943

– – – – German front line, end February

────── German front line, 10 March

────── German front line, 23 March

◀━━━━ German attacks

Belgorod

XXXX
69

Trostyanets

Akhtyrka

XXX
II SS

Bogodukhov

XXXX
3

0   100 km

0   100 miles

N

Lyubotin   Kharkov

Merafa   Chuguyev

XXXX
6

Kupiansk

XXXX
Southwestern Front
VATUTIN

Poltava

XXXXX
Army Group Don
MANSTEIN
(from
13 Feb)

Krasnograd

Balakleya

Svatova

XXXX
1   Guards

Isyum

XXXX
4
HOTH

U   k   r   a   i   n   e

Lozovaya

Kremennaya

Slaviansk

XXXX
5   Shock

Kramatorsk

Novomoskorsk

Popasnaya

XXX
LVIII

Druzhkovka

Artemovsk

Dnepropetrovsk

Konstantinovka

XXX
III

XXXX
1

XXXX
1
MACKENSEN

Dzerzhinsk

Yenskiyevka

Yasinovataya

200
100
0 m

Zaporozhe

Stalino

Khartsyzsk

Makeyevka

as a whole – comparative strengths of the two sides were:

■ Axis – 2.7 million men, 2209 AFVs and 6360 guns
■ Soviet – 6 million men, 15,000 AFVs and 33,000 guns

Despite the massive losses sustained by Axis forces since the opening of Operation Barbarossa, they were actually winning the battle of attrition. Although Soviet reserves of manpower were easily double those of Germany and her allies, Red Army casualties were several times greater than this in 1941/42 and even in 1943, the casualty ratio was 4:1 in favour of the Axis. It was a similar story as far as AFVs were concerned – Soviet tank production was more than twice that of German factories, but the loss ratio stood at more than 3:1 in the Germans' favour.

Why Kursk?

The Kursk salient was very much 'unfinished business' left over from von Manstein's counter-offensive. Von Manstein had fully intended to eliminate the salient in March, but Soviet reinforcements, the spring thaw and the exhaustion of his forces had compelled him to halt operations before this could be achieved.

To the Germans, the salient measuring 200 kilometres (120 miles) from north to south with a depth of up to 150 kilometres (90 miles) was a potential 'springboard for the Soviet reconquest of the Ukraine'. Something would clearly have to be done to eliminate the threat that it posed, but there was initial uncertainty over just what that 'something' should be.

As early as February 1943, von Manstein had proposed a 'backhand' offensive for the coming summer – this was essentially a large-scale version of his successful winter counter-offensive. His plan envisaged concentrating a powerful armoured reserve around Kiev before luring the Red Army into a series of advances deep into the Ukraine as far as the Dneiper. The panzers would then be unleashed in a massive attack with the aim of trapping and destroying the Soviet spearheads between the Sea of Azov and the Dneiper.

As von Manstein put it: '…if the Russians did as we anticipated and launched a pincer attack on the Donets area from the north and south, an operation which would sooner or later be supplemented by an offensive around Kharkov, our arc of front along the Donets and Mius should be given up in accordance with an agreed time-table in order to draw the enemy westwards towards the Lower Dnieper. Simultaneously, all the reserves that could possibly be released, including the bulk of the armour, were to assemble [in the vicinity of Kiev], first to smash the enemy assault forces which we expected to find there and then to drive into the flank of those advancing in the direction of the Lower Dnieper. In this way the enemy would be doomed to suffer the same fate on the Sea of Azov as he had in store for us on the Black Sea.'

This plan had the potential to inflict a stunning defeat on the Red Army, but it was far too unorthodox for Hitler who instinctively hated the thought of voluntarily surrendering any territory. He was also highly suspicious of any plan such as this which would give such wide-ranging freedom of action to a single commander in contravention of his aim of exercising the greatest possible control of his generals' conduct of the war.

'FOREHAND' OFFENSIVE

Unsurprisingly, Hitler rejected the plan, opting for the much more conventional 'forehand' offensive – pincer attacks from north and south to surround and destroy the forces defending the salient which were estimated at 60 divisions and five or six tank corps. It was confidently expected that their loss would cripple the Red Army and yield up to 700,000 prisoners – potentially invaluable slave labour for German war industries. (The elimination of the salient would also significantly shorten the German front line, releasing up to 20 divisions to reinforce other key sectors.) The planning for the offensive received top priority following the issue of

Hitler's Operational Order No. 6 on 15 April – the definitive directive for the Kursk offensive, designated *Zitadelle* (Citadel). This stressed the urgency of the operation, which was scheduled for 3 May, stating that it 'must succeed rapidly' – this urgency was partly due to the military risks of the offensive, but also recognized the political imperative to restore the confidence of Germany's increasingly reluctant Italian, Rumanian and Finnish allies.

As Operational Order No. 6 was being drafted, Stalin was reluctantly deciding that he had to ignore his instinctive preference for a pre-emptive offensive and follow his commanders' advice not to attack until the Germans had weakened themselves in assaults against properly prepared Soviet defences in the Kursk salient. The question was how much time the Red Army would be given to prepare those defences.

WHY PROKHOROVKA?

Although the German offensive was a two-pronged attack, the south was the *Schwerpunkt* – the focal point of the operation. The assault was to be spearheaded by Colonel General Hoth's Fourth Panzer Army of two panzer corps fielding a total of 1100 tanks and assault guns, the most powerful German armoured force to be assembled during the entire war. Operational Order No. 6 had stated that the attack in this sector would be made: '...with strongly concentrated forces from the Belgorod-Tomarovka line, break through the Prilepy-Oboyan line and link up with the attacking armies of Army Group Centre east of Kursk'.

This was the direct route, but when von Manstein and Hoth began detailed operational planning, it became clear that it was unlikely to be the quickest or the surest way of securing its

RIGHT: Kursk was such an obvious objective that the Soviets began fortifying it almost as soon as the Germans decided to attack it. As early as March, Marshal Georgi Zhukov and his Front commanders were presenting Stalin with their expectations of likely German plans for the coming campaigning season. Their predictions proved to be remarkably accurate when the battle started in July.

In addition, the Red Army planned new offensives of its own, scheduled to open the moment the German attack stalled. Stalin and his most senior commanders gambled that they could hold Kursk against the elite Panzer divisions, absorb the full strength of the German blow, then unleash a multi-Front offensive that would liberate the Ukraine.

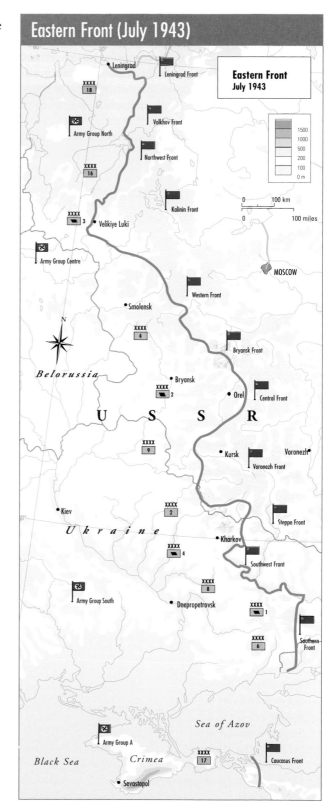

Eastern Front (July 1943)

Eastern Front
July 1943

objectives. They identified the following drawbacks to this route:

■ The terrain south of Oboyan was poor tank country – much of the area was marshy and strewn with minor water obstacles in addition to the River Psel which would have to be crossed in the teeth of strong Soviet defences.

■ The importance of Oboyan was so obvious that it was almost certain to be one of the main concentration points for Red Army armoured formations being brought in to reinforce the salient.

■ It was believed that the main Soviet strategic armoured reserve (including Fifth Guards Tank Army) was assembling around Korocha and that it would intervene as soon as Fourth Panzer Army was committed to fighting its way across the Psel. The obvious Soviet approach route was across the land bridge between the rivers Psel and Donets, through the town of Prokhorovka. There was real risk that following Operational Order No. 6 would allow a

Soviet Ground Forces, July 1943

UNIT TYPE	STRENGTH
Headquarters	
Fronts	18
Armies	81
Rifle Corps	82
Cavalry Corps	9
Tank Corps	24
Mechanized Corps	13
Infantry	
Rifle Divisions (inc Mountain & Motorized)	462
Rifle Brigades	98
Ski Brigades	3
Tank Destroyer Brigades	6
Separate Rifle Regiments	6
Fortified Regions	45
Ski Battalions	–
Cavalry	
Cavalry Divisions	27
Armour	
Tank Divisions	2
Motorized Divisions	–
Armoured Car Brigades	–
Tank Brigades	182
Assault Gun Brigades	–
Mechanized Brigades	42
Motor Rifle Brigades	21
Motorcycle Brigades	–
Separate Tank Regiments	118
Separate Assault Gun Regiments	57
Motorcycle Regiments	8
Separate Tank Battalions	45
Separate Aerosan Battalions	57
Special Motorized Battalions	–
Armoured Train Battalions	66
Separate Armoured Car & Motorcycle Btns	44

Soviet Ground Forces, July 1943

UNIT TYPE	STRENGTH
Airborne	
Airborne Divisions	10
Airborne Brigades	21
Artillery	
Artillery Divisions	25
Rocket Divisions	7
Anti-Aircraft Divisions	63
Separate Artillery Brigades	17
Separate Anti-Aircraft Brigades	3
Separate Mortar Brigades	11
Separate Rocket Brigades	10
Anti-Tank Brigades	27
Separate Artillery Regiments	235
Separate Mortar Regiments	171
Separate Anti-Tank Regiments	199
Separate Rocket Regiments	113
Separate Anti-Aircraft Regiments	212
Separate Artillery Battalions	41
Separate Anti-Aircraft Battalions	112
Separate Rocket Battalions	37
Separate Anti-Tank Battalions	44
Separate Mortar Battalions	5
PVO Stranyi	
PVO Stranyi Corps Region HQ	5
PVO Stranyi Division Region HQ	13
PVO Stranyi Brigade Region HQ	11
Anti-Aircraft Regiments	106
Anti-Aircraft Machine Gun Regiments	14
Searchlight Regiments	4
Anti-Aircraft Battalions	168
Anti-Aircraft Machine Gun Battalions	21
Searchlight Battalions	13

mass of Soviet armour to smash Hoth's right flank as he was struggling to force a crossing of the River Psel, creating a situation which he felt could '…quickly turn into a disaster'.

Hoth therefore proposed that on approaching the Psel, Fourth Panzer Army should change its line of advance and swing northeast to intercept the Soviet armoured reserves around Prokhorovka. (Another important factor in the equation was III Panzer Corps which was to spearhead the advance of Army Detachment *Kempf* covering Hoth's right flank. Its line of advance should bring it into action just south of Prokhorovka, with a good chance of trapping the Soviet armour between the two forces.)

After eliminating this threat, the German forces would again swing north, cross the Psel east of Obayan and resume the drive on Kursk. The proposal was readily accepted by von Manstein and formed the basis of all future operational plans for this sector of the front.

THE SOVIET 'CITADEL'

The Red Army began to build field defences in the Kursk salient as soon as the front lines stabilised in late March 1943, but these were insignificant in comparison with the massive construction programme which began in April as soon as the

decision had been taken to await the German offensive rather than attempt a pre-emptive strike. Eight defensive zones were completed with a total depth of roughly 160 kilometres (100 miles). Their positioning was carefully selected to cover all eventualities – only five were built in the salient itself, the remainder were constructed across its 'neck' so that the area could be sealed off if the Germans succeeded in breaking through to Kursk.

The scale of the construction work was staggering – whilst the first two defence lines were built by military units, the remainder were largely completed by a workforce of impressed local civilians which may well have totalled 300,000. (A high proportion of these were women as most remaining men of military age were hastily conscripted to bring the units defending the salient up to strength.)

The defences were optimised for the anti-tank role as it was recognized that the German offensive would almost certainly rely on armoured strength to compensate for the heavy losses which had seriously weakened their infantry formations. The forward

Tank train – a trainload of T-34 Model 1943 tanks en route to the front, in Spring 1943. The Soviet rail network was vital for strategic redeployments of major armoured formations.

BELOW: Each Soviet defence line was a deep complex of trenches, minefields, barbed wire entanglements and anti-tank positions designed to slow the progress of German armoured attacks. The expectation was that such defences would severely weaken the German assault forces, which could then be destroyed in a series of counter-attacks by the armoured reserves of the Central and Voronezh Fronts. These counter-attacks were intended to pave the way for the major Soviet offensives to take Orel, Belgorod and Kharkov. The defence of the northern sector of the salient was successful enough to allow the offensive against Orel to be launched as planned. In contrast, the attacks on Belgorod and Kharkov were delayed by the alarming progress of Fourth Panzer Army in the south, which was only contained by drawing on Fifth Guards Tank Army and other reserves intended for these offensives.

edge of each defence line was a maze of barbed wire entanglements, anti-tank obstacles and minefields, all of which were covered by artillery fire.

MINES

The Red Army laid a total of 640,000 mines of all types in defence of the salient. These were positioned in front of the main defence lines and in depth to channel attacking armour into 'killing zones'. The commander of the Sixty-Fifth Army recalled that they posed a real risk to the defenders as they '…stretched from the front line far into the

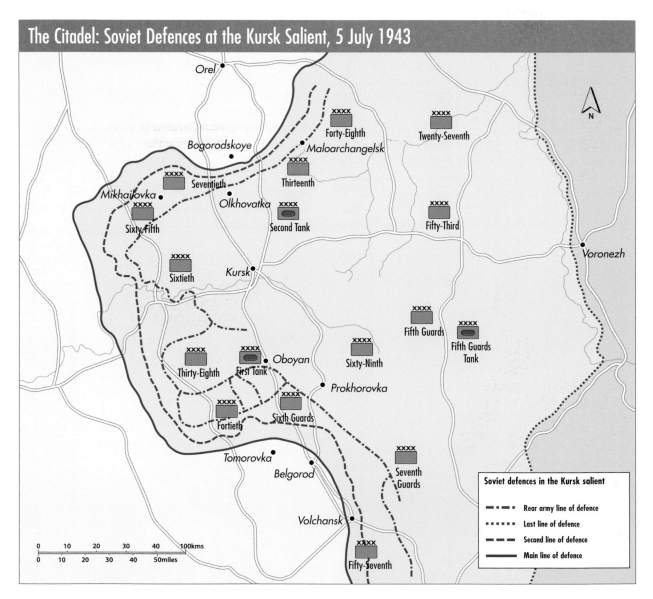

The Citadel: Soviet Defences at the Kursk Salient, 5 July 1943

Soviet defences in the Kursk salient	
‑ ‑ ‑ ‑	Rear army line of defence
⋯⋯⋯	Last line of defence
‑ ‑ ‑ ‑	Second line of defence
⎯⎯⎯	Main line of defence

rear...They were so extensive that we had to post warning pickets and mark the mined areas with signs.' Throughout the offensive, the main minefields were supplemented by mobile mine laying detachments who could rapidly be deployed to any threatened sector.

The density of the minefields was well in excess of anything previously encountered by the Germans – Sixth Guards Army which was to bear the brunt of Hoth's attack held a 60-kilometre (37-mile) front. It laid 69,688 anti-tank and 64,340 anti-personnel mines in its first defence line, backed up by a further 20,200 anti-tank and 9097 anti-personnel mines in the second defence line. Mine laying was concentrated along the anticipated German lines of advance where mine densities averaged between 1400 and 2000 anti-tank mines per kilometre of front.

Minefields played an important role in the Soviet defences in the south of the salient, where the defenders laid a total of 292,000 anti-tank mines and 306,000 anti-personnel mines in the sector held by the Voronezh Front. During the battle Soviet engineers laid more than 55,000 additional mines, primarily by mobile obstacle detachments operating under the command of 5th Engineer Sapper Brigade and 42nd Engineer Brigade, in addition to the detachments formed by divisional engineer units An estimated 113 German tanks, 30 assault guns and 73 other vehicles were destroyed in the minefields laid by mobile obstacle detachments during the battle. According to Soviet sources, the Germans lost a total of about 630 AFVs in all the Soviet minefields on the south face of the salient during the period 5–17 July.

Mines were a particularly important weapon against the Tigers whose armour made them invulnerable to most of the Red Army's tank and anti-tank guns, except at very close range. Minefields were also responsible for inflicting a significant number of casualties – Soviet sources claimed that these were the equivalent of two infantry battalions (approximately 450 men) on the first day of the offensive on the south face of the salient. (The toll included a senior officer – Lieutenant General Schäfer, commander of the 332nd Infantry Division of XLVIII Panzer Corps.)

In addition to conventional mines, the defenders made extensive use of artillery shells – these were fitted with pressure fuses and buried nose-up. The heaviest of these, such as the 43.5kg (96lb) 152mm (6in) and 98.7kg (217lb) 203mm (8in) shells were capable of destroying rather than simply disabling most German AFVs. (Fortieth Army alone used 6377 shells to supplement its 130,000 anti-tank and anti-personnel mines.) Other unconventional devices included incendiary mines of up to 20 petrol-filled bottles surrounding an anti-personnel mine which were ignited when the mine detonated.

ARTILLERY

As always, the Red Army gave a high priority to deploying artillery in defence of the salient and had brought in a total of 31,000 guns and mortars by the time that the German offensive began. Whilst

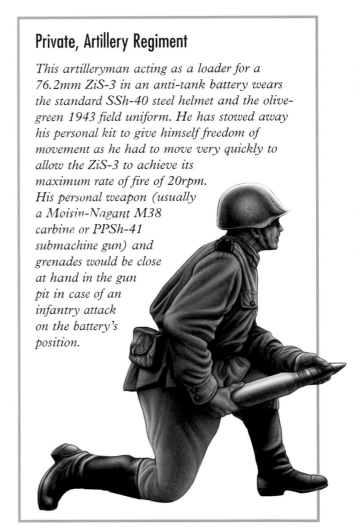

Private, Artillery Regiment

This artilleryman acting as a loader for a 76.2mm ZiS-3 in an anti-tank battery wears the standard SSh-40 steel helmet and the olive-green 1943 field uniform. He has stowed away his personal kit to give himself freedom of movement as he had to move very quickly to allow the ZiS-3 to achieve its maximum rate of fire of 20rpm. His personal weapon (usually a Moisin-Nagant M38 carbine or PPSh-41 submachine gun) and grenades would be close at hand in the gun pit in case of an infantry attack on the battery's position.

Anti-tank Brigade, July 1943

37mm (1.45in) 61-K M1939 AA Gun: 4
45mm (1.8in) Model 1942 Anti-tank Gun: 12
76mm (3in) ZiS-3 Field/Anti-tank Gun: 16

Anti-tank brigades were a key part of the Soviet defences in the Kursk salient, forming what the Germans termed *Pakfronten*. These were tank-killing zones protected by extensive minefields in which massed anti-tank guns would concentrate their fire to destroy the nearest or most threatening AFV, before swiftly targeting the next.

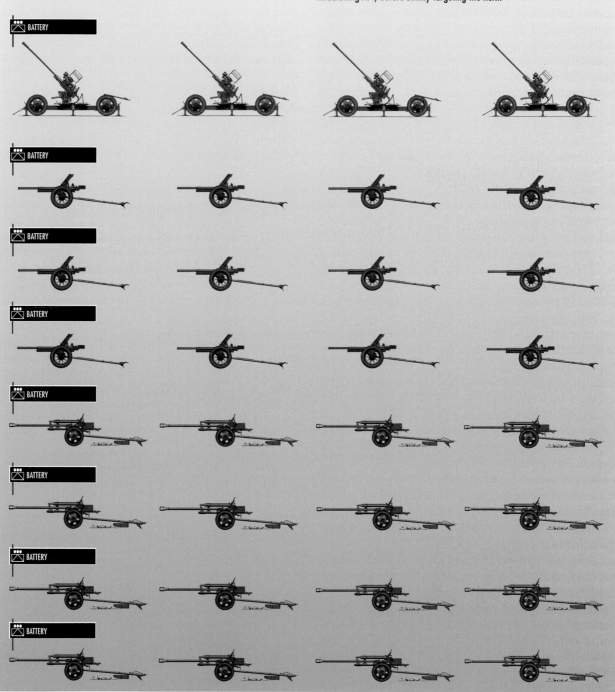

the heaviest concentrations were in the north of the salient, Sixth Guards Army in the south deployed 1682 guns and mortars – 316 guns and howitzers (122mm and 152mm – 4.8in and 6in), 573 anti-tank guns of all calibres and 793 mortars (82mm and 120mm – 3.2in and 4.7in). These were supported by 88 *Katyusha* salvo rocket launchers.

The anti-tank guns were a key element in the defence lines – many were deployed in mutually-supporting anti-tank strongpoints (ATSPs) designed for all-round defence. These were supported by infantry detachments and sappers with anti-tank mines. Each ATSP contained:

■ Four to six anti-tank guns (usually 45mm and 76.2mm – 1.8in and 3in).
■ Six to nine anti-tank rifles.
■ Two to three medium or heavy machine guns.
■ Three or four light machine guns.

All Soviet artillery was integrated into the overall anti-tank defence plan and was positioned to provide the maximum possible fire support for the anti-tank strongpoints. In the event of a German breakthrough, all 122mm (4.8in) and 152mm (6in) guns and howitzers in the threatened sector were to be used in the direct-fire anti-tank role. (Although the majority of these were low-velocity weapons which were too inaccurate to make ideal anti-tank weapons, their heavy shells were effective against most German AFVs at close range.) In similar fashion, all AA guns were earmarked to operate in the anti-tank role if necessary.

The most powerful artillery concentrations are useless without adequate ammunition and stockpiling sufficient supplies to meet the anticipated demand was a massive task which placed a heavy strain on the limited rail network serving the salient. In this respect, as in many other aspects of defence preparations, the repeated delays in launching the German offensive were of immense value to the Red Army.

ARMOUR

Stavka appreciated that the German offensive could not be defeated solely by even the most formidable fixed defences and ensured that substantial armoured forces totalling almost 3500 AFVs were deployed within the salient. Some were positioned in direct support of the defence lines, but a high proportion of the available armour was concentrated in the First and Second Tank Armies. These formations were intended to defeat the main German thrusts, leaving the 1600 plus AFVs of the Steppe Front (including Fifth Guards Tank Army) to spearhead the subsequent counter-offensives.

Operation Citadel

Although Hitler's Operational Order No. 6 had stressed the need for the swift elimination of the Kursk salient, the offensive was repeatedly postponed, to the growing alarm of many German commanders.

Hitler's motive for ordering these repeated delays was primarily a belief that the new Panthers and Ferdinands just entering service were essential for the success of the offensive. His belief that they could be rushed into service to ensure a decisive breakthrough of the ever-improving Soviet defences prompted an outburst from Guderian: 'I don't regard the new Panther or Ferdinand as ready for active service. They are still suffering from numerous teething troubles as is perfectly natural with such new types – and we can't possibly clear these up in five or six weeks!'

Despite the protests from Guderian and other senior officers, Hitler was adamant that the offensive would not be launched until both new types were available in significant quantities, thus giving the Soviets more invaluable time to strengthen their defences. (Ironically, the 200 Panthers and 90 Ferdinands committed to the operation proved to be more trouble than they were worth, suffering appalling mechanical problems and depressingly frequent breakdowns. All too many broken-down vehicles had to be abandoned due to the difficulties in recovering these heavy AFVs with

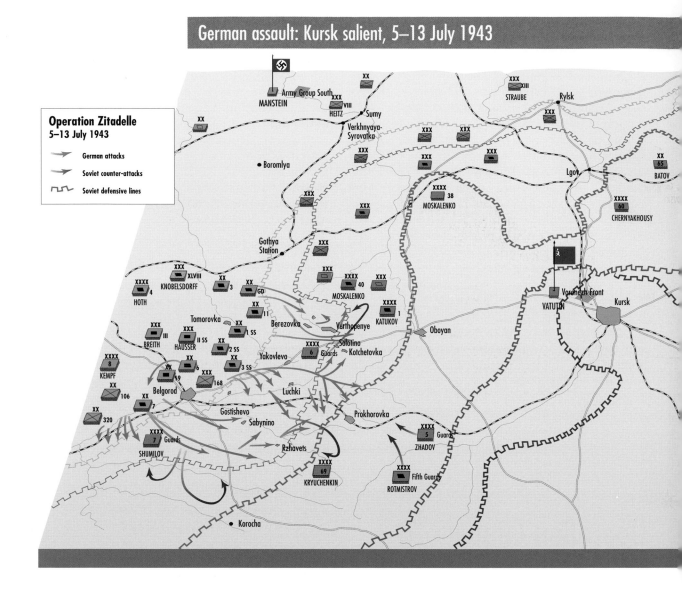

German assault: Kursk salient, 5–13 July 1943

Operation Zitadelle
5–13 July 1943

→ German attacks

→ Soviet counter-attacks

⌐⌐⌐ Soviet defensive lines

ABOVE: The German attacks on both sides of the salient were crippled by the lack of good infantry formations to support the panzers. Even during the spectacular victories of 1941–42, the German infantry had sustained huge casualties – as early as May 1942, almost all units in the Soviet Union were under strength, reporting a total shortage of 635,000 men. By mid-1943, the situation had worsened, forcing the use of panzer and panzer grenadier units in roles which should have been carried out by infantry. (The problem had even more widespread effects as the *Luftwaffe* was frequently called upon to provide emergency assistance for the hard-pressed infantry instead of attacking key targets.) During the Kursk offensive German commanders were repeatedly forced to divert armoured units to support weak infantry formations. The effect of this was most serious in the southern sector, where it may have been instrumental in preventing a decisive breakthrough by Fourth Panzer Army.

equipment designed for the much lighter Panzer IV and StuGs.)

INTO ACTION

The much delayed German offensive finally opened on 5 July – *Generaloberst* Model's Ninth Army attacked the northern face of the salient, whilst Hoth's Fourth Panzer Army and Army Detachment *Kempf* assaulted the first Soviet defence line in the south.

Despite the support of all the serviceable Ferdinands, Model's attacks quickly bogged down. In part this was due to the sheer strength of the

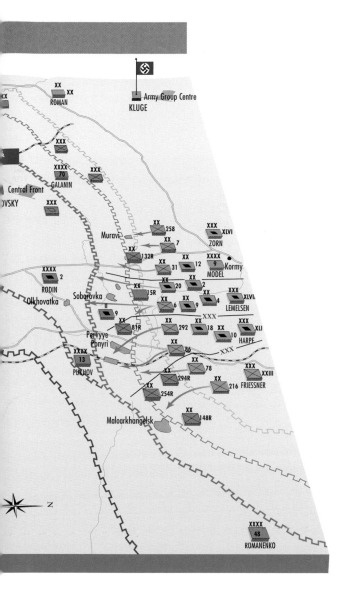

defences in this sector, but Model's tactics were also partly responsible. He had decided to use his infantry to assault the Soviet lines with the panzers following up to exploit the breakthrough. This prevented the attacks from developing any real impetus, reducing them to a process of slow, grinding attrition reminiscent of World War I. The painfully slow German advance was finally halted on 10 July after achieving a maximum penetration of no more than 17 kilometres (10.5 miles).

Hoth had adopted very different tactics for the attacks in the south – these were to be carried out by massed panzer formations acting as armoured battering rams, with the infantry following on to hold the newly-won ground. His Fourth Panzer Army was able to exploit the shock of these massed armoured assaults and *Luftwaffe* air superiority to achieve a far deeper penetration of the Soviet defences than had been possible on the north face of the salient.

PLAN OF ATTACK

The operational level plan was that west of Belgorod the two panzer corps of Fourth Panzer Army would attack northwards towards Oboyan before swinging to the northeast to intercept and defeat the Soviet armoured reserves around Prokhorovka before resuming the drive on Kursk. These two corps, XLVIII and II SS Panzer Corps, fielded a total of two panzer, four panzer grenadier divisions and two infantry divisions.

Similarly, the III Panzer Corps with its three panzer divisions would lead the attack of Army Detachment *Kempf* southwest of Belgorod. Three all-infantry corps were assigned to defend the flanks of the penetrations – LII Corps was to cover the west flank of Fourth Panzer Army, whilst XI and XLII Corps protected the flanks of Army Detachment *Kempf*.

Army Group South had 135 Tiger tanks -- the equivalent of three battalions. During the attack on the south face of the salient these were not employed en mass, as General Guderian had recommended, or even by battalions. Instead, they were employed as individual companies in support of the panzer divisions. This tactical employment was favoured by the TOE – each of the SS divisions and Panzer Grenadier Division *Grossdeutschland* had a company of Tigers. (The independent Heavy Panzer Battalion 503 was used by III Panzer Corps in the same way to support its panzer divisions.) However, the 200 Panthers of Panzer Battalions 51 and 52 (Panzer Regiment 39) were employed en masse in support of Panzergrenadier Division *Grossdeutschland*.

Whenever the terrain and the Soviet minefields on the south face permitted, the Germans attacked in *Panzerkeil* or arrow formation with tanks in the lead. The panzers usually advanced in roughly battalion strength with about 50 tanks deployed on a frontage of about 1200 metres (4000ft). The first wave was formed by two lead companies, preferably including a Tiger company at the point of the arrowhead. Each lead company deployed two platoons of five tanks in a 500-metre (1640ft) line with the tanks spaced at roughly 50-metre (164ft) intervals. The two remaining platoons and the HQ section followed in column.

The primary function of the first wave was to suppress the enemy anti-tank defences. The Tigers were especially effective in this role as their 88mm (3.45in) guns significantly out-ranged the Soviet tanks and 76.2mm (3in) anti-tank guns. The second wave included a tank company to provide covering fire for the first wave before attacking the enemy positions together with one or two companies of the division's panzer grenadiers in SdKfz 251 halftracks. The panzer grenadiers would dismount as close as possible to their objectives before dismounting for the final attack covered by fire from assault guns. A third wave, with the remaining tank company and the bulk of the panzer grenadiers, would eliminate any remaining resistance. The flanks were protected by anti-tank guns, operating by platoons and moving by bounds to cover each other's advance.

These were essentially standard German tank-infantry tactics, except for the integration of Tigers in the first wave. Once the attack broke into the Soviet front line company strong points, the tactical drill was to eliminate the defensive positions one by one. Each strong point was an essential link in the chain of interlocking fire, dependent on its neighbours to lay down a curtain of fire across its front. Thus, immediately after capturing each strong point, the Germans intended to widen the breach by 'rolling up' the neighbouring strong points from each flank. The Soviets were well aware of the German tactics and attempted to forestall them by:

■ Preparing deep defensive belts rather than thin defence lines.
■ Providing defence in depth totalling eight defence belts.
■ Deploying massed artillery and anti-tank guns
■ Holding reserves in readiness for counter-attacks.
■ Laying extensive minefields to hinder the German ability to manoeuvre.

ACTIONS ON THE 'ROAD TO PROKHOROVKA'

Although Fourth Panzer Army's advance was slowed by the extensive Soviet defences, its progress was during the first few days of the offensive caused considerable alarm at the HQ of General Vatutin's Voronezh Front which was responsible for the defence of the southern sector of the salient. On the evening of 6 July, Vatutin sent a report on the situation to Stalin, with a request for reinforcements totalling four tank corps and substantial additional air support. Marshal Vasilevsky, Stavka's representative at the Front HQ, strongly backed this assessment and actually went further, recommending that two additional tank corps should be sent if the Front was to '...conduct further active operations'.

Stalin accepted the recommendations and ordered the transfer of Fifth Guards Tank Army from General Konev's Steppe Front to the Voronezh Front. (The Army was also substantially reinforced by the addition of XVIII Tank Corps to its original XXIX Tank Corps and V Guards Mechanized Corps.) As Hoth had foreseen, Stavka's intention was to concentrate Rotmistrov's command around Prokhorovka and attack Fourth Panzer Army's right flank as it attempted to force its way across the River Psel. Konev was unhappy at what he feared was the first of a series of moves which would gradually whittle away the strategic reserves and threaten the success of the offensives which were scheduled to be launched after the German attack had been defeated. Konev argued his case so forcefully that Stalin phoned him with an abrupt order to get Fifth Guards Tank Army moving immediately.

After speaking to Konev, Stalin contacted Rotmistrov to discuss the details of the redeployment. He agreed to Rotmistrov's proposals to move the entire force by road in a series of forced marches with air cover being provided from dawn to dusk. The move was made along three routes in a 30–35 kilometre (19–22 mile) sector – even spread over two or three routes, each tank corps occupied 20–30 kilometres (12–19 miles) of road.

Even if the redeployment could be carried out with textbook precision, Fifth Guards Tank Army could not reach the front line for several days and the Red Army formations defending the south of the salient were in desperate need of more immediate armoured support. Stavka therefore ordered that II Tank Corps should be released from the Southwestern Front, whilst Voronezh Front was to commit II Guards Tanks Corps from its reserves. Both formations would be attached to Fifth Guards Tank Army at Prokhorovka, but, as summarised in the following chronological notes, they were involved in heavy fighting throughout much of the preceding week.

II TANK CORPS

7 July - Additional heavy tank battles took place between Kalinin and Teterevino, including an attack

Several T-34 Model 1942s negotiate the Soviet rear area at Prokhorovka. The wet ground was a result of the stormy weather in the afternoon of 12 July. The log, behind the external fuel tank, was used for crossing ditches.

at 10:30 by II Tank Corps. *Das Reich* successfully beat off these attacks and by the end of the day had advanced over 10 kilometres (6 miles), reaching Teterevino on the road to Prokhorovka. This represented a significant gain after a hard day's fighting, but it was still 10 kilometres (6 miles) short of the third defence line, the objective for the day.

8 July – During the morning, II Tank Corps moved into position south of Prokhorovka just behind the third defence line before launching a series of attacks against the infantry units of *Das Reich* south of Teterevino. Throughout the afternoon it was involved in further attacks at Teterevino, North Luchki and Kalinin. In one of

these attacks 20 Soviet tanks broke through and dispersed the divisional artillery. The German infantry received unexpected help from *Totenkopf*'s reconnaissance battalion, which happened to be passing through on the way north. To meet the simultaneous heavy attacks from the northwest, the northeast, and the east, II SS Panzer Corps had to use all its reserves. In a typical emergency *Das Reich* formed a battle group comprising its engineer battalion, 627th Engineer Battalion, and 818th Artillery Regiment's 3rd Battalion to plug a dangerous gap opening up between it and *Totenkopf*, which was still defending the corps' east flank.

9 July – On the corps' east flank, *Das Reich*, with one regiment of 167th Infantry Division attached, spent the day fending off tank-supported attacks from the north and northeast by elements of V Guards Mechanized Corps and II Tank Corps. Some of the attacks from the direction of Prokhorovka were substantial affairs including up to 100 tanks. Further south other elements of II Tank Corps attacked two regiments of 167th Infantry Division defending Fourth Panzer Army's east flank.

11 July – Two regiments of *Das Reich* attacked II Tank Corps south of Prokhorovka at 09:30. The struggle lasted more than three hours, as the German tanks were picked off by anti-tank guns. Finally the Soviets were forced to withdraw northeast toward Prokhorovka. Further to the south at Ivanovka other elements of *Das Reich* had to fight off several attacks by II Tank Corps and were able to advance only about a kilometre to the east.

II GUARDS TANK CORPS

The corps was moved to the area south of Prokhorovka during the night of 5/6 July in preparation for attacks against the right flank of II SS Panzer Corps.

6 July – During the afternoon the corps counter-attacked *Das Reich* east of Luchki in conjunction with 96th Tank Brigade, temporarily halting the German advance on the west bank of the Lipovyi Donets River.

7 July – II Guards Tank Corps and 375th Infantry Division attacked elements of *Totenkopf* which were protecting the eastern flank of Fourth Panzer Army's advance. These prevented *Totenkopf* from adding its full strength to the advance of II SS

Panzer Corps, but were ultimately beaten off with the loss of 50 T-34s.

8 July – The corps was ordered to attack the right flank of II SS Panzer Corps in an attempt to relieve the pressure on Sixth Guards and First Tank Army. The primary objective was to cut the Belgorod-Orel road which was the main German supply route for this sector of the front. This seemed to be a promising operation as *Totenkopf* was in the process of handing over the defence of the area to the newly arrived 167th Infantry Division.

Moreover, Soviet operational security had been very good and the Germans did not suspect that II Guards Tank Corps was in the area. All this careful preparation was ruined by pure chance – a flight of Hs 129 'tank busters' led by Hauptmann Bruno Meyer, the commander of *Panzerjagdkommando Weiss*, sighted the corps' lead elements.

Meyer radioed a sighting report to the Kommando's base at Mikoyanovka and the unit's four Staffeln, each with 16 Henschels, took off in relays to keep II Guards Tank Corps under constant attack. They were joined by the Fw 190s of Major Druschel's *Schlachtgeschwader* 1 in a textbook display of air power.

The Fw 190s targeted the AA guns and infantry with SD-2 cluster bombs and strafing runs, allowing the Hs 129s to attack the Soviet tanks with their 30mm (1.18in) MK 103 cannon. The tungsten-cored 30mm (1.18in) APCR rounds easily penetrated the engine decks and rear armour of the T-34s and T-70s and the *Luftwaffe* claimed a total of at least 50 tanks destroyed in three hours of attacks which halted II Guards Tank Corps without the involvement of any German ground forces.

OPPOSITE: Von Manstein's decision to commit his panzers en masse from the beginning of the offensive allowed his forces to make good progress through the Soviet defences in the south of the Kursk salient. His initial attacks also benefitted greatly from the *Luftwaffe*'s highly effective close air support. However, the chronic shortage of German infantry meant that armoured divisions were constantly being held back to protect the flanks of the penetration, which in turn fatally slowed the rate of advance. However, the sheer tactical skill of elite formations such as II SS Panzer Corps very nearly succeeded in overcoming even these crippling problems – by 10/11 July, the Soviet position was so critical that Stalin was demanding hourly situation reports. Even in the immediate aftermath of the fighting at Prokhorovka, he was so concerned at the possibility of a German breakthrough that he appointed Zhukov as Stavka representative to oversee future operations in that sector.

German Assault: Southern Sector, Kursk salient, 5–17 July 1943

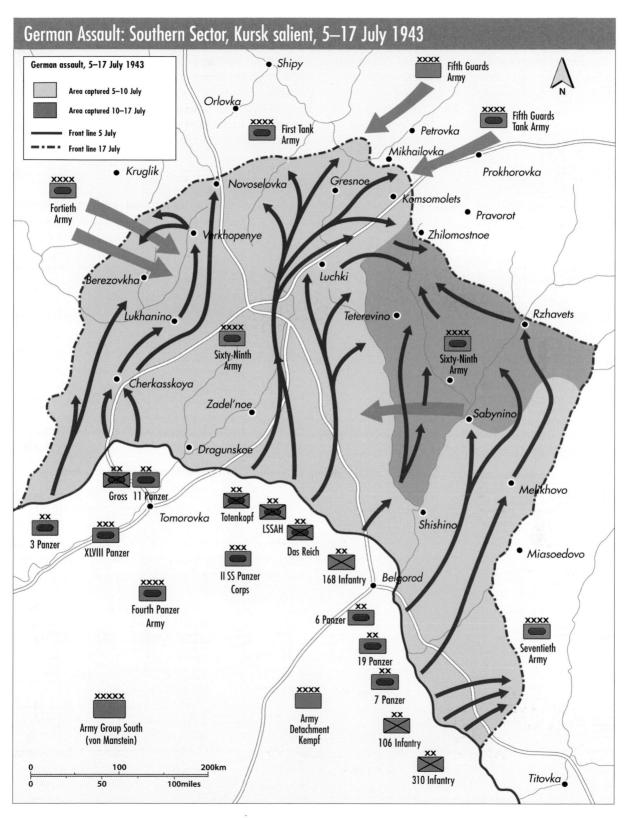

German assault, 5–17 July 1943

- Area captured 5–10 July
- Area captured 10–17 July
- Front line 5 July
- Front line 17 July

Shipy

Orlovka

Kruglik

Fifth Guards Army

Fifth Guards Tank Army

First Tank Army

Petrovka

Mikhailovka

Prokhorovka

N

Novoselovka

Gresnoe

Komsomolets

Pravorot

Fortieth Army

Verkhopenye

Zhilomostnoe

Berezovkha

Luchki

Teterevino

Rzhavets

Lukhanino

Sixty-Ninth Army

Sixty-Ninth Army

Cherkasskoya

Zadel'noe

Sabynino

Dragunskoe

Melikhovo

Gross

11 Panzer

Totenkopf

Shishino

Tomorovka

LSSAH

Miasoedovo

3 Panzer

Das Reich

XLVIII Panzer

168 Infantry

Belgorod

II SS Panzer Corps

Fourth Panzer Army

6 Panzer

Seventieth Army

19 Panzer

7 Panzer

Army Group South (von Manstein)

Army Detachment Kempf

106 Infantry

310 Infantry

Titovka

0   100   200km
0   50   100miles

9–11 July – Although German and Soviet sources fail to agree on the degree of damage suffered by II Guards Tank Corps on 8 July, it is likely that it was substantial as the formation does not seem to have been involved in any significant actions during this period. This implies that it may well have been temporarily withdrawn to act as a local reserve whilst undergoing at least limited refitting.

BELOW: German forces faced the daunting challenge of assaulting formidable defences, manned by a fully prepared enemy, a situation in which the attacker would normally be expected to suffer far heavier losses than defending forces. However, the Germans still retained a vital advantage in tactical skill and professionalism which allowed them to inflict many more casualties on the Red Army. (It seems likely that in the fighting in the north of the salient Soviet losses were about 1.5 times higher than German casualties, whilst in the south the Soviets lost 4.6 times as many men as von Manstein's forces.)

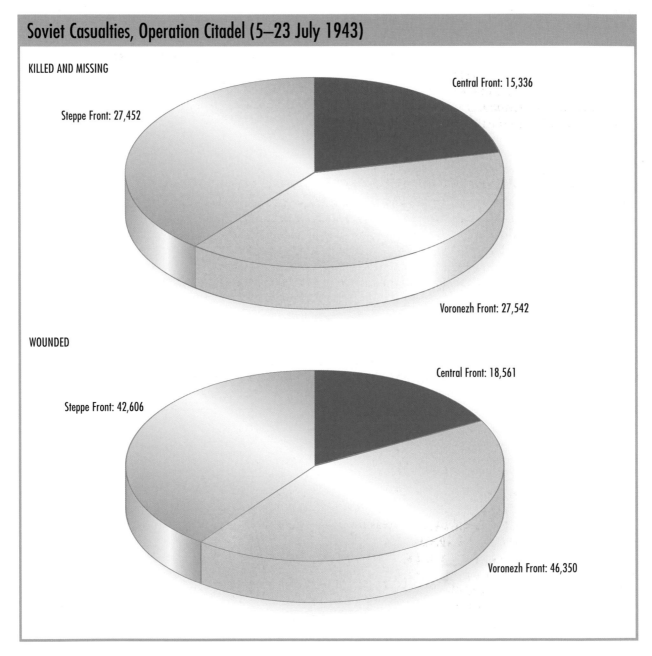

Soviet Casualties, Operation Citadel (5–23 July 1943)

KILLED AND MISSING

Central Front: 15,336

Steppe Front: 27,452

Voronezh Front: 27,542

WOUNDED

Central Front: 18,561

Steppe Front: 42,606

Voronezh Front: 46,350

Prelude to Prokhorovka

By mid-1943 the Red Army was becoming an increasingly professional and formidable force. However, its staff work and communications were still prone to failures, one of which could have led to the destruction of Fifth Guards Tank Army as it arrived at Prokhorovka.

Rotmistrov and his HQ staff arrived at Prokhorovka in the early hours of 11 July, well ahead of the main body of Fifth Guards Tank Army to receive Vatutin's orders that by 10:00 the next morning he was to: '…deliver a counterstroke in the direction of Komsomolets State Farm and Pokrovka and, in conjunction with Fifth Guards Army and First Tank Army destroy the enemy in the Kochetovka, Pokrovka and Greznoye regions and do not permit him to withdraw in a southerly direction.'

However, these orders were rapidly overtaken by events as II SS Panzer Corps had managed to continue its advance on 11 July and actually occupied the ground to the west and southwest of Prokhorovka which Rotmistrov had earmarked as the jumping-off areas for his attacks. There was a potentially disastrous breakdown in the Soviet command and control system at this stage as it seems that no one informed Voronezh Front HQ or Fifth Guards Tank Army of the rapidly changing situation. Rotmistrov had been informed that II Tank Corps and II Guards Tank Corps would be under his command and intended to deploy them in his first echelon, alongside XVIII and XXIX Tank Corps. V Guards Mechanized Corps would form the second echelon, leaving only a small task force under his deputy, Major General Trufanov, to act as a reserve.

FRONT VISIT

Having completed his deployment plans, Rotmistrov was visited by Marshal Vasilevsky at about 19:00 who was keen to inspect the areas from which Fifth Guards Tank Army would attack. They set off with a small escort in a convoy of jeeps. Rotmistrov later recalled that:

'Our route passed through Prokhorovka to Belenikhino and the quick-moving Willys [jeeps], bobbing up and down over the potholes, skirted around vehicles with ammunition and fuel which

were heading to the front. Transports with wounded slowly went past us. Here and there, destroyed trucks and smashed transports stood by the roadside.

'The road passed through wide fields of yellowing wheat. Beyond them began a forest which adjoined the village of Storozhevoe.

"There, along the northern edge of the forest are the jumping off positions of XXIX Tank Corps. XVIII Tank Corps will attack to the right." I explained to A.M. Vasilevsky.

'He intently peered into the distance and listened to the ever-growing rumble of battle. One could divine the front lines of our combined arms armies from the clouds of smoke and the explosions of aerial bombs and shells. The agricultural installations of the Komsomolets State Farm could be seen two kilometres distant to the right.

'Suddenly, Vasilevsky ordered the driver to stop. The vehicle turned off the road and abruptly halted amid the dust-covered roadside brush. We opened the doors and went several steps to the side. The rumble of tank engines could be clearly heard. Then the very same tanks came into sight.

'Quickly turning to me, and with a touch of annoyance in his voice, Aleksandr Mikhailovich asked me, "General! What's going on? Were you not fore-warned that the enemy must not know about the arrival of our tanks? And they stroll around in the light of day under the Germans' eyes…"

'Instantly I raised my binoculars. Indeed, tens of tanks, firing from the march from their short-barrelled guns, were crossing the field and stirring up the ripened grain.

"However, Comrade Marshal, they are not our tanks. They are German…"

"So the enemy has penetrated somewhere. He wants to pre-empt us and seize Prokhorovka."

"We cannot permit that" I said to A.M. Vasilevsky, and by radio I gave the command to General Kirichenko to move without delay two tank brigades to meet the German tanks and halt their advance. Returning to my command post, we knew that the Germans had launched operations against almost all of our armies. Thus the situation suddenly became complicated. The jumping-off positions that we had earlier selected for the counterstroke were in the hands of the Hitlerites.'

The unexpected German advance meant that Rotmistrov had to hastily revise his plans for the following day – as he wrote: '…we had to prepare for the offensive anew; in particular select artillery firing positions and deployment and attack lines. In the compressed time, we had to refine missions, organise cooperation between corps and units, revise the schedule for artillery support, and do all to facilitate the precise command and control of forces in combat.'

It seems that both Rotmistrov and Vasilevsky had assumed that the German advance towards Prokhorovka had been virtually halted and were working on the basis that Fifth Guards Tank Army would be the spearhead of a counter-offensive to at least retake the territory lost since 5 July. These

comfortable assumptions were abruptly shattered by their uncomfortably 'close encounter' with *Leibstandarte* on the evening of 11 July. Suddenly, it was apparent that II SS Panzer Corps was still a force to be reckoned with and was still quite capable of taking Prokhorovka.

This realisation prompted Rotmistrov to issue tactical instructions based on earlier discussions with Vatutin and Vasilevsky at Voronezh Front's HQ. He recalled Vasilevsky's question: '…the German tank divisions possess new heavy Tiger tanks and Ferdinand self-propelled guns. Katukov's tank army has suffered considerably from them. Do you know anything about this equipment and how do you feel about fighting them?

'We know, Comrade Marshal,' he replied. 'We have received tactical and technical information about them from the Steppe Front staff. We have also thought about means for combating them…The fact is that the Tigers and Ferdinands not only have strong frontal armour, but also a powerful 88mm gun….. In that regard they are superior to our tanks which are armed with 76mm guns. Successful struggle with them is possible only in circumstances of close combat, with exploitation of the T-34's greater manoeuvrability and by flanking fire against the side armour of the heavy German machines.'

A platoon of T-34 Model 1942 tanks waits before moving off. The infantry are the *tankodesantniki* who will shortly be riding into action on the backs of the T-34s. The slogan on the nearest tank reads, 'For the Motherland.'

Musing on this, Vatutin had commented: 'In other words, engage in hand-to-hand fighting and board them.'

Ironically, much of this discussion was based on the false premise that, as an elite formation, II SS Panzer Corps must be equipped with large numbers of Tigers and Ferdinands. The reality was very different – even at the beginning of Operation Citadel, the corps fielded a total of just 57 Tigers and not a single Ferdinand. (All 90 of the latter were assigned to support Ninth Army's assault on the north of the salient.) It is likely that the *schurzen* – skirting armour – fitted to the majority of the German tanks and assault guns was partly responsible for the confusion, but there is an equally strong possibility that Soviet commanders were keen to report masses of Tigers and Ferdinands to justify their own heavy losses and inability to halt the German advance.

Whilst not going so far as Vatutin's comment had implied, the orders sent out to all Roymistrov's units emphasised the need to advance swiftly against the German armour and close the range as quickly as possible so that massed fire from the T-34s and T-70s could 'swamp' the panzers. If they could achieve tactical surprise, most would have a reasonable chance of surviving for the five minutes or so that it would take to get into close combat. In order to give his units the best chance of achieving that surprise, Rotmistrov brought forward his attack to 06:30 local time in the hope of catching the Germans whilst they were still forming up.

ATTACK FROM THE SOUTH

However, II SS Panzer Corps was not his only problem as away to the south, III Panzer Corps spearheading the advance of Army Detachment *Kempf* was finally making real progress towards Prokhorovka. During the night of 11/12 July III Panzer Corps seized the bridge over the Donets at Rzhavets and pushed north to within 20 kilometres (12 miles) of Prokhorovka, endangering Fifth Guards Tank Army's left flank. Rotmistrov now had to face the strong possibility that he would have to fight both panzer corps. In order to counter this threat, Major General Trufanov was assigned V Guards Mechanized Corps, together with most of the smaller units from the Army's second echelon. This was a well-balanced force with about 120

AFVs which provided a powerful reinforcement for the ten anti-tank regiments fielding a total of at least 200 guns (a mixture of 45mm and 76.2mm – 1.8in and 3in – weapons) which were being deployed in the attempt to halt III Panzer Corps.

THE BATTLEFIELD

For both sides the best terrain for the attack was a relatively narrow strip of land southwest of Prokhorovka, which formed a corridor of good tank country. (Its importance had been recognized well before the German offensive began and a huge anti-tank ditch forming part of the third line of Soviet defences ran southeast from the Oktabrisky State Farm, cutting across the southern half of the corridor.) The area was bounded on the north by the River Psel and to the south by the embankment of the Belgorod to Kursk railway line, which formed a significant obstacle for tanks.

The area was flat and largely covered with standing crops of wheat and maize, broken by gullies where the ground sloped down to the river and the villages of Mikhailovka, Prelestnoye and Petrovka which straggled along its southern bank. A further village, Polyzhaev, lay on the northern bank – all four settlements had been heavily fortified and were occupied by infantry, artillery and *Katyusha* rocket batteries.

The terrain north of the Psel was also relatively good going for tanks, but the river itself was a serious obstacle, especially in its swollen state after the rain of the last few days. However, *Totenkopf* had seized a small bridgehead on the far bank on 10 July and had completed one bridge capable of carrying medium tanks by the following day. South of the railway embankment the terrain was less favourable for armoured units, with scattered woodland, marshes and small ravines.

At dawn on 12 July, both sides were occupying less than ideal positions. II SS Panzer Corps certainly had its problems – on the left, *Totenkopf* was still penned into a small bridgehead across the Psel, whilst in the centre *Leibstandarte*'s advance of the previous evening had left it in a narrow salient west of Prokhorovka. Its left flank was uncomfortably exposed to fire and counter-attacks from the fortified villages along the banks of the Psel. *Das Reich* was unable to add its weight to the advance on Prokhorovka as it was committed to

Tank Battle at Prokhorovka: German and Soviet Forces Compared

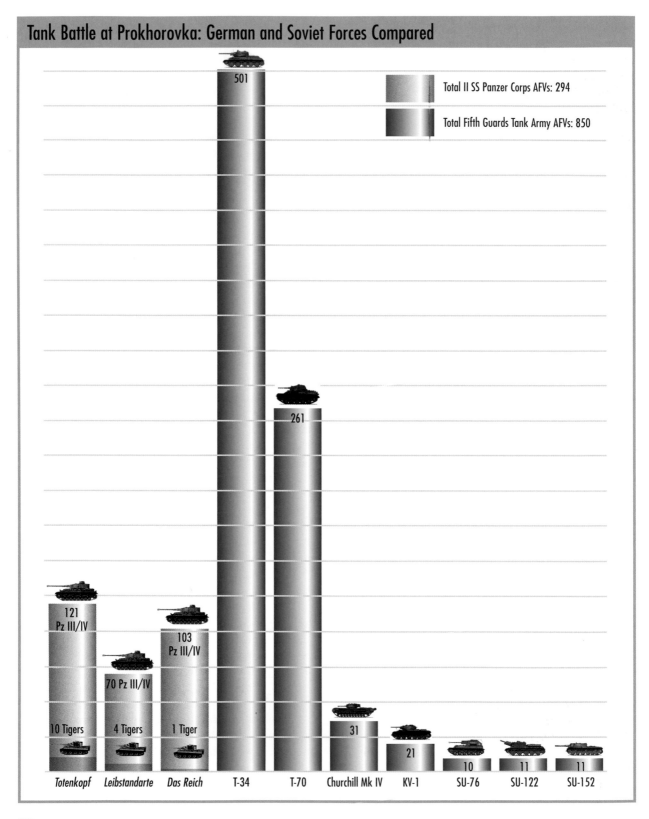

Total II SS Panzer Corps AFVs: 294

Total Fifth Guards Tank Army AFVs: 850

501									
261									
121 Pz III/IV		103 Pz III/IV							
	70 Pz III/IV								
10 Tigers	4 Tigers	1 Tiger			31	21	10	11	11
Totenkopf	Leibstandarte	Das Reich	T-34	T-70	Churchill Mk IV	KV-1	SU-76	SU-122	SU-152

holding the corps' right flank against repeated Soviet attacks. (Its positions ran south from the area of Storozhevoe, roughly parallel to the Belgorod-Kursk highway.)

The Red Army's positions were equally problematic – in the north, all attempts to crush the German bridgehead on the east bank of the Psel had failed and there was a real risk that *Totenkopf* might break through the defences of the badly-battered 52nd and 95th Guards Rifle Divisions to threaten Fifth Guards Tank Army's right flank. In the centre, the forward positions of *Leibstandarte* were little more than 3 kilometres (1.8 miles) from Prokhorovka itself, confining the bulk of Rotmistrov's forces to cramped deployment areas to the northwest and north of the town.

A German breakthrough in this sector would open up the possibility of a swift advance along the Belgorod-Kursk highway. By taking this route, II SS Panzer Corps would only have to breach a single further defence line before reaching Kursk. Rotmistrov's left flank was held by the depleted II Guards Tank Corps and II Tank Corps. They were in the unenviable situation of trying to attack *Das Reich* whilst their left flank was under increasing threat from the advance of III Panzer Corps, which was now barely 20 kilometres (12 miles) south of Prokhorovka.

THE CORRELATION OF FORCES

For many years after the war, the accepted wisdom was that Prokhorovka was a truly epic tank battle with huge forces deployed on each side. Soviet sources claimed that the total German strength was in the order of 600 AFVs including 100 Tigers and Ferdinands. The reality was very different – by 12 July, II SS Panzer Corps deployed no more than 294 operational tanks and assault guns. The likely breakdown being:

- *Totenkopf* – 121, including 10 Tigers
- *Leibstandarte* – 70, including 4 Tigers
- *Das Reich* – 103, including (possibly) 1 Tiger

Rotmistrov's forces probably fielded a total of approximately 850 AFVs, including: 501 T-34s, 261 T-70s, 31 Churchill Mark IVs and 21 KV-1s, plus 10 SU-76s, 11 SU-122s and 11 SU-152s (see graph opposite). This total was reduced to perhaps 730 tanks and assault guns by the detachments sent to halt the advance of III Panzer Corps, but still gave Fifth Guards Tank Army an overall numerical superiority of almost 2.5:1.

The Battle

Traditionally, the battle has been described in terms of the fighting in the centre where Rotmistrov's XVIII and XXIX Tank Corps, supported by elements of V Guards Mechanized Corps, clashed with *Leibstandarte*.

However, this was only one element in an inter-related series of actions which would have a major impact on the outcome of the German offensive in the southern sector of the salient. In order to give a clearer impression of the scale of the fighting which began on the morning of 12 July, each sector of the battlefield will be examined in turn, starting in the north.

12 JULY: NORTH OF THE PSEL

On the morning of 12 July, *Totenkopf* was holding what was still a very constricted bridgehead no more than 4 kilometres (2.5 miles) wide across the Psel. By dawn, engineers had finally completed a Class 60 bridge to allow the division's 10 serviceable Tigers to cross. Except for a small detachment of assault guns and infantry guarding the bridges, the bulk of the division was now concentrated on the north bank ready to renew attacks on the remnants of the 52nd and 95th Guards Rifle Divisions which were supported by the equally battered XXXI Tank Corps.

Both sides recognized the importance of Hill 226 which dominated the terrain in this sector. The hill and the surrounding area were a maze of minefields and field fortifications, but throughout the morning, its already weakened garrison was subjected to a series of air attacks, followed by artillery and rocket bombardments. *Totenkopf*'s infantry began the assault on the hill with armoured support at 12:00 and despite fanatical resistance had taken the position in little more than an hour's fighting. Attempts to follow up this success with an immediate advance northeastwards bogged down in further Soviet defences.

Totenkopf regrouped during the late afternoon and called in a major strike by the *Luftwaffe*, which was made with great effect in the early evening despite the rapidly worsening weather, with thunderstorms and heavy rain sweeping across the battlefield. Following up this success, the Tiger company led an all-out attack which by dusk had taken the village of Polyzhaev and was poised to cut the Kursk-Belgorod highway.

Rotmistrov was understandably alarmed by this advance which threatened to outflank his positions. Although Fifth Guards Army was steadily reinforcing the units fighting north of the Psel, it was weak in artillery and had no tanks as its sole armoured formation, X Tank Corps, had been transferred to the command of Voronezh Front on 7 July. Faced with what could rapidly develop into a real catastrophe, Rotmistrov had no choice but to use his own small reserve force and ordered V Guards Mechanized Corps to deploy the remnants of its 24th Tank Brigade around the Voroshilov State Farm astride the Kursk-Belgorod highway with orders to stop *Totenkopf*'s advance at all costs.

12 JULY: PROKHOROVKA

The action around Prokhorovka itself began at about dawn when Soviet armour made a reconnaissance in force, probing *Leibstandarte*'s positions. This was rapidly driven off without loss and the Germans were able to complete refuelling and loading ammunition in preparation for their own attack which was scheduled for 06:00. (Having filled their ammunition racks, most experienced tank and assault gun crews stowed extra ammunition in any available space. This proved to be a wise precaution and was one of the factors contributing to the day's very high Soviet losses.)

As these preparations were completed, the Soviet tank crews were also carrying out their final checks. Rotmistrov had decided to set up his HQ at the command post of XXIX Tank Corps which was hidden in a large orchard on the slopes of Hill 230.5

just south of Prokhorovka. He recalled that: 'Fragments of bombs and shells pitted the trunks of apple trees. The rods of aerials were protruding from holes dug beside the currant bushes. The quiet of the morning was broken by the roar of Messerschmitts. Columns of smoke soared into the sky from the German bombers.'

The position gave a clear view of the enemy deployment and just as the pre-planned 15 minute Soviet artillery and *Katyusha* bombardment began at 06:00, the German guns opened up and *Leibstandarte*'s armour started its advance. In response to the hail of incoming fire, the panzers fanned out into open order as the 290 tanks of XVIII and XXIX Tank Corps forming the first wave of the Soviet attack started their engines, the clouds of exhaust smoke clearly visible to the German tank crews.

Rotmistrov realized that there was no chance of achieving tactical surprise and that his attack would have to go in quickly, before the panzers overran his tanks in their assembly areas. As the Soviet bombardment ended, he gave the codeword *Stal* (Steel) to order the assault and the mass of T-34s and T-70s moved off. *Shturmoviks* bombed and strafed the German forces in the few minutes before it became impossible to identify targets as the two tank forces closed with each other.

The panzer crews were understandably temporarily shocked at the sight of the rapidly approaching mass of almost 300 Soviet tanks firing on the move despite being festooned with infantry. The training and experience of *Leibstandarte*'s tank crews quickly kicked in and they halted to select their targets as the Soviet armour came within effective range. Rudolf von Ribbentrop, the son of the Reich Foreign Minister, who commanded a company of Panzer IVs, recalled that: 'As we drove down the forward slope, we spotted our first T-34s, which were apparently trying to outflank us from the left. We halted on the slope and opened fire, hitting several of the enemy. A number of Russian tanks were left burning. For a good gunner 800 metres was the ideal range.'

TIGER COMPANY

Whilst von Ribbentrop's company were dealing with XXIX Tank Corps, the remnants of the Tiger company, numbering just four serviceable tanks,

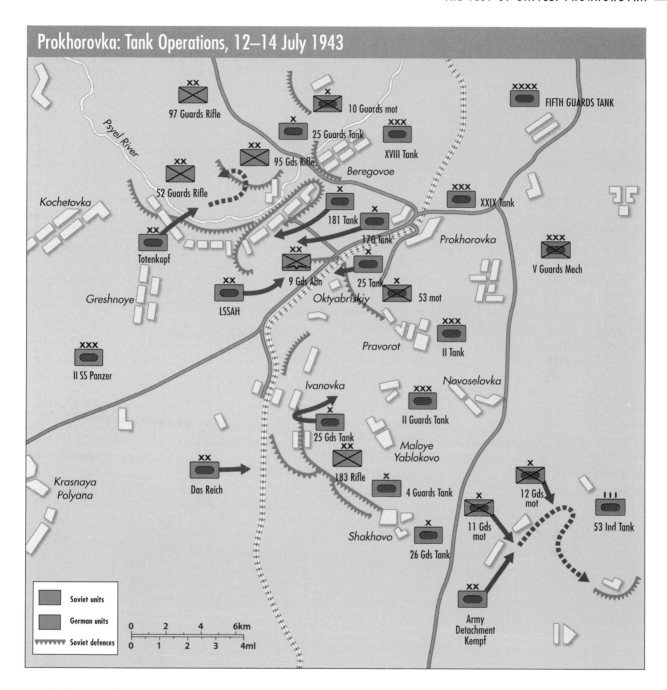

Prokhorovka: Tank Operations, 12–14 July 1943

97 Guards Rifle

10 Guards mot

25 Guards Tank

95 Gds Rifle

XVIII Tank

52 Guards Rifle

Beregovoe

FIFTH GUARDS TANK

Psyel River

Kochetovka

181 Tank

170 Tank

Prokhorovka

XXIX Tank

Totenkopf

9 Gds Abn

25 Tank

V Guards Mech

Greshnoye

LSSAH

Oktyabriskiy

53 mot

Pravorot

II Tank

II SS Panzer

Ivanovka

Novoselovka

II Guards Tank

25 Gds Tank

Maloye Yablokovo

183 Rifle

4 Guards Tank

12 Gds mot

Krasnaya Polyana

Das Reich

53 Ind Tank

11 Gds mot

Shakhovo

26 Gds Tank

Army Detachment Kempf

Soviet units

German units

Soviet defences

0   2   4   6km
0   1   2   3   4ml

ABOVE: By 11 July, II SS Panzer Corps had achieved a deep penetration of the Soviet defence lines in the south of the Kursk salient. However, the sheer strength of these defences prevented the three Waffen-SS divisions from generating sufficient momentum to overcome the resistance of 9th Guards Airborne Division and take Prokhorovka before the arrival of Fifth Guards Tank Army. Even so, Rotmistrov was badly shaken by the extent of the German advance which turned Fifth Guards Tank Army from the spearhead of a decisive counter-attack into a sacrificial attack force. It was now a question of saving Prokhorovka at all costs as its loss would fatally undermine the Soviet defence of the entire southern half of the Kursk salient. In a series of meeting engagements on 12 July, Fifth Guards Tank Army did indeed halt *Leibstandarte*, but at the price of horrendous losses. Even as it did so, *Totenkopf*'s continued progress northwest of Prokhorovka, combined with Army Detachment *Kempf*'s belated approach from the south, threatened to outflank Rotmistrov's battered forces. *Totenkopf*'s advance was only halted after fierce fighting on 13 July, at which point Hitler closed down the offensive in order to free forces to meet the Allied invasion of Sicily.

were deployed near the Oktabrisky State Farm. They were suddenly confronted by the 100 or so T-34s and T-70s of the XVIII Tank Corps' 170th and 181st Tank Brigades, which were attempting to break through the German lines between the river and the state farm to destroy the pontoon bridges and isolate *Totenkopf* on the north bank of the Psel. The Tigers halted and opened fire at 1800 metres (5900ft) to inflict as much damage as possible before the T-34s could close to within 500 metres (1640ft) where the fire of their 76.2mm (3in) guns would begin to take effect. One of the Tigers was commanded by Michael Wittmann who was already gaining a reputation as a particularly talented tank commander. He noted that by the time that the Russian tanks came within 1000 metres (3280ft), the Tigers were hitting with every shot.

The Tiger's 88mm (3.5in) L/56 gun was theoretically capable of penetrating the frontal armour of the T-34 Model 1943 at well over 2000 metres (6560ft), but in practice, experienced crews would not open fire against moving targets at ranges above 1800 metres (5900ft) to give a reasonable chance of scoring hits. The effect of a hit from an 88mm (3.5in) armour piercing round on a T-34 was devastating, often detonating the poorly-protected ammunition, whilst a similar hit on a T-70 would frequently rip the vehicle apart, even if it did not cause an ammunition explosion. As von Ribbentrop's company demonstrated, even the Panzer IV's 75mm (2.95in) could routinely penetrate a T-34 at 800 metres (2625ft). The effectiveness of German weapons was enhanced by the poor quality of much of the Soviet armour plate, which had a low nickel content and was prone to spalling (internal chipping and splintering) when hit, even if the round failed to penetrate. This spalling was a frequent cause of crew casualties and could also inflict sufficient damage to disable the tank.

It was soon apparent that the sheer number of Soviet tanks advancing on narrow frontages was causing its own problems. The very limited room for manoeuvre meant that many vehicles collided as they tried to avoid the burning victims of German fire. (The fate of the hapless infantry carried on the T-34s and T-70s was even worse – those that survived the hits which destroyed their tanks were frequently run down by the milling mass of armour.)

SECOND WAVE

The initial Soviet attacks were finally beaten off by about 09:00, after almost three hours of fierce fighting, but there was only a brief lull before Rotmistrov launched another series of attacks across the entire front. Fierce artillery bombardments covered the advance of more Red Army tanks from Prokhorovka and Jamki. *Leibstandarte*'s divisional history vividly described the action: 'Four of the seven panzers [of 6th Panzer Regiment] were put out of commission at a distance of only about 220 metres. The remaining three panzers joined the ranks of advancing Russian tanks and moved with the pack of them [towards 2nd Panzer Regiment] located about 800 metres to the rear. These three could fire at the Russians from a

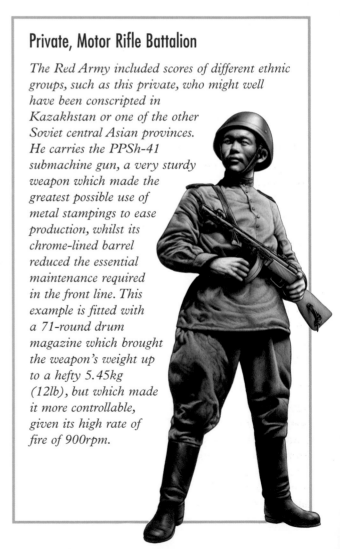

Private, Motor Rifle Battalion

The Red Army included scores of different ethnic groups, such as this private, who might well have been conscripted in Kazakhstan or one of the other Soviet central Asian provinces. He carries the PPSh-41 submachine gun, a very sturdy weapon which made the greatest possible use of metal stampings to ease production, whilst its chrome-lined barrel reduced the essential maintenance required in the front line. This example is fitted with a 71-round drum magazine which brought the weapon's weight up to a hefty 5.45kg (12lb), but which made it more controllable, given its high rate of fire of 900rpm.

distance of 10 to 30 metres and make every shell a direct hit because the Russians could not see through the dust and smoke that there were German tanks rolling along with them…There were already 19 Russian tanks standing burning on the battlefield when [2nd Panzer Regiment] opened fire… [it] destroyed about 62 T-70s and T-34s in a three-hour long battle that could almost be termed hand-to-hand tank combat.'

At 11:00, a small group of four T-34s took advantage of the confusion to attack *Leibstandarte*'s thinly-stretched reconnaissance battalion screening the division's left flank and broke through. They then charged the divisional artillery positions, knocking out two 150mm (5.9in) guns before they were destroyed by infantry anti-tank teams supported by field artillery firing over open sights. Scarcely had this fighting died away when another series of Soviet attacks were made at about 11:30. These achieved a local breakthrough near Hill 252 before being repulsed with the usual heavy losses.

Despite the intensity of the morning's fighting, *Leibstandarte* was able to reorganise and resume its advance on Prokhorovka during the afternoon. By this time, XVIII and XXIX Tank Corps had suffered such heavy losses that they were no longer effective combat formations. In desperation, Rotmistrov scraped together a force totalling perhaps 120 T-34s and T-70s drawn from V Guards Mechanized Corps, 10th Guards Mechanized Brigade and 24th Guards Tank Brigade – a scratch force which proved just sufficient to halt the German advance. As the fighting petered out in mutual exhaustion during the evening, the bulk of Fifth Guards Tank Army pulled back to defensive positions in and around Prokhorovka, whilst the majority of *Leibstandarte*'s units found themselves in much the same positions that they had held at the start of the day.

12 JULY: THE EASTERN BATTLEFIELD

The sector to the east of the railway embankment was largely held by *Das Reich*, which was primarily committed to a defensive role, protecting II SS Panzer Corps' long right flank. (III Panzer Corps, which should have been acting as flank guard, had been badly delayed by strong Soviet field defences and was still 20 kilometres (12 miles) to the south on the morning of the 12th.)

The first Soviet attacks in this sector were made against *Das Reich*'s positions at about 08:30 by elements of II Tank Corps and II Guards Tank Corps totalling perhaps 120 tanks. These were not beaten off until mid-morning, delaying Das Reich's *Deutschland* Regiment's attack in support of *Leibstandarte*'s assault on the heavily fortified village of Storozhevoe which was finally taken during the afternoon.

Soviet pressure in this sector was so unremitting that *Deutschland*'s attack was the only significant offensive action that the division was able to undertake throughout 12th July. In a typical attack just after 14:00, 50-plus T-34s advanced from Vinogradovka towards Yasnaya Polyana, but were intercepted by a force of 25 captured T-34s which had been taken into service with *Das Reich*, forming the 3rd Company of SS *Panzer Jager Abteilung* 2. The scene was witnessed by Sylvester Stadler, commanding the division's *Der Fuhrer* Regiment, who recalled that: 'In a short period of time all 50 tanks…were set ablaze by shells from the captured tanks with German crews. The Soviet tanks each had a barrel of fuel attached to its back. These could be set on fire by a well-aimed shot, and shortly after the whole tank exploded. Of the Soviet tanks only the command tank…was equipped with a radio. For this reason, that tank was knocked out first. The other crews were perplexed; obviously they did not recognize the T-34s on the hill as their enemy.'

As in the other sectors of the battlefield, the fighting gradually died down during the evening as mutual exhaustion set in, with the front line almost where it had been that morning.

'SO ENDS THE BLOODY BUSINESS OF THE DAY' – THE OUTCOME OF THE 12TH

Soviet propaganda was quick to claim that the 12th had been a great victory, issuing wildly inflated claims that the Germans had sustained losses of anything up to 300 AFVs, including 70 Tigers. The truth was embarrassingly different – the daily divisional strength returns prepared for II SS Panzer Corps indicate that a total of 294 AFVs were serviceable at dawn on 12 July, 24 hours later, the corresponding total stood at 251. On the basis of these figures, Rotmistrov's tank crews had knocked out no more than 43 German AFVs, including 11 Tigers – all 10 of *Totenkopf*'s and a single vehicle belonging to *Leibstandarte*. (German 'write-offs' were significantly lower as all these Tigers and many of the other AFVs were repairable.)

In contrast, the Soviet losses were horrendous – Fifth Guards Tank Army had approximately 850 serviceable AFVs immediately before the battle, but had at best 200 combat-ready tanks and assault guns on 13 July, indicating the loss of at least 650 in one day's fighting. German reports of the massive casualties which they had inflicted seemed so exaggerated that *Obergruppenfuhrer* Paul Hausser commanding II SS Panzer Corps visited *Leibstandarte*'s sector of the front to see the situation for himself. His initial scepticism was quickly dispelled when he saw the mass of wrecked Soviet armour and he counted over 100 knocked-out Soviet tanks, marking each with chalk to keep an accurate tally.

In accordance with standing orders, the senior Soviet commanders phoned Stalin to report on the day's actions. Vasilevsky reported first in his capacity as Stavka representative and had the unenviable task of breaking the news of Fifth Guards Tank Army's losses, which was only slightly mitigated by the fact that II SS Panzer Corps' advance had been halted. When Rotmistrov phoned with a more detailed report, Stalin allegedly rounded on him, shouting 'What have you done to your magnificent tank army?'

Always paranoid, Stalin seems to have become highly suspicious of the competence of the entire senior command structure of the Voronezh Front. Zhukov, his most trusted 'trouble-shooter', was at the HQ of the Bryansk Front overseeing the preparations for Operation Kutuzov (the Soviet offensive to eliminate the Orel salient). Stalin abruptly ordered him to fly out to the Prokhorovka sector and take over from Vasilevsky as the Stavka representative.

The losses sustained by Fifth Guards Tank Army left Rotmistrov with little option but to go over to the defensive for the next few days. The surviving tanks of the most badly-battered armoured units were dug in to support the anti-tank strongpoints which were hurriedly constructed to protect Prokhorovka. The stronger tank units were held in reserve to counter-attack if a renewed German assault breached the defences.

Rotmistrov had to carefully deploy his remaining strength to counter three main threats:
■ The possibility that *Totenkopf* might continue its drive along the north bank of the Psel and outflank his position.
■ A renewed frontal attack by *Leibstandarte* with the aim of breaking through to Prokhorovka.
■ The belated arrival of III Panzer Corps from the south.

(The 'nightmare scenario' was that *Leibstandarte* might pin his forces in place whilst *Totenkopf* and III Panzer Corps closed in from north and south to carry out a classic encirclement of the entire army.)

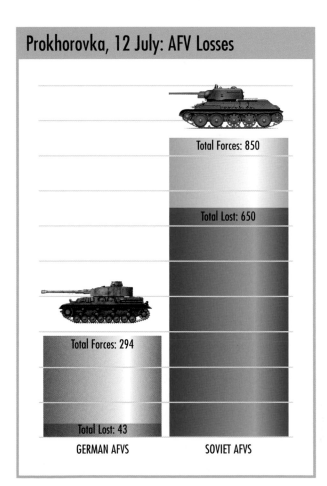

Prokhorovka, 12 July: AFV Losses

Total Forces: 850

Total Lost: 650

Total Forces: 294

Total Lost: 43

GERMAN AFVS   SOVIET AFVS

LEFT: Soviet losses for a single day's fighting at Prokhorovka were horrendous, but ultimately sustainable. With so few AFVs available for immediate offensive action, Rotmistrov was forced to go on the defensive until losses were replaced and damaged tanks repaired. German recovery and repair rates were far superior, partly explaining why so many SS AFVs were ready for combat on 13 July.

13 JULY: THE BATTLE RENEWED

During the night of 12/13 July, von Manstein, Hoth and Hausser agreed that exploitation of *Totenkopf*'s advance offered the best chance of unhinging the Soviet position at Prokhorovka. The division was accordingly ordered to continue its attacks on the 13th with the objective of cutting the Belgorod-Kursk highway north of the Psel. At the same time, *Leibstandarte* would resume its assault on Prokhorovka, whilst *Das Reich* advanced south of the town to make contact with III Panzer Corps.

Rotmistrov had identified *Toptenkopf* as the primary threat and moved 10th Guards Mechanized Brigade to reinforce XXXIII Guards Rifle Corps which would bear the brunt of any German attacks in this sector. *Totenkopf* could only commit 54 serviceable panzers to spearhead its renewed offensive as its 20 or so assault guns were still needed to guard the bridges across the Psel. Despite its reduced strength, the division was able to reach its objective by late morning in the face of repeated Soviet attacks. (*Leibstandarte* made limited attacks to coincide with this offensive which were unable to make much impression on the defence positions covering Prokhorovka. These attacks did give limited assistance to *Totenkopf* by forcing the Soviets to divide their fire.)

However, constant attacks against the long northern flank of the German salient which had now formed north of the Psel made it impossible to hold the position and *Totenkopf* was forced to withdraw to a more readily defensible line during the afternoon.

Leibstandarte's main effort was made in the early afternoon when it launched a two-pronged attack against the XVIII and XXIX Tank Corps with its remaining 50 panzers and 20 assault guns. The principal attack was directed at Soviet positions northeast of the Oktabrisky State Farm, whilst the reconnaissance battalion made a probing attack along the south bank of the Psel near the villages of Andreyevka and Mikhailovka. Both attacks broke down after an hour or so in a maze of newly constructed Soviet defences, with minefields causing the greatest damage.

On the southern sector of the front, *Das Reich* was able to make some progress with its attacks along the line Ivanovka-Vinogradovka. It was helped by the defenders having to divert units to face the advance of III Panzer Corps which was now only 12 kilometres (7.5 miles) away from the southern outskirts of Prokhorovka.

WINNERS & LOSERS

The day's actions had exhausted *Totenkopf* and *Leibstandarte* to such a degree that they simply defended their positions. However, *Das Reich* and III Panzer Corps retained a significant offensive capability and von Manstein believed that there was still a realistic prospect of at least destroying Fifth Guards Tank Army and the remaining Soviet armoured forces in this sector.

Zhukov, Vatutin and Rotmistrov were far from convinced that they had weathered the storm – the

A T-34 Model 1942 heads a column that includes a Model 1940 (second in line, with the single large turret hatch). Fifth Guards Tank Army's journey to Prokhorovka necessitated running repairs such as checking the track tension as the crewman is carrying out on the lead vehicle.

day's fighting had inflicted further heavy losses on their formations – XVIII Tank Corps had lost 30 per cent of its strength, whilst XXIX Tank Corps' losses now stood at a crippling 60 per cent.

However, the key decisions were being made far away from the battlefield in East Prussia at Hitler's Rastenburg HQ. The Allied invasion of Sicily had begun on 9/10 July with very little effective resistance from the Italian forces on the island. Hitler was convinced that Mussolini's regime was on the point of being overthrown by a military coup after which Italy would make a separate peace with the Allies or possibly even change sides.

On 13 July, von Manstein and von Kluge, the commanders of Army Groups South and Centre, arrived at Rastenburg for a conference with Hitler who announced that the critical situation in Italy compelled him to call off Operation Citadel so that II SS Panzer Corps could be rushed to Italy to bolster Mussolini's position. Whilst von Kluge was relieved at the decision which would free his forces to counter the Red Army's attacks on the Orel

salient, von Manstein was appalled at what he saw as the premature abandonment of the chance to decisively defeat the First Tank Army and Fifth Guards Tank Army around Prokhorovka which he believed were the entire Soviet armoured reserves. He emphasised Fourth Panzer Army's successes since 5 July – it had taken 24,000 prisoners and virtually annihilated up to 10 tank and mechanized corps, with the destruction or capture of 1800 AFVs, 267 field guns and 1080 anti-tank guns.

Despite his concerns about the looming crisis in Italy, Hitler was sufficiently impressed by von Manstein's arguments to authorize a temporary continuation of the attacks around Prokhorovka, whilst closing down Ninth Army's offensive against the northern face of the Kursk salient. (However, shortly afterwards he robbed the operation of any real chance of success by overruling von Manstein and ordering XXIV Panzer Corps to defend the Donets Basin against an anticipated Soviet offensive instead of reinforcing III Panzer Corps for its renewed attack on Fifth Guards Tank Army.)

14–17 July: Operation Roland

Although bitterly disappointed at the absence of XXIV Panzer Corps, von Manstein believed that there was still a good chance of mauling Rotmistrov's forces. He and Hoth agreed that *Totenkopf* and *Leibstandarte* should remain on the defensive, whilst *Das Reich* and III Panzer Corps concentrated their attacks south of Prokhorovka, encircling the Soviet forces deployed between the Lipovyi Donets and the North Donets.

The first stage of the operation began at 04:00 on 14 July with an attack by *Das Reich* against the village of Belenikhino which fell to the *Der Führer* Regiment after air attacks followed by fierce hand-to-hand fighting. The division's panzer regiment then led an assault on the village of Ivanovka which was taken that afternoon and inflicted further heavy losses on the already weakened II Guards Tank Corps which was forced to withdraw eastwards.

At the same time, III Panzer Corps was attacking northwards in an attempt to break through the network of strongpoints set up by the newly arrived 31st and 32nd Anti-Tank Brigades and link up with *Das Reich*. These attacks were costly and frustrating,

although the defenders were under orders to fall back steadily to avoid encirclement and lost substantial numbers of anti-tank guns which could not be withdrawn in time.

The following day, *Das Reich* resumed its advance in driving rain against fierce opposition, but was heartened by a report that III Panzer Corps was now making real progress and the two formations finally made contact early that afternoon. Despite this success, *Das Reich* was unable to break through the maze of minefields, anti-tank ditches and strongpoints defending the town of Pravorot.

Throughout this period, there was no respite for Fifth Guards Tank Army, which Zhukov ordered to maintain pressure on *Totenkopf* and *Leibstandarte* to prevent any advance or redeployment which might yet jeopardise the defence of Prokhorovka. Between 14 and 17 July, both formations were subjected to repeated artillery and air bombardments. Soviet tank losses had been so heavy that only small-scale company or battalion strength probing attacks could be made, all of which were beaten off.

The German failure to take Pravorot on the 15th finally convinced von Manstein and Hoth that there was no longer any realistic chance of Operation Roland succeeding and on 17 July the order was given to prepare for a phased withdrawal to the positions held before the start of Operation Citadel.

WHO WON?

For many years after the war, the Soviet propaganda version of the battle was generally accepted by most historians. It certainly generated some memorable phrases such as 'the Tigers are burning' and 'the death ride of the panzers', but these had very little basis in fact. Each side's losses for 12 July have already been given, but those for the entire period are even more revealing.

Documents held by the office of the Inspector General of Panzer Troops indicate that just 33 tanks and assault guns of II SS Panzer Corps were totally destroyed during the period 5–17 July. Comparable figures for Fifth Guards Tank Army are far higher – on 17 July 1943 Major General Baskakov, the Army's Chief of Staff, reported that its 'irretrievable losses' for the period from 12 to 16 July totalled 334 tanks and assault guns, approximately 40 per cent of its AFVs.

II SS Panzer Corps certainly demonstrated immense professionalism and expertise in inflicting 11 times its own tank losses whilst attacking a powerful enemy force which benefitted from elaborate field defences, but the crucial point was that the Red Army could afford such losses. In July and August 1943 Soviet factories completed roughly 4000 tanks, more than sufficient to replace the 1600 or so which it had lost during the entire Kursk Offensive.

Significantly, the Red Army was able to deploy a total of 2832 AFVs in early August for the offensive which re-took Belgorod and Kharkov (Operation Polkovodets Rumyantsev), giving it a 5:1 superiority over the defending German forces.

BELOW: Documents issued by the chief of staff of the Fifth Guards Tank Army, Major General Baskakov, show that 222 T-34s, 89 T-70s, 12 Churchills and 11 assault guns were irretrievably lost between 12–16 July in actions around Prokhorovka. Totalling 334 tanks and assault guns, this indicates a loss of around 40 per cent for Fifth Guards Tank Army. The loss rate was very similar for First Tank Army, who began Operation Citadel with 634 tanks, but after 10 days of fighting had only 321 operational tanks, indicating a 51 per cent loss of initial strength.

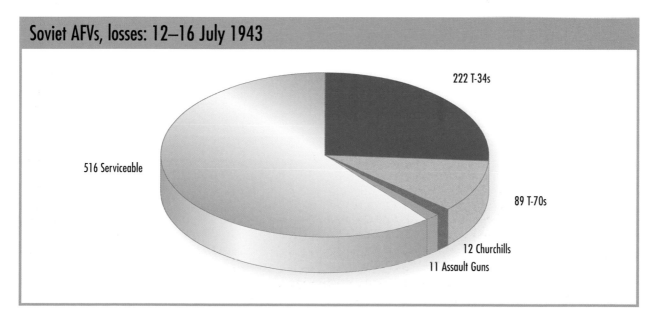

Soviet AFVs, losses: 12–16 July 1943

222 T-34s

89 T-70s

12 Churchills

11 Assault Guns

516 Serviceable

Chapter 5
Aftermath:
1943–44

Stavka had planned its counter-offensives well before the Germans finally launched Operation *Zitadelle*. There were two principal attacks, Operation *Kutuzov*, aimed at Orel, and Operation *Polkovodets Rumyantsev*, which was intended to recapture Belgorod and Kharkov. Neither of these would prove to be easy, as all their objectives were well fortified, but the defeat of the German summer offensive well short of Kursk had instilled the Red Army with a new sense of confidence and a steadily increasing degree of professionalism.

Fifth Guards Tank Army was to be heavily involved in the attacks on Belgorod and Kharkov, but these were only the beginning of advances which would take it through the Ukraine and Belorussia to end the war in northern Germany.

OPPOSITE: In an obviously staged Soviet propaganda shot, Soviet civilians welcome Soviet tank crews after being liberated somewhere in western Russia, 1943. In the background stands a T-34 Model 1942.

Soviet Counter-Offensives, 1943–44

Soviet forces in the north of the Kursk salient recovered quickly from the German attack and launched their own offensive Operation *Kutuzov* against Orel on 12 July.

Orel was strongly defended – only falling on 3/4 August after Third Guards Tank Army and Fourth Tank Army had been committed to the assault. Further south, the battering that Hoth's Fourth Panzer Army had inflicted on Fifth Guards Tank Army and other Soviet formations meant that Operation *Polkovodets Rumyantsev*, the Soviet attack on Belgorod and Kharkov, could not begin until 3 August.

The attacks on Belgorod showed the mixture of professionalism and brute force which was to characterise Soviet offensives for the remainder of the war. The Red Army's artillery laid down a 'wall of fire' 1500 metres (500ft) deep to neutralise the German defences, whilst a corps of *Shturmoviks* was assigned to each attacking army to provide close air support.

At 05:00 on 3 August the Soviet artillery fired a very short initial bombardment against the German defences around Belgorod, before switching to prolonged shelling of specific targets such as artillery positions. Finally at 07:35 the artillery and mortars resumed a general bombardment, followed ten minutes later by massed *Katyusha* fire. Air support was equally lavish – in the first 24 hours, aircraft of the Second Air Army flew 2670 close air support sorties. The weight and precision of the attacks ensured the swift recapture of Belgorod, which fell on 5 August.

TOUGH NUT

However, Kharkov was a far tougher proposition, as it was protected by much stronger defences. In addition, its garrison had been reinforced by *Das Reich* with 96 Panthers, 32 Tigers and 25 assault guns. When Rotmistrov's newly re-equipped Fifth Guards Tank Army attacked on 17 August in an attempt to encircle the city, its assaults were clumsily delivered without proper air, artillery or infantry support against well-prepared defences held by XI Infantry Corps and *Das Reich*. With excellent *Luftwaffe* support, the defenders were able to give a 'text book' demonstration of all-arms co-

operation in marked contrast to the poorly co-ordinated Soviet attacks.

General Raus commanding XI Infantry Corps described how '...the Russian tanks had been recognized while they were still assembling in the villages and flood plains of a brook valley. Within a few minutes heavily laden Stukas came on in wedge formation and unloaded their cargoes of destruction in well timed dives on the enemy tanks caught in this congested area. Dark fountains of earth erupted skyward and were followed by heavy thunderclaps and shocks that resembled an earthquake. These were the heaviest, two-ton bombs, designed for use against battleships, which were all that *Luftflotte* 4 had left to counter the Russian attack. Soon all the villages occupied by Soviet tanks lay in flames. A sea of dust and smoke clouds illuminated by the setting sun hung over the brook valley, while dark mushrooms of smoke from burning tanks stood out in stark contrast. This gruesome picture bore witness to an undertaking that left death and destruction in its wake, hitting the Russians so hard that they could no longer launch their projected attack that day, regardless of Stalin's order. Such a severe blow inflicted on the Soviets had purchased badly needed time for XI *Armeecorps* to reorganise.

'On 20th August the Russians avoided mass groupings of tanks, crossed the brook valley simultaneously in a number of places, and disappeared into the broad cornfields that were located ahead of our lines, ending at the east-west

OPPOSITE: Work on the Dnieper defence line, which formed part of the Panther-Wotan Line or the Eastern Wall, had begun as early as 11 August 1943. Although in theory fortifications were to be erected along the length of the Dnieper River, resources were totally inadequate for such a massive project and defence works were concentrated in sectors where Soviet assault crossings were most likely to be attempted. On 15 September 1943, Hitler finally authorized Army Group South to fall back to the Dnieper defence line and a deadly race ensued with the Red Army attempting to cut off the German line of retreat to the river. Despite the odds, von Manstein managed to get the bulk of Army Group South safely across the Dnieper.

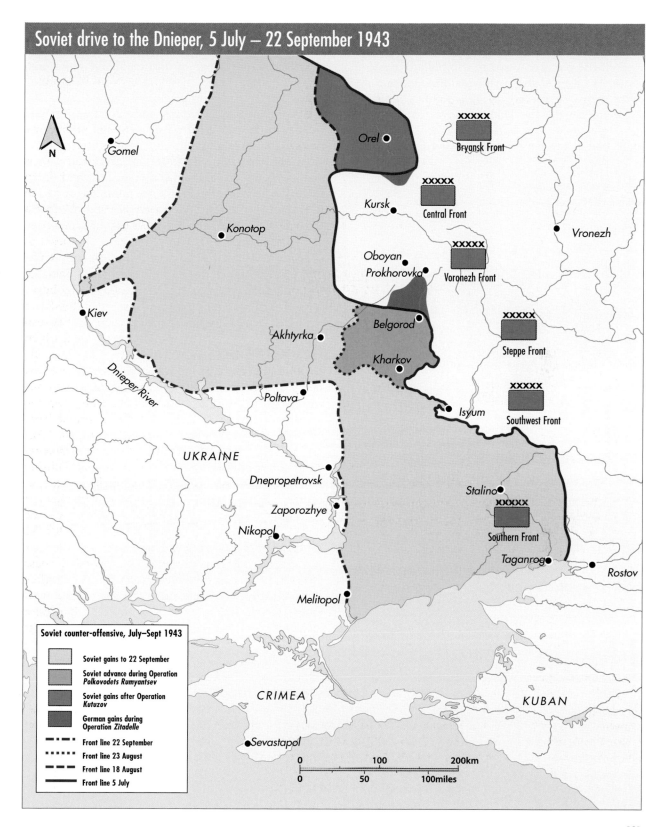

Soviet drive to the Dnieper, 5 July – 22 September 1943

Soviet counter-offensive, July–Sept 1943

- Soviet gains to 22 September
- Soviet advance during Operation *Polkovodets Rumyantsev*
- Soviet gains after Operation *Kutuzov*
- German gains during Operation *Zitadelle*

- ·—·—· Front line 22 September
- ········· Front line 23 August
- ——— Front line 18 August
- ——— Front line 5 July

Gomel

Orel

XXXXX
Bryansk Front

XXXXX
Central Front

Kursk

Konotop

Oboyan
Prokhorovka

XXXXX
Voronezh Front

Vronezh

Kiev

Akhtyrka

Belgorod

Kharkov

XXXXX
Steppe Front

Dnieper River

Poltava

Isyum

XXXXX
Southwest Front

UKRAINE

Dnepropetrovsk

Stalino

Zaporozhye

XXXXX
Southern Front

Nikopol

Taganrog

Rostov

Melitopol

CRIMEA

KUBAN

Sevastapol

N

0   100   200km
0   50   100miles

rollbahn several hundred metres in front of our main battle line. Throughout the morning Soviet tanks worked their way forward in the hollows up to the southern edges of the cornfields, then made a mass dash across the road in full sight. *Das Reich*'s Panthers caught the leading waves of T-34s with fierce defensive fire before they could reach our main battle line. Yet wave after wave followed, until

Russian tanks flowed across in the protecting hollows and pushed forward into our battle positions. Here a net of anti-tank and flak guns, Hornet 88mm tank destroyers, and Wasp self-propelled 105mm field howitzers trapped the T-34s, split them into small groups, and put large numbers out of action. The final waves were still attempting to force a breakthrough in concentrated masses when the Tigers and StuG III self-propelled assault guns, which represented our mobile reserves behind the front, attacked the Russian armour and repulsed it with heavy losses. The price paid by the Fifth Guards Tank Army for this mass assault amounted to 184 knocked out T-34s.'

Rotmistrov then attempted night attacks on two consecutive nights, again without success, bringing his total tank losses to 420 for five days of combat. It was only on 22 August that the defenders withdrew from Kharkov to avoid being cut off.

THE KORSUN POCKET

By 24 December 1943, the Fourth Ukrainian Front had sealed off the 150,000 German and Rumanian troops in the Crimea. As the New Year began, cavalry of the First Ukrainian Front crossed the 1939 Polish frontier and turned southwards in an attempt to trap the German forces in the Dnieper bend south of Kiev.

The bulk of these forces (elements of 11 divisions of the Eighth Army) held a salient centred on Korsun, west of Cherkassy. Stavka quickly

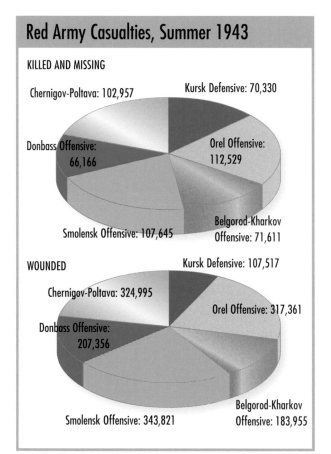

Red Army Casualties, Summer 1943

KILLED AND MISSING

Chernigov-Poltava: 102,957
Kursk Defensive: 70,330
Donbass Offensive: 66,166
Orel Offensive: 112,529
Smolensk Offensive: 107,645
Belgorod-Kharkov Offensive: 71,611

WOUNDED

Kursk Defensive: 107,517
Chernigov-Poltava: 324,995
Orel Offensive: 317,361
Donbass Offensive: 207,356
Smolensk Offensive: 343,821
Belgorod-Kharkov Offensive: 183,955

LEFT AND BELOW: As the tables show, the defensive part of the Kursk battle was much less costly in casualties and equipment for the Red Army than the consequent offensives at Orel and Belgorod-Kharkov, with the Soviets losing 177,847 men between 5–23 July, but another 1.8 million in operations up to the end of September 1943.

Red Army Equipment Losses, Summer 1943

OPERATION	DATE	SMALL ARMS WEAPONS	TANKS AND ASSAULT GUNS	GUNS AND MORTARS
Kursk defensive	5–23 July	70,800	1614	3929
Orel offensive	12 July–18 August	60,500	2586	892
Belgorod-Kharkov offensive	3–23 August	21,700	1864	423
Smolensk offensive	7 August–2 October	33,700	863	234
Donbass offensive	13 August–22 September	37,900	886	814
Chernigov-Poltava	26 August–30 September	48,000	1140	916

Soviet Advance to Dnieper

Soviet Advance to Dnieper
5 July – 1 December 1943

- —— Soviet front line, 5 July
- ← Soviet movements to 1 September
- —— Soviet front line, 1 September
- ← Soviet movements to 1 October
- —— Soviet front line, 1 October
- ← Soviet movements to 1 December
- —— Soviet front line, 1 December
- → German counter-attacks
- ⌐⌐ Wotan defensive line

appreciated the salient's vulnerability, assigning Vatutin's First Ukrainian Front and Konev's Second Ukrainian Front to strike at its flanks. By this stage of the war, both were powerful formations, with each fielding three tank armies, plus three to four other armies.

Konev's Fifth Guards Tank Army and Sixth Tank Army sealed off the salient on 3 February despite appalling weather conditions (intense cold spells broken by brief thaws which turned the region's dirt roads to thick, clinging mud.) Roughly 60,000 men under General Stemmermann (of *Gruppe Stemmermann*) were trapped in this newly-formed Korsun Pocket. A rescue attempt was made by First Panzer Army, which managed to seize small bridgeheads across the River Gniloy Tikich on 11 February, but was unable to break through to the pocket 30 kilometres (18 miles) away to the east. During the next few days, First Panzer Army was locked in fierce combat with Sixth Tank Army, but the relief force could do no more than hold its ground in the face of such strong opposition.

LEFT: 5 JULY – 1 DECEMBER 1943
After the recapture of Kiev, the Red Army was content to clear the rest of the Dnieper in the south, and recapture a few significant places to the north. Now the ground was frozen, the Russian winter again chilled the hearts of the German forces. The Steppe and Southwestern Fronts drove across the river and formed a wide and deep penetration pointing at Krivoi Rog and Kirovograd. Southern Front reached the mouth of the Dnieper and effectively shut off all German forces left in the Crimea. To the north, Generals Vatutin and Rokossovsky had driven their fronts as far as Korosten and the eastern edge of the Pripet Marshes, and Sokolovsky had taken – at great cost – the massive defensive bastion that the Germans had made of Smolensk.

Operation *Bagration*: June–July 1944

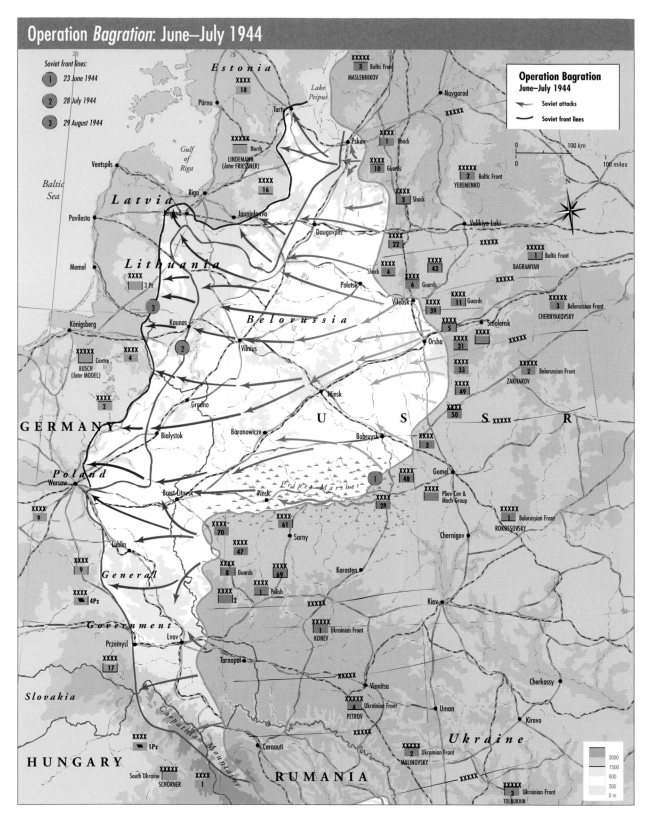

Soviet front lines:

1. 23 June 1944
2. 28 July 1944
3. 29 August 1944

Operation Bagration
June–July 1944

⟵ Soviet attacks

⟋ Soviet front lines

Estonia

XXXX
18

XXXXX
3 Baltic Front
MASLENNIKOV

Pärnu

Lake Peipus

Novgorod

Tartu

XXXX
1 Shock

Pskov

Gulf of Riga

XXXXX
North
LINDEMANN
(later FRIESSNER)

XXXX
10 Guards

XXXXX
2 Baltic Front
YEREMENKO

Ventspils

XXXX
16

XXXX
3 Shock

Baltic Sea

Riga

Jelgava

Jaunjelgava

Daugavpils

Volikiye Luki

Pavilosta

Latvia

XXXX
22

XXXXX
1 Baltic Front
BAGRAMYAN

Memel

Lithuania

XXXX
3 Pz

3

Polotsk

XXXX
4 Shock

XXXX
43

XXXX
6 Guards

XXXXX
3 Belorussian Front
CHERNYAKOVSKY

Königsberg

Kaunas

2

Belorussia

Vitebsk

XXXX
39

XXXX
11 Guards

XXXXX
Centre
BUSCH
(later MODEL)

XXXX
4

Vilnius

Orsha

XXXX
5

XXXX
31

Smolensk

XXXX
2

Grodno

Minsk

XXXX
33

XXXXX
2 Belorussian Front
ZAKHAROV

GERMANY

Baranowicze

U S S R

XXXX
49

Bialystok

Bobruysk

XXXX
50

XXXX
3

Poland

Warsaw

Gomel

XXXX
48

1

Pripet Marshes

Pinsk

XXXX
28

Pliev Cav &
Mech Group

XXXX
9

Brest-Litovsk

Chernigov

XXXXX
1 Belorussian Front
ROKOSSOVSKY

XXXX
70

XXXX
61

Sarny

Lublin

XXXX
47

XXXX
9

XXXX
8 Guards

XXXX
69

Korosten

General

XXXX
2

XXXX
1 Polish

Kiev

XXXX
4 Pz

XXXXX

Government

Lvov

XXXXX
1 Ukrainian Front
KONEV

Przemysl

XXXX
17

Tarnopol

Slovakia

XXXXX
Vinnitsa

XXXX
1 Pz

XXXXX
4 Ukrainian Front
PETROV

Uman

Cherkassy

Ceraauti

Ukraine

Kirovo

HUNGARY

South Ukraine
SCHÖRNER

XXXX
1

RUMANIA

XXXXX
2 Ukrainian Front
MALINOVSKY

XXXXX

XXXXX
3 Ukrainian Front
TOLBUKHIN

0   100 km
0   100 miles

3000
1500
600
300
0 m

By 15 February, it was clear that the trapped forces would have to attempt a breakout. They had already edged to within closer to the stalled relief force and launched their main effort on the night of 16/17 February. Elements of three Soviet tank armies lay between *Gruppe Stemmermann* and the forward elements of First Panzer Army only 12 kilometres (7.5 miles) away.

Konev reacted furiously to the German breakout attempts – he had rashly promised Stalin a second Stalingrad – and threw in all available units, including the new JS-2s of XX Tank Corps. Although as many as 35,000 German troops eventually fought their way clear after abandoning all their artillery and heavy equipment, Eighth Army had been badly mauled and First Panzer Army had lost large numbers of AFVs, which were increasingly difficult to replace.

OPERATION *BAGRATION*:
DESTROYING ARMY GROUP CENTRE

Throughout April and May 1944, Stavka planned Operation *Bagration*, a massive offensive intended to destroy Army Group Centre and drive German forces from Soviet territory.

Elaborate deception measures were employed to convince the Germans that the forthcoming offensive would be launched away to the south against Army Group North Ukraine. These were highly successful and the offensive achieved complete surprise when it opened on 22 June, on the third anniversary of the start of Operation *Barbarossa*. In crucial sectors of the front, the Soviets had local numerical superiority of up to

OPPOSITE: JUNE–JULY 1944

The Soviet summer offensive of 1944 was the most decisive single campaign of World War II. Launched three years to the day after the German invasion, and three weeks after the Western Allies landed in Normandy, it involved the largest military force in history: more than 2.4 million men smashed into the German front lines. More than one million men attacked Army Group Centre alone, crushing the army group within a matter of weeks.

By the end of August, Soviet forces were in the Baltic states, across the Polish border and about to cross into Rumania. Army Group Centre had been virtually annihilated. Of the 97 German divisions and 13 separate brigades that had been in place in Army Group Centre, or which had been rushed into action as reinforcements throughout the two-month operation, 17 divisions and three brigades were destroyed completely. Another 50 divisions lost 60–70 per cent of their manpower.

10:1 and quickly broke through the German defences.

Within days, Fifth Guards Tank Army and the two other tank armies assigned to the operation were able to exploit the breakthroughs and advance deep into the German rear areas, whilst a cavalry-mechanized group moved through the Pripet Marshes in Belorussia to cut off the German Ninth Army's line of retreat.

VITEBSK SURROUNDED

On 25 June, Vitebsk was surrounded by a second cavalry-mechanized group and Soviet forces pressed on, cutting off Mogilev, Bobruisk and Minsk by 3 July. (Minsk was taken the following day and the pockets of German troops trapped around the city were destroyed by 11 July.) Army Group Centre had now lost 25 of its 63 divisions (including the bulk of the Ninth Army).

Rotmistrov's forces had played a key role in this phase of the operation and were instrumental in completing the encirclement of Minsk, but his III Guards Mechanized Corps alone lost 295 AFVs in heavy fighting against 5th Panzer Division and the Tigers of sPzAbt. 505, whilst the remainder of Fifth Guards Tank Army also sustained heavy casualties.

HEAVY LOSSES

The main phase of Operation *Bagration* ended with the capture of Vilnius, Pinsk and Grodno in the period 13–16 July. Army Group Centre had been practically annihilated with 2000 AFVs and 57,000 other vehicles destroyed or captured. German casualties may have been as high as 300,000 dead, 250,000 wounded and about 120,000 prisoners.

Red Army losses were also high, with 60,000 killed, 110,000 wounded and about 8000 missing. In terms of equipment, Soviet forces lost 2957 tanks, 2447 guns and 822 aircraft, but Soviet war production and Lend-Lease supplies meant that they could readily be replaced.

Despite this success, Rotmistrov's reputation was damaged by the heavy losses suffered by Fifth Guards Tank Army and in August 1944 he was ordered to relinquish command and take up a new post as Deputy Commander of Red Army Armoured and Mechanized Forces, which he retained for the remainder of the war.

Bibliography

BOOKS

Armstrong, Richard N. *Red Army Tank Commanders: The Armored Guards*. Schiffer Publishing Ltd, 1994.

Bergstrom, Christer. *Kursk, the Air Battle: July 1943*. Ian Allan Publishing Ltd, 2007.

Forczyk, Robert. *Panther versus T-34: Ukraine 1943*. Osprey Publishing, 2007.

Glantz, David M. & Orenstein, Harold S. *The Battle for Kursk 1943: The Soviet General Staff Study*. Frank Cass Publishers, 2002.

Healy, Mark. *Zitadelle, the German Offensive Against the Kursk Salient, 4–17 July 1943*. Spellmount, The History Press Ltd, 2010.

Kershaw, Robert. *Tank Men: The Human Story of Tanks at War*. Hodder & Stoughton Ltd, 2009.

Merridale, Catherine. *Ivan's War: The Red Army 1939–45*. Faber and Faber Limited, 2006.

Nafziger, George F. *The German Order Of Battle: Waffen SS And Other Units In World War II*. Da Capo Press, 2000.

Porter, David. *The Essential Vehicle Identification Guide: Soviet Tank Units, 1939–45*. Amber Books Ltd, 2009.

Porter, David. *Order of Battle: The Red Army in WWII*. Amber Books, 2009.

Rottman, Gordon L. and Gerrard, Howard. *Soviet Rifleman 1941–45*. Osprey Publishing, 2007.

Sharp, Charles C. *Red Storm: Soviet Mechanized Corps and Guards Armored Units, 1942–1945*. George F. Nafziger, 1995.

Sharp, Charles C. *Soviet Armor Tactics in World War II*. George F. Nafziger, 1999.

Vanags-Baginskis, Alex and Watanabe, Rikyu. *Aggressors Volume 1: Tank Buster Vs. Combat Vehicle*. Airlife Publishing Ltd, 1990.

Zaloga, Steven J. & Ness, Leland S. *Red Army Handbook 1939–1945*. Sutton Publishing Ltd, 1998.

Zetterling, Niklas & Frankson, Anders. *Kursk 1943: A Statistical Analysis*. Frank Cass Publishers, 2000.

WEBSITES

Engines of the Red Army in WW2:
http://www.o5m6.de/
Oliver Missing's superb website, which is the source of many of the illustrations in this book.

Kursk – July 1943:
http://dspace.dial.pipex.com/town/avenue/vy75/kursk.htm

Soviet Hand and Rifle Grenades:
http://lexpev.nl/grenades/sovietbalkan/russia/index.html

Soviet Mines:
http://lexpev.nl/minesandcharges/sovietbalkan/russia/index.html

The Kursk Battle:
http://rkkaww2.armchairgeneral.com/battles/kursk43.htm#Oleinikov
A part of the excellent 'RKKA in World War II' website.

The Russian Battlefield:
http://www.battlefield.ru/en/home.html

World Guns:
http://world.guns.ru/
A good source of information on the small arms of the Red Army.

Guide to Symbols

UNITS SIZE

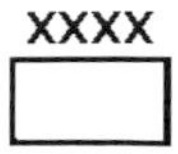

ARMY

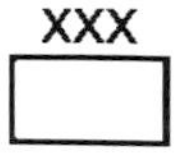

CORPS

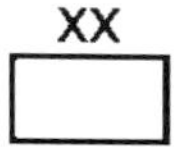

DIVISION

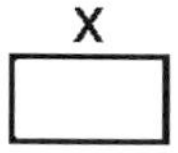

BRIGADE

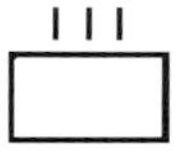

REGIMENT

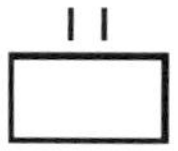

BATTALION

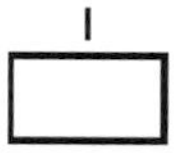

COMPANY

PLATOON

SECTION

SQUAD/TEAM

UNIT TYPE

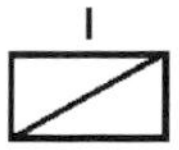

CAVALRY

INFANTRY

MOTORIZED INFANTRY

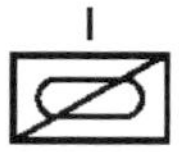

RECONNAISSANCE

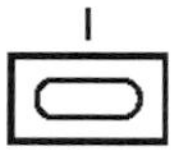

ARMOUR/TANK

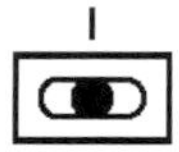

SELF-PROPELLED ARTILLERY

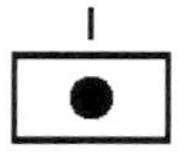

ARTILLERY

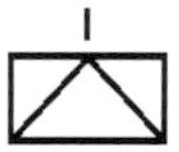

ANTI-TANK

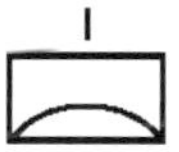

AIR DEFENCE

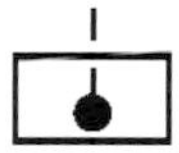

MORTAR

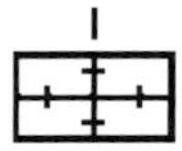

MEDICAL

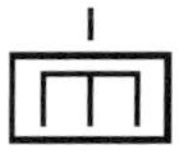

ENGINEERS

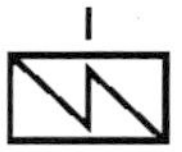

SIGNALS

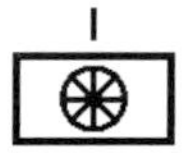

TRANSPORT

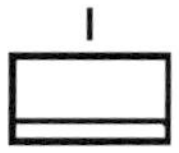

SUPPLY

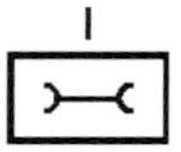

MAINTENANCE

Index

Page numbers in *italics* refer to illustrations.

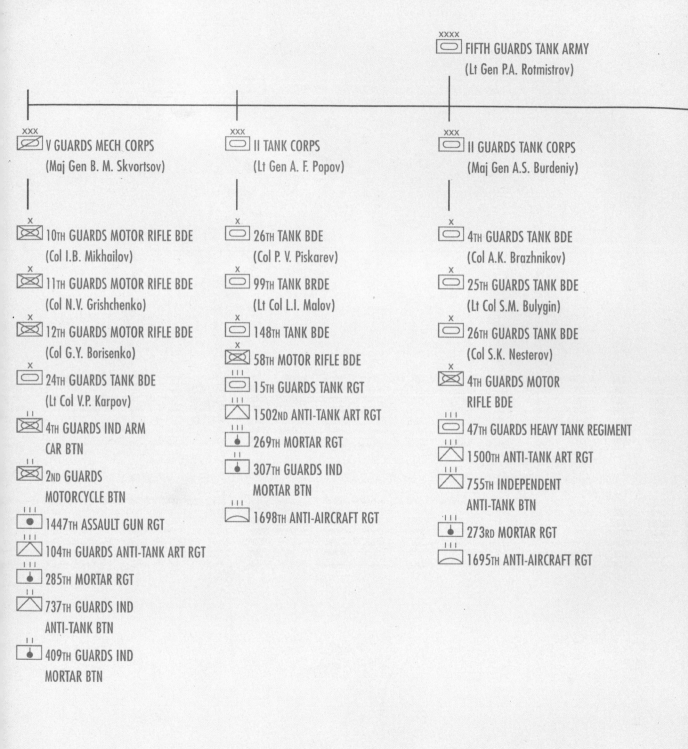

FIFTH GUARDS TANK ARMY
(Lt Gen P.A. Rotmistrov)

V GUARDS MECH CORPS
(Maj Gen B. M. Skvortsov)

10TH GUARDS MOTOR RIFLE BDE
(Col I.B. Mikhailov)

11TH GUARDS MOTOR RIFLE BDE
(Col N.V. Grishchenko)

12TH GUARDS MOTOR RIFLE BDE
(Col G.Y. Borisenko)

24TH GUARDS TANK BDE
(Lt Col V.P. Karpov)

4TH GUARDS IND ARM
CAR BTN

2ND GUARDS
MOTORCYCLE BTN

1447TH ASSAULT GUN RGT

104TH GUARDS ANTI-TANK ART RGT

285TH MORTAR RGT

737TH GUARDS IND
ANTI-TANK BTN

409TH GUARDS IND
MORTAR BTN

II TANK CORPS
(Lt Gen A. F. Popov)

26TH TANK BDE
(Col P. V. Piskarev)

99TH TANK BRDE
(Lt Col L.I. Malov)

148TH TANK BDE

58TH MOTOR RIFLE BDE

15TH GUARDS TANK RGT

1502ND ANTI-TANK ART RGT

269TH MORTAR RGT

307TH GUARDS IND
MORTAR BTN

1698TH ANTI-AIRCRAFT RGT

II GUARDS TANK CORPS
(Maj Gen A.S. Burdeniy)

4TH GUARDS TANK BDE
(Col A.K. Brazhnikov)

25TH GUARDS TANK BDE
(Lt Col S.M. Bulygin)

26TH GUARDS TANK BDE
(Col S.K. Nesterov)

4TH GUARDS MOTOR
RIFLE BDE

47TH GUARDS HEAVY TANK REGIMENT

1500TH ANTI-TANK ART RGT

755TH INDEPENDENT
ANTI-TANK BTN

273RD MORTAR RGT

1695TH ANTI-AIRCRAFT RGT